A Genealogy of Modernism

A Genealogy of Modernism

A study of English literary doctrine 1908–1922

MICHAEL H. LEVENSON

University of Virginia

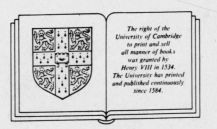

CAMBRIDGE UNIVERSITY PRESS

Cambridge

New York   New Rochelle

Melbourne   Sydney

Published by the Press Syndicate of the University of Cambridge
The Pitt Building, Trumpington Street, Cambridge CB2 1RP
32 East 57th Street, New York, NY 10022, USA
10 Stamford Road, Oakleigh, Melbourne 3166, Australia

First published 1984
First paperback edition 1986
Reprinted 1988

Printed in Great Britain at the
University Press, Cambridge

Library of Congress catalogue card number: 83-15220

British Library Cataloguing in Publication Data
Levenson, Michael H.
The genealogy of modernism.
1. Modernism (Literature)
2. English literature – 20th century – History and criticism
I. Title
820′.9′00912   PR 478.M/

ISBN 0 521 25010 2 hard covers
ISBN 0 521 33800 X paperback

SE

Contents

CONTENTS

Preface

Vague terms still signify. Such is the case with "modernism": it is at once vague and unavoidable. Anything more precise would exclude too much too soon; anything more general would be folly. As with any blunt instrument, the best that can be done is to use it for the rough tasks and to reserve the finer work for finer tools. As a rough way of locating our attention, "modernism" will do.

The problem of naming is apposite, since my subject is the emergence of a literary movement one of whose own problems was how to name itself. The movement is that associated with Pound, Hulme, Ford, Lewis and Eliot; Joyce, Woolf and Lawrence loom on the periphery. These are large and unwieldy figures, but that is undisturbing, since it is not with the careers of figures that we will be concerned. The study does not occupy itself with biography, nor with the elucidation of much-elucidated texts. The interest lies in the structure of English modernism, as it slowly assumed coherence, as aesthetic concepts received new formulation, as those concepts were worked into doctrine. Among the concepts were image, symbol, tradition, expression, objectivity. The doctrines were successively called Impressionism, Imagism, Vorticism and Classicism.

As for the dates, they, too, are a preliminary convenience. In 1908 Pound arrived in London; Ford began to edit the *English Review*; and T. E. Hulme joined the short-lived Poets' Club. In 1922 *The Waste Land*, *Ulysses* and the *Later Poems* of Yeats were published; the *Criterion* was founded. In 1914, the year that divides the study, Eliot met Pound and showed him "Prufrock." Joyce began serializing *A Portrait of the Artist as a Young Man*. It was the year of the first Imagist anthology and the

Vorticist journal *Blast* – also, of course, the year the war began. There is no need to quibble over these dates. They are only boundary stones; what is interesting is the terrain.

Still, as a contribution to the history of English modernism, this work encounters a number of difficulties that should be acknowledged. First, its principals keep changing. No one figure appears in every phase of the narrative, because no one figure followed all the turnings of the literary movement. T. S. Eliot emerges late in the study, but then immediately occupies the foreground. Ford Madox Ford and Wyndham Lewis are conspicuous for a time, and then drop from consideration. This is not because their later work or Eliot's early work is without interest. It is only because the book follows the thread of concepts, not the thread of lives; what will provide continuity are the constituent ideas of English modernism; these are the characters whose destinies will unfold.

Second, although modernist literary doctrine is the subject, its boundaries are not secure. On one frontier, the critical work became entangled in the creative work, and thus the model of text and context will not serve. Literary texts were often explained before they were written, and they themselves were often eloquent critical acts. On another frontier, the literary doctrine did not remain distinct from other forms of discursive writing – not from theories of painting and sculpture, nor from philosophic or religious speculation. One of the most notable features of the period was the continuity between genres and between disciplines, the self-conscious attempt to construct a unified theory of modernity. Any effort to isolate literary doctrine would only impoverish it, and one need not be ashamed to pursue the study of aesthetic concepts into the imaginative work that they describe and into the related disciplines that frame them.

Finally, there is the issue of the rhetoric of literary change. By temperament as well as by their cultural position, the English modernists were inclined to definitive opinions expressed in vehement tones. Literary attitudes were not offered as tentative hypotheses subject to revision, but as final judgments. However, in the course of very few years, final judgments succeeded one another at an alarming rate. Beliefs changed markedly, only the tone of conviction was unchanged. It is therefore well to consider at the start that the critical pronouncements were not the insights of Olympian minds, but more often the hasty formulae of polemicists.

> What Mr. Murry does show is that there are at least two attitudes toward literature and toward everything, and that you cannot hold both.
>
> (T. S. Eliot, "The Function of Criticism")[1]

Eliot's remark is infelicitous. If there are "at least" two attitudes, then there can be no question of "both." Nor is this the cavil it may appear. The lapse is symptomatic, marking the strength of the modernist urge towards dualistic opposition and radical polarities. "Good" and "evil" may disappear from the modernist vocabulary, but the Manichean habit remains. In the essay on "Dante," Eliot writes that "Dante and Shakespeare divide the modern world between them; there is no third." In the modernist polemic, no *tertium quid* is allowed. Thus Pound separates the modern movement into "two camps," while Ford distinguishes "two distinct strains." Hulme concurs, arguing that "there are two kinds of art . . . absolutely distinct in kind from one another," that each "corresponds to a certain general attitude towards the world," and that each race is "inclined to one of these two tendencies." Moreover, Hulme regards the difference between the two attitudes as "simply the difference between true and false."[2]

The effect of such a dualism is to suggest a thorough historical discontinuity. Victorian poetry has been soft; modern poetry will be hard (Pound's terms). Humanist art has been vital; the coming geometric art will be inorganic (Hulme's terms). Romanticism was immature; the new classicism will be adult (Eliot's terms). "We have got clean out of history," wrote Lewis. "We are not to-day living in history."[3]

George Eliot, in a deft phrase, speaks of the "suppressed transitions which unite all contrasts."[4] That provides a convenient way for me to identify my approach, for in one of its aspects this study is the attempt to establish the continuity of a movement which repeatedly announced a clean break with the immediate past. Such an aim will require a close look at the minute changes which would be lost within too broad a vista. Accordingly, at the centre of the book is a detailed history of some transformations in modernist thought between the years 1908 and 1914. But for transitions to have meaning, they must be linked to contrasts, and the first and third sections attempt to construct a wider angle of vision. The book begins by approaching Conrad in the context of late Victorian ideology, and it concludes by locating T. S. Eliot as the heir to English modernism. Between the two it follows the increasingly tangled series of attempts to formulate a successful definition of modernity.

Within a decade and a half, a movement that set out to change the theory and practice of literature changed its own theory and practice. During this brief period, it may or may not have swept out "the last century the way Attila swept across Europe," but it certainly swept away most of its earlier assumptions.[5] This process of change was not homogeneous or thoroughgoing, no stately changing of the literary guard: romanticism withdrawn, classicism attendant. It was a complex interaction of literary forces, passing through a series of distinct phases – a product of gradual and sometimes obscure developments, and of conflicting and sometimes contradictory values.

This is a study in literary transition, then, which attempts to recover some of the intricacy of the period. It hopes to take modest steps towards some finer conceptual distinctions and towards a greater historical precision. To do this, it must avoid loose appeals to the spirit of the age; it must consider the literary change not as something that descended but as something that was made; it must follow the determinate acts that accumulated to alter a sensibility; and it must, regrettably, exclude some writers of the first rank. This is only "a" not "the" genealogy of modernism. It is evident that Yeats, Lawrence, Woolf and Joyce belong in any comprehensive history of modern literature. But this is not a comprehensive history. It is the account of a recognizable lineage in a specific geographic centre during a confined period. Hulme, Pound, Lewis, Ford and Eliot did not just inhabit London within the same few years; they engaged in active debate and frequent interchange; they formulated positions with one another and then against one another; they quarrelled and were reconciled; and the line of intellectual development connecting them is the axis on which the book turns.

Unlike these English modernists, I am happy to acknowledge my immediate predecessors. A study like this could be written only because previous scholars have interpreted difficult texts, uncovered lost manuscripts and traced complicated lives. Because of these efforts it is now possible to pursue the history of modernist doctrine more rigorously, to see the false starts, reversals, hesitations, resolutions. Part of the difficulty with modernism is that it has suppressed its origins. As it became an established cultural presence, it revised its history in line with its present inclinations. This is a "genealogy," then, whose aim is not to establish pedigree, but to redeem certain lines of development which have been obscured or neglected, and which, once traced, may help restore modernity to history.

Acknowledgements

My scholarly debts are acknowledged in the notes, but let me mention here my personal gratitude: to Ian Watt, who taught me by terse precept and eloquent example and who steered with such care; to Albert Guerard, who so deftly improved whatever he read; to Joel Porte and J. C. La Driere, who tended this project when it was young; to Robert Langbaum and J. C. Levenson, who read the manuscript so attentively and who made many valuable suggestions; to Ralph Cohen and Austin Quigley, who taught me that any worthy idea must be strong enough to withstand both fire and ice; to Anthony Winner, who showed me that it was possible to stand on the boundary between Victorian and Modern and still keep one's balance; to John Powers, who so often talked me into thought; to Gordon Braden, whose lucubrations inspired mine. I also owe a great deal to my students at the University of Virginia, who will see much that is familiar in these pages, but all of it better for their sensitive and generous responses. I hope that my family realizes that I can never acknowledge enough their love and trust. I save my last and first and deepest thanks for my closest colleague, Karen Chase.

I. Progenitors

CHAPTER I

Consciousness

The modernist narrator on the Victorian sailing ship

In the first lines of the preface to The Nigger of the "Narcissus," Conrad defines art as "a single-minded attempt to render the highest kind of justice to the visible universe . . ."[1] This is reasonable and reasonably straightforward: it squares nicely with the stipulation that art "make its appeal through the senses," with the proposal to show life's "vibration, its color, its form" and with Conrad's oft-quoted summary of his aim: "to make you hear, to make you feel . . . before all, to make you *see*."[2] Moreover, it conforms to a prevailing view of Conradian Impressionism which Ford Madox Ford was among the first to underscore and which emphasizes attention to physical, especially visual, immediacy.

But early in the preface Conrad pursues definition in another direction. Unlike the scientist or the thinker, he tells us, the artist "descends within himself, and in that lonely region of stress and strife, if he be deserving and fortunate, he finds the terms of his appeal."[3] The remark represents a sufficiently familiar romantic gesture, but in the context of the preface it provokes an immediate strain. If the aim is fidelity to the visible universe, then the inner life of the artist would seem beside the point. If the aim is "before all to make you see," then why should Conrad invoke that part of our nature "kept out of sight"? This tension appears throughout. On the one hand, Conrad makes a rousing rhetorical call for the sensory apprehension of life's surfaces; on the other, he demands inwardness and depth – thus his return to notions such as the "fundamental," the "essential," the "permanently enduring."

But this is a tension, not a contradiction, and Conrad's

I

resolution of the issue is telling if indirect. Fiction, he goes on to say, "appeals to temperament": "And in truth it must be, like painting, like music, like all art, the appeal of one temperament to all the other innumerable temperaments whose subtle and resistless power endows passing events with their true meaning, and creates the moral, the emotional atmosphere of the place and time."[4] The central notion here is that of temperament "endowing" events with their "true meaning." The implication, of course, is that such meaning is not intrinsic, that the significance of events remains incomplete without further adumbration. And this attitude goes some distance towards clarifying matters. For given the devaluing of mere appearances, Conrad's insistence on an inner artistic descent now becomes intelligible. It by no means marks a retreat from the programme of rendering "the highest kind of justice to the visible universe"; indeed it constitutes that justice. The "subtlety" of human consciousness is the source of meaning and artistic "justice"; against the evanescent flux of the phenomenal world, it provides permanence, pattern and significance.

This aspect of the preface is characteristically neglected. But once the meaning-giving function of temperament is recognised, then it becomes apparent why Conrad enjoins the artist to hold up a fragment of life "in the light of a sincere mood," or why he insists on a "light of magic suggestiveness" to play over the "commonplace surface of words."[5] It is because words, like events, are in themselves speechless; they depend for their meaning on an animating subjectivity.

The preface has been taken – rightly, I think – as the central statement of Conrad's artistic position. Samuel Hynes has written that it contains his "whole aesthetic,"[6] and Ian Watt calls it "the most reliable, and the most voluntary, single statement of Conrad's general approach to writing."[7] Here, however, it will be taken as an entrance not into Conrad's thought, at least not only to his thought, but into the general situation of early modernism; it will serve as a representative text. In particular, I intend to show how the tensions in the preface point to certain widespread and fundamental literary tensions.

If we are to consider the preface, we must consider that to

which it is prefatory; the text of *The Nigger of the "Narcissus"* becomes illustrative. Among the values endorsed in the novel, there has been broad critical consensus that the steadfastness of Old Singleton is foremost. We are never to forget that he "steered with care" or that he is "the lonely relic . . . of the everlasting children of the mysterious sea." Where the younger sailors have grown swollen with egoism, Singleton "had never given a thought to his mortal self."[8] In the face of social crisis, the stirrings of mutiny, he holds to his place in the ship's hierarchy. In the face of natural crisis, he holds to the wheel. Singleton is an exemplar of Conradian "Fidelity" and possesses the virtues peculiar to his type: persistence, self-denial, subordination to authority. Such, in any case, is the accepted view of the novel, which it is not my purpose to dispute. My aim is to indicate another dominant value, which is not subject to explicit thematic treatment, which was most likely not part of Conrad's avowed intention and which stands in opposition to the values that Singleton exemplifies. This is the value of consciousness, about which I have already had something to say.

The novel's intermittent first-person narration has provoked its share of critical controversy. It has been considered whimsical and capricious; the consistency of its point of view has been challenged.[9] But rather than pursue discussion within such a normative context, we will do better to analyse the use of the narrator as part of the subjectivist perspective, which underlies Conrad's method here as elsewhere. For it is precisely the character of Singleton's heroism that it is a mute heroism. His taciturnity is as unbroken as his reliability. Such a conjunction is familiar in Conrad, particularly in this period: the capacity for work implies an abandonment of self-consciousness, a submergence of the intellectual function in the practical task at hand. Thus Singleton is the survivor of a generation which had been strong "as those are strong who know neither doubts nor hopes"; they were "voiceless men," "inarticulate and indispensable," "strong and mute." Of Singleton himself, we learn that the "thoughts of all his lifetime could have been expressed in six words."[10] We are not told which six.

Plainly, such a figure does not satisfy all the requirements identified in the novel's preface – he does not provide the registering temperament which might endow "passing events with their true meaning." But the novel's narrator does just that. The narrator, that is to say, is the fictional manifestation of the preface's demand for "temperament" or "a sincere mood." His appearance places incidents within the context of a perceiving subject, and this makes possible a more direct apprehension of meanings. The significance of an event need no longer be imputed or inferred; it is immediately accessible to the narrating consciousness. These are points that can be best elaborated through example. I quote at length a passage from the opening of the third chapter:

> They watched the weather and the ship as men on shore watch the momentous chances of fortune. Captain Allistoun never left the deck, as though he had been part of the ship's fittings. Now and then the steward, shivering, but always in shirt sleeves, would struggle towards him with some hot coffee, half of which the gale blew out of the cup before it reached the master's lips. He drank what was left gravely in one long gulp, while heavy sprays pattered loudly on his oilskin coat, the seas swishing broke about his high boots; and he never took his eyes off the ship. He kept his gaze riveted upon her as a loving man watches the unselfish toil of a delicate woman upon the slender thread of whose existence is hung the whole meaning and joy of the world. We all watched her. She was beautiful and had a weakness. We loved her no less for that. We admired her qualities aloud, we boasted of them to one another, as though they had been our own, and the consciousness of her only fault we kept buried in the silence of our profound affection. She was born in the thundering peal of hammers beating upon iron, in black eddies of smoke, under a grey sky, on the banks of the Clyde. The clamorous and sombre stream gives birth to things of beauty that float away into the sunshine of the world to be loved by men. The *Narcissus* was one of that perfect brood. Less perfect than many, perhaps, but she was ours, and, consequently, incomparable. We were proud of her. In Bombay, ignorant landlubbers alluded to her as that "pretty grey ship." Pretty! A scurvy meed of commendation! We knew she was the most magnificent sea-boat ever launched.[11]

Close reading of the passage should open large issues. Of most interest is the sudden appearance of the narrator and its consequences. The early part of the paragraph (before the shift to the first person) reveals Conrad's familiar descriptive virtues: the close attention to physical detail, the sensitivity to motion, the eye for the telling gesture. The prose is restrained, the narrative tone detached. Moreover, the sentences are of almost identical syntactic and rhetorical structure: a human subject ("they," "Captain Allistoun," "the steward") performs a physical action ("watched," "drank," etc.), and the subject or the action is then qualified – either through supplementary physical detail ("while heavy sprays pattered loudly") or through simile ("as though he had been part of the ship's fittings").

Indeed, the reliance on simile in the first half of the paragraph is striking. And this is a standard Conradian mannerism in third-person narration. Conrad depends then on metaphor or simile to *suggest* psychological attitudes or states, while he scrupulously avoids direct psychological speculation. Thus there are no explicit statements of attitude or emotion until the appearance of the first-person "we"; instead, simple actions (the way, for instance, the men watch the ship) are embellished with similes designed to *evoke* the intended psychological quality. We are not told that the crew "anguished" over the weather, only that they watched it "as men on shore watch the momentous chances of fortune." Nor are we told that the captain "loved" the ship, only that his gaze resembled the way "a loving man watches the unselfish toil," etc. Conrad here clings fastidiously to externals: he is reluctant to assign emotions directly to characters. Whereas his Victorian predecessors had allowed themselves unrestrained access to a character's consciousness, Conrad here inclines to restrict his attention to the directly available sensory surface. Precise devotion to physical detail becomes a way of defining a character's sensibility, as Captain Allistoun is defined through his movements and his glance. Ford would later describe this as a move towards a more scientific and realistic fiction, whose dictum was "Never state: present." [12] Whether Conrad formulated the issue in these terms is unclear. In any case, it is plain that the conventions of omniscience were breaking down, and that one result was an increased dependence on evocative physical description.

But the resources of description are only so great, and as the passage proceeds and emotion deepens, there is a complicating of prose strategies. Sentences become longer, their connotations more intricate. In the description of Allistoun's gaze, which occurs just before the shift to the first person, Conrad is obliged to resort to a highly complex and intellectualized comparison in order to suggest the depth of emotion: Allistoun is like a lover, the ship is like a woman, the woman is like a thread, and on the thread hangs meaning and joy.

Just at this moment, when there is a straining after emotion, the perspective abruptly alters: "We all watched her." The effect is of a sudden relaxing of tension. The measured restraint in the prose disappears; the dependence on simile disappears; sentence length begins to vary. Conrad employs a greater range of prose effects: on the one hand, the grandiloquence of phrases in series ("in the thundering peal . . . in black eddies . . . under a grey sky, on the banks of the Clyde") and an increased use of adjectives ("the clamorous and sombre stream"); on the other hand, the casualness of colloquial speech ("ignorant landlubbers"). In Conrad's hands, the first person exercises great rhetorical flexibility, and in general he abandons the explicit narrating consciousness (as, for instance, in *The Secret Agent*) only when he is not primarily interested in such flexibility, when he is content to maintain a consistent tone, especially of irony.

Once the leap into consciousness is made, no need remains for the painstaking *reconstruction* of subjectivity by means of accumulated detail or evocative metaphor. Psychology, emotion, attitude become immediately accessible. There need be no scruples about the text penetrating a consciousness, because the text has become identical with a consciousness. Where an author may not go, the narrator is entitled to tread because, as a fictional character, he may quite plausibly give utterance to his beliefs, perceptions, inferences. Conrad no longer hesitates to make direct statements of attitude or to use psychological verbs (e.g. "admired," "loved").

A passage from George Eliot will provide a useful context for these issues. What follows are the concluding paragraphs from chapter 61 of *Middlemarch*, when the banker Nicholas Bulstrode offers Will Ladislaw money, as a way of atoning for his mistreatment of Ladislaw's mother.

Bulstrode was going to speak, but Will with determined quickness was out of the room in an instant, and in another the hall-door had closed behind him. He was too strongly possessed with passionate rebellion against this inherited blot which had been thrust on his knowledge to reflect at present whether he had not been too hard on Bulstrode – too arrogantly merciless towards a man of sixty, who was making efforts at retrieval when time had rendered them vain.

No third person listening could have thoroughly understood the impetuosity of Will's repulse or the bitterness of his words. No one but himself then knew how everything connected with the sentiment of his own dignity had an immediate bearing for him on his relation to Dorothea and to Mr. Casaubon's treatment of him. And in the rush of impulses by which he flung back that offer of Bulstrode's, there was mingled the sense that it would have been impossible for him ever to tell Dorothea that he had accepted it.

As for Bulstrode – when Will was gone he suffered a violent reaction, and wept like a woman. It was the first time he had encountered an open expression of scorn from any man higher than Raffles; and with that scorn hurrying like venom through his system, there was no sensibility left to consolations. But the relief of weeping had to be checked. His wife and daughters soon came home from hearing the address of an Oriental missionary, and were full of regret that papa had not heard, in the first instance, the interesting things which they tried to repeat to him.

Perhaps, through all other hidden thoughts, the one that breathed most comfort, was that Will Ladislaw at least was not likely to publish what had taken place that evening.[13]

Part of every fiction is *physis*, the elaboration of an external physical space, and part is *psyche*, the construction of an internal psychological space. For George Eliot, as this passage reveals, the two regions open readily into one another: both submit to her narrating eye. As Ladislaw leaves the room, and the door closes behind him, the narrative does not follow him outside, but follows him, as it were, *inside*, to the interiority of consciousness. One enclosure gives way to another. A physical movement, located by walls and doors, becomes suddenly a psychological movement, marked out by "passionate rebellion," "impetuosity," "the rush of impulses." Casually, and without hesitation, George Eliot passes from externality to internality, from behaviour to consciousness, from a public to a private realm. Moreover, she does not restrict herself to Will's emotional architecture. With an abrupt transition – "As for Bulstrode" – she paces the length of the banker's psyche. What is noteworthy is the narrative licence. The text passes easily through space and time, over the boundaries of pesonality, into the recesses of emotional intimacy. Indeed George Eliot insists on the intimacy. "No third person listening," she writes, could have understood Will's bitterness. "No one but himself" can recognize the force of the incident. Here, then, is an exemplary private truth outside the reach of public knowledge.

But here also is irony. The very narrating voice which denies knowledge has knowledge. In the last paragraph Bulstrode's thoughts are described as "hidden thoughts," but they are not hidden from the narrator, who proceeds immediately to describe one: ". . . the one that breathed most comfort was that Will Ladislaw at least was not likely to publish what had taken place that evening." Ladislaw may be unlikely to publish it, but the narrator has just done so. The narrator, that is to say, is precisely the "third person listening" whose understanding is denied – then exemplified.

If George Eliot ignores such ironies, it is because she places her narrator above irony, in a different fictional region, where such considerations cease to apply. The narrator is not another character, but a disembodied presence, moving freely over the dramatic scene, and granted prerogatives not allowed to mere mortals. Without becoming implicated in the recorded scene, the narrator becomes an assimilating, amalgamating force who makes transparent the opacities between individuals, who lets moral evaluation mingle freely with description, who sees hidden thoughts quite as clearly as natural landscapes, who hears distinctly the faintest whispers of introspection.

George Eliot, of course, in seizing such privileges for the narrator, is following a well-established convention; what become distinctive in Conrad are the changes he works on that convention. In *The Nigger of the "Narcissus"* he makes what amounts to a division of narrative labour. The third-person narrator provides the precision of physical detail but hesitates to penetrate the individual psyche which George Eliot had so remorselessly invaded. Only with the shift to the first person is there a comfortable indulgence in moral and psychological speculation. Where George Eliot maintains the consistency of a single omniscient voice, Conrad here draws upon distinct voices, distinguishable points of view. While he is by no means systematic in his alternation between them, the shifts reveal the pressures upon an omniscience no longer confident that it knows all.

The rejection of omniscience was a complicated matter. Here, the point is not its causes but its immediate narrative consequences, and these, we can begin to see, lead in two directions, represented in the Conrad passage by the third-person and first-person perspectives. One tendency is toward a physical description confined to sensory detail, the other toward the creation of characters who can assume the traditional functions of the omniscient narrator (though, of course, on a more modest scale): to direct attention, to interpret incidents, to evaluate behaviour.

The passage from *The Nigger of the "Narcissus"* repeats, then, the tension in the novel's preface and implicitly attains the same conclusion. Devotion to the visible universe stands at some point in need of a witnessing consciousness which can organize surface reality and ratify its meanings. This may explain why the first person appears most often in the novel in contexts of emotional or moral stress (Wait's first malingering, the storm, the parting of the crew), for in just these instances does narrative by physical detail become most limiting. The fiction seems to require an explicit conscious agent, whose responses can validate the progression of events. Nowhere is this more apparent than in the novel's final pages, when the generalized "we" becomes the more obtrusive, though still unnamed, "I":

Outside, on Tower Hill, they blinked, hesitated clumsily, as if blinded by the strange quality of the hazy light, as if discomposed by the view of so many men; and they who could hear one another in the howl of gales seemed deafened and distracted by the dull roar of the busy earth. "To the Black Horse! To the Black Horse!" cried some. "Let us have a drink together before we part." They crossed the road, clinging to one another. Only Charley and Belfast wandered off alone. As I came up I saw a red-faced, blowsy woman, in a grey shawl, and with dusty, fluffy hair, fall on Charley's neck.[14]

This is the first time in the novel that the "I" (as opposed to the "we") "comes up" – and Conrad's choice of phrase is apt. For in a sense, here and elsewhere, the narrator indeed "comes up," ascending from the midst of events. Invariably he appears in the middle or at the end of a paragraph, delicately altering perspectives; with his appearances, the text struggles towards self-consciousness, towards a reflecting human presence which will ensure due consideration for the unreflecting, the unconscious, the merely factual. In this last case, the crew is dispersing, and the novel is threatened with a premature and understated conclusion. The return to the narrator makes possible a sustained moral summary which guarantees appropriate depth of emotion and provides the coherence of an individual perspective. "The permanence of memory," wrote Conrad, is "the only possible form of permanence in this world of relative values."[15] Singleton has a "vast empty past." The narrator, on the other hand, has the past alone, and in the last paragraphs of The Nigger of the "Narcissus" he effects the passage from event into sanctifying memory, from fact into consciousness.

Arnold, Huxley, Pater: toward a small world and a large self

Before going forward, let us retreat slightly further back – this is the occupational hazard of genealogy – in order to place modernist clangour against a Victorian harmony, or what would pass for harmony in the later, more dissonant, age. For reasons soon to be apparent, we might begin with Arnold on religion. Though the details of his position are intricate, even baroque, the main lines of argument are accessible and clear. Arnold himself managed to give succinct expression to his aim: "The object of Literature and Dogma is to re-assure those who feel attachment to Christianity, to the Bible, but who recognise the growing discredit befalling miracles and the supernatural."[16]

This represents a familiar Victorian concern, but the striking thing about Arnold's contribution is his willingness to revise Christianity in order to retain it. Science had been the great contemporary antagonist of religion but, rather than contest the scientific worldview, Arnold chooses to appropriate it: "Whatever is to stand must rest upon something which is verifiable, not unverifiable."[17] Arnold, that is to say, concedes without argument the root empirical premise, the principle of verifiability. He makes the concession, because he denies that it is a concession. Properly conceived, properly defined, science is to be religion's stay. The goal becomes the grounding of religion on a sound empirical basis, and the method of Literature and Dogma is then to show that, when we come to put the right construction on the Bible, we give to the Bible a real experimental basis, and keep on this basis throughout; instead of any basis of unverifiable assumption to start with, followed by a string of other unverifiable assumptions of like kind, such as the received theology necessitates.[18]

Such is Arnold's project. It is perhaps the blithest and most ingenuous of the Victorian efforts towards synthesis. In the name of science, dogma is to be abandoned, miracles are to be abandoned, a personal divinity is to be abandoned – they exceed the bounds of "experiment." The supernatural and the miraculous are obsolete: "belief in them has given way": to restore the Bible "in the literal sense" would be "as impossible as to restore the feudal system, or the belief in witches." "By the sanction of miracles Christianity can no longer stand; it can stand only by its natural truth."[19]

And where lies this natural truth? – in the human consciousness of certain psychological experiences, in "personal experience." The true meaning of religion implies nothing otherworldly; it is, in Arnold's formulation, simply "morality touched by emotion."[20] Religion must be based upon human experience. Indeed experience, as Trilling rightly says, "is the key-word to Arnold's religious discussion."[21] It makes possible the desired *rapprochement* with science, for religion, much like physics, is now to rest – not on an "axiomatic basis," not on "false notion-work" – but on immediate perception.[22] If Christianity can be translated into these terms – as an aspect of "personal experience" rather than as a supernatural apparatus – then, thinks Arnold, its foundation will be secured. Unquestionably, this means the abandonment of much once deemed essential. But "if we want here, as we do want, to have what is admittedly certain and verifiable, we must content ourselves with very little."[23]

The task, then, which Arnold sets for himself, is one of redefinition; religion must be "recast." Of a Personal First Cause we can have no genuine acquaintance. But we have an immediate perception of certain primary religious categories: "Eternal," "Righteousness," "not ourselves." These are verifiable data, insists Arnold, and we would profit by making our conceptions of deity correspond to such incontestable perceptions. Accordingly, he suggests that we redefine divinity in the light of these concepts. We are no longer to speak of an identifiable personal God but of "*the Eternal Power not ourselves, that makes for righteousness.*" [24]

This, in outline, is Arnold's argument. Though its occasion, its context and its point are religious, its significance extends further. Most noteworthy for our present purposes is the way that a formerly extra-individual category (the God of creation) has been located on grounds of individual consciousness. Any transcendent character has been abandoned; religious force is now to be derived from human psychology. And here two tendencies must be distinguished. The first has to do with the rejection of transcendence, the abandonment of religious supernaturalism. This, of course, was a predominant tendency in nineteenth-century thought. Ludwig Feuerbach was an early and avid exponent, and Feuerbach's translator, George Eliot, was an eager defender of that attitude:

My books have for their main bearing a conclusion . . . without which I could not have cared to write any representation of human life – namely, that the fellowship between man and man which has been the principle of development, social and moral, is not dependent on conceptions of what is not man: and that the idea of God, so far as it has been a high spiritual influence, is the ideal of a goodness entirely human.[25]

Here is religion secularized, humanized and modernized. George Eliot is boldly confident of the result, as is Arnold when he intimates the superseding of religion by poetry:

The future of poetry is immense, because in poetry, where it is worthy of its high destinies, our race, as time goes on, will find an ever surer and surer stay. There is not a creed which is not shaken, not an accredited dogma which is not shown to be questionable, not a received tradition which does not threaten to dissolve. Our religion has materialized itself in the fact, in the supposed fact; it has attached its emotion to the fact, and now the fact is failing it. But for poetry the idea is everything; the rest is a world of illusion, of divine illusion. Poetry attaches its emotion to the idea; the idea *is* the fact. The strongest part of our religion to-day is its unconscious poetry.[26]

But the secularizing process, as now seems to us inevitable, carried further than it knew. A second and allied tendency began to emerge in the latter half of the century. This was the retreat, not just to this world, but to individual psychology, personal experience, "religious consciousness." Arnold entertains the question: "How are we to *verify* that there rules an enduring Power, not ourselves, which makes for righteousness?" To this he immediately responds: "as you verify that fire burns, – by experience!"[27] Religion is thus assimilated to the most elementary cognitive process, the trial and error of individual contact with reality. Secularizing is thus radicalized into psychologizing.

This second part of the process is worth stressing because it represents an increasingly pronounced tendency in Victorian thought. It appears, for instance, in Mill's attempt in *Utilitarianism* (by way of patently fallacious reasoning) to derive an altruistic morality from an egoistic basis: "No reason can be given why the general happiness is desirable, except that each person, so far as he believes it to be attainable, desires his own happiness . . . each person's happiness is a good to that person, and the general happiness, therefore, a good to the aggregate of all persons."[28] It appears likewise in Tennyson's persistent attempt to conjoin the expression of self and of community, to identify the poet with the good citizen. Thus of *In Memoriam* he would comment: "'I' is not always the author speaking of himself, but the voice of the human race speaking through him."[29]

Taken together, these attitudes constitute an almost poignant moment in English cultural history, when a loss was made to seem a gain. Traditional justifications of value had lapsed, but this is seen less as a cause for regret than as an opportunity. Value will be given a firmer grounding, more in line with inevitable historical development: human subjectivity will become the foundation and support for a range of threatened institutions. If religion has lost its dogmatic basis, that is so much the better as far as Arnold is concerned, because dogma can provide only a spurious foundation, and its deterioration makes possible a return to roots of religion within consciousness. So, too, if morality cannot maintain its traditional dogmatic character, then Mill (following Bentham) is quite willing to ground it on psychological principles – most notably the desire for individual happiness. Large areas of traditional conviction are abandoned without regret.

What is striking among these figures (though certainly not among others) is that neither secularism nor subjectivism is conceived as an abandonment of perennially valued human activity. The notion is rather that cultural forces will achieve a new balance, in a humanism which does not threaten religion and an individualism that does not jeopardize community. All meanings are to derive from immediately given facts of human experience. There are to be no autonomous bodies of knowledge or belief; systems of thought achieve significance only as organized by human psychology. No effort is made to *replace* religion, morality or aesthetics – they are to be translated into psychological terms without losing their force.

It may already be apparent how the mid-century ascendancy of science ratified this displacement in the direction of subjectivity. For the rigour of science depended on the scrupulous attention to what appears directly to perception. All that we can ever know of things, wrote T. H. Huxley, is "under the shape of a bundle of our own consciousness." Matter and motion "are known to us only as forms of consciousness"; indeed, "all the phænomena of Nature are, in their ultimate analysis, known to us only as facts of consciousness." The business of science is certainty, and "unquestionable certainty," in brief, belongs only "to the existence of a state of consciousness so long as it exists."[30]

From where we now stand, we can recognize revolutionary implications in such an extreme empiricist position. But Huxley saw it as new stability. "[S]cience and her methods," he once wrote to Kingsley, "gave me a resting-place independent of authority and tradition."[31] "Resting-place" will sound strange. What rest did Victorian culture receive when it exchanged traditional authority for aggressive empiricism? But Huxley envisioned none of the crises toward which his cult of scientific subjectivism so clearly points. He was decided, unwavering, polemical. Praising David Hume's attack on metaphysics, he wrote:

Near a century and a half has elapsed since these brave words were shaped by David Hume's pen; and the business of carrying the war into the enemy's camp has gone on but slowly. Like other campaigns it long languished for want of a good base of operations. But since physical science, in the course of the last fifty years, has brought to the front an inexhaustible supply of heavy artillery of a new pattern, warranted to drive solid bolts of fact through the thickest skulls, things are looking better.[32]

Within this configuration of individualizing tendencies, one further element demands notice: the self-celebrating independence of the middle-class at mid-century. The phenomenon has been much remarked; we need only to emphasize a single aspect: the sense of personal emancipation from obsolete external constraints. Samuel Smiles' *Self-Help*, an immense popular success, provides the classic statement of the attitude. In its opening paragraph appears the following remark:

Help from without is often enfeebling in its effects, but help from within invariably invigorates. Whatever is done *for* men or classes, to a certain extent takes away the stimulus and necessity of doing for themselves; and where men are subjected to over-guidance and over-government, the inevitable tendency is to render them comparatively helpless.[33]

Smiles' distinction here is exactly to the point. "Within" is celebrated at the expense of "without": to rely on external sanction, guidance, authority is to be reduced to abject dependence. Smiles' book becomes a catalogue of achievements in self-help, from Richard Arkwright to Wellington and Disraeli. Such boundless complacency was a target which Arnold, for one, would mercilessly attack. But the manifest differences between an Arnold and a Smiles ought not to obscure some fundamental similarities in outlook. For Smiles, in his rough-and-ready way, gives expression to the same impulse we have been charting in other areas, the desire to dismiss external and traditional norms and to make the independent individual the ground of value.

This Victorian perspective has been worth articulating, because it represents a particular intellectual equilibrium, short-lived but influential, which stands at the antipodes from the developed modernist programme. Much modernist antipathy was directed at this ideology: it is therefore worth keeping in the background. Moreover, its disintegration opened the way for a new play of forces.

"The gospel of Pater follows naturally upon the prophecy of Arnold."[34] T. S. Eliot is here characteristically unfair to

Arnold. It would be as accurate to lay blame at the feet of Mill,
Tennyson, Ruskin or Rossetti. But Eliot is no doubt right in
seeing Pater as the heir to Victorian compromise: his work
represents the undoing of the mid-century synthesis. He
accepts Mill's psychological hedonism without the system of
morality which it generates. He attends to Arnold's literature
but neglects his dogma. What he does – in short and decisively –
is to oversee the withdrawal of subjectivity from the realm of
fact. The point is worth elaborating, and we may best do so by
considering Pater's most celebrated piece of writing, the
conclusion to *The Renaissance*.

The conclusion of the "Conclusion" is well known: "to burn
always with this hard, gem-like flame," "to be for ever
curiously testing new opinions and courting new impressions,"
"to set the spirit free for a moment."[35] These need no
reiteration. Nor do their consequences for late-century aestheticism. If this were all that were at issue, Pater would occupy only
a peripheral place in the tradition. But it is the generally
neglected opening of the argument, the conclusion's premise,
which has more immediate bearing.

Pater, like Arnold, begins with science. He, too, acknowledges its irrefutable empirical claims. But where Arnold welcomes this as an opportunity for certainty, Pater underscores the
sceptical and destructive vision, the undermining of principles
of constancy, the rigorous theoretical analysis of physical life
into "a combination of natural elements." His "Conclusion"
opens by arguing that the external world is "flamelike," the
"concurrence, renewed from moment to moment, of forces
parting sooner or later on their ways." Any pattern which we
perceive is "but an image of ours." At first sight, says Pater,
"experience seems to bury us under a flood of external objects,
pressing upon us with a sharp and importunate reality." But the
moment "reflexion" comes into play, such objects "are
dissipated under its influence."[36]

Although expressed in more obviously sceptical terms,
Pater's attack is compatible with Arnold's "dissipating" of
traditional religion, the conversion of God into a collection of
concepts: "The Eternal Not Ourselves That Makes for Righteousness." Pater, however, carries the destructive process still

further. Having dismissed the external world, he turns attention to the "inward world of thought," where the whirlpool becomes "still more rapid, the flame more eager and devouring." "The whole scope of observation is dwarfed into the narrow chamber of the individual mind." In a famous phrase, he continues: "Every one of those impressions is the impression of the individual in his isolation, each mind keeping as a solitary prisoner its own dream of a world." [37] The process is not yet complete; analysis "goes a step farther still." The mental impressions themselves exhibit no constancy or integrity; they are in "perpetual flight," "limited by time" and "infinitely divisible": "To such a tremulous wisp constantly reforming itself on the stream, to a single sharp impression, with a sense in it, a relic more or less fleeting, of such moments gone by, what is real in our life fines itself down." [38]

It was this limiting, this "fining down," of reality that Arnold and Mill had resisted even as they prepared it. But Pater welcomes a process which will confine attention to sensation, perception and reflection, and which (in his interpretation) will ignore the obligation of theorizing. "We shall hardly have time," he writes, "to make theories about the things we see and touch." [39]

In the set of attitudes so far described, subjectivity had existed in equilibrium with the large world beyond it. Though certainty was allowed to exist only within the self, this was a cause for little distress, since the self was to contain the ground of morality, religion, even the construction of external reality. Pursue happiness, Mill had said, and you will pursue morality. Restrict yourself to "personal experience," advised Arnold, and you will experience religion. But Pater saw, or perhaps merely felt, that such restriction was not without consequence. He recognized, and no doubt correctly, that to redefine traditional values as phases of the self was to weaken traditional sanctions. Like others, he was intent on restricting attention to the psychologically verifiable, but he had no illusions (or scruples) about rescuing morality, religion or the external world. Pater followed relentlessly the logic of immediacy, acknowledging the primacy of the subjective but denying its necessary connection with extrasubjective concerns. The consequence was a bifurcation into a realm of fact and a realm of subjective consciousness. Value was to reside within consciousness, and all other value became derivative: "The service of philosophy, of speculative culture, towards the human spirit, is to rouse, to startle it to a life of constant and eager observation."[40]

The human spirit is now served, rather than serving philosophy and culture reduced to mental stimulants. Pater, we might say, not only took the subjectivist tendency seriously: he recognized what it would portend. If subjectivity was indeed the locus of experience, and hedonism the pre-eminent psychological fact, then connections to morality and religion became strained and factitious.

Arnold had looked to scientific subjectivism as the occasion for a new religious certainty. In pursuit of cultural stability, traditional belief was to be reinterpreted in terms of personal experience; and although, as Arnold admitted, such reinterpretation had less imaginative force, it offered the security of a verifiable truth which could withstand the pressure of scientific standards. Subjectivity and subjective mental processes became the historically appropriate justification. But subjectivity was a double-edged sword. In the hands of Pater, it was used not only to cut away the metaphysical, but also the traditionally moral, the traditionally religious, the objective and the permanent. For if these are simply shorthand appellations for psychological phenomena, then it is but a small step towards the discarding of such categories altogether. Pater took a series of such steps.

In the essay on "Style" Pater writes that "just in proportion as the writer's aim, consciously or unconsciously, comes to be the transcribing, not of the world, not of mere fact, but of his sense of it, he becomes an artist, his work *fine* art."[41] This is the literary application of the distinction outlined above: on the one side fact, on the other side sensation, perception or consciousness. Aesthetic value resides in the latter region, as an attribute of the perceiving or conceiving subject, and so becomes distinct from "mere fact," from the quotidian, the mechanical, the objective.

What is new here, however, is not the opposition but its imbalance. In *Culture and Anarchy* Arnold had introduced his well-known distinction between Hebraism and Hellenism – the aim of the former being "conduct and obedience" and that of the latter "to see things as they really are."[42] Hebraism, according to Arnold, was the dominant contemporary perspective, and much of his purpose in *Culture and Anarchy* was to vindicate the claims of the countervailing Hellenic impulse. But he is intent to avoid the error of disproportion; though he acknowledges ineffaceable differences in method and perspective, he denies any need to choose between the two: "Hebraism and Hellenism are, neither of them, the *law* of human development, as their admirers are prone to make them; they are, each of them, *contributions* to human development."[43]

Arnold, then, arrives at a calculated balance between extremes. But for Pater, as we have seen, the equilibrium has come undone; the Hebraist principle recedes into irrelevance, and hope lies with the Hellenes. "Not the fruit of experience," writes Pater, "but experience itself, is the end," and the "theory or idea or system which requires of us the sacrifice of any part of this experience, in consideration of some interest into which we cannot enter, or some abstract theory we have not identified with ourselves, or of what is only conventional, has no real claim upon us."[44]

The step is a critical one. It is not a move (not primarily, not most notably) in the direction of aestheticism. It is towards what we would better call psychologism: not life for art's sake, but life *and* art for the sake of a "quickened multiple consciousness" – consciousness as a source of value and a refuge from experience. Quite evidently, such a position has literary consequences more profound than the aestheticism of *The Yellow Book*.

The moment is opportune for a return to Conrad, whose work after *The Nigger of the "Narcissus"* reveals the increasingly dominant ascendancy of consciousness, an ascendancy which will become a matter of explicit thematic concern. "Facts" become a specific literary target. Thus in *Lord Jim*, Jim's first response to the trial is described in this way: "They wanted facts. Facts! They demanded facts from him, as if facts could explain anything!"[45] And later Marlow continues:

"There was no incertitude as to facts – as to the one material fact, I mean . . . Yet, as I've told you, all the sailors in the port attended, and the waterside business was fully represented. Whether they knew it or not, the interest that drew them there was purely psychological – the expectation of some essential disclosure as to the strength, the power, the horror, of human emotions."[46]

The point worth reiterating is that, in the opposition between fact and psychology, deeper interest lies on the psychological side. It would distort matters to claim that Conrad formulated an established position on this issue or that his sympathies were consistently on the side of consciousness. For every one of Marlow's jibes at unthinking complacency, there is an example, such as the Malay helmsman, where heroism precludes introspection. At the thematic level the conflict between work and consciousness remains persistent and unresolved.

More interesting are the developments in literary method. These comprise a number of narrative features, but the stratagem of "Marlow" is paramount. About his role much has been said; I will restrict myself to pointing out his place within the development I have been following: for in Paterian terms, he confirms the triumph of "sense of fact" over "fact." He completes what was inchoate in The Nigger of the "Narcissus" and embodies the psychologistic premise, namely that the meaning of a phenomenon is its presence to a mind. Part of his role in Lord Jim is to redeem Jim from sudden moral deterioration – he is a guardian of the personality. But at another and more general level of analysis, his position is to redeem the tale from moral simplicity – he is a proprietor of meanings. His first sentence in Lord Jim is revealing in its directness: "Oh yes." Not description, not self-identification, no positing of dramatic principles – simply the abrupt contact between subject and world.

Ford liked to claim that the justification for a narrator was realism. To this claim I will return. But what I am arguing is that there is another criterion than verisimilitude, a criterion of significance. And though James and Conrad differed widely on a range of aesthetic and moral principles, on this issue they converged. A few details of that convergence will make for useful recapitulation.

The preface to The Ambassadors echoes Conrad's preface of a decade earlier. "Art deals with what we see," writes James there; "it must first contribute full-handed that ingredient; it plucks its material, otherwise expressed, in the garden of life . . . ."[47] The parallel would be slight if it went no further. But James, having acknowledged the importance of "what we see," immediately insists on a further and supplementary process: "the expression, the literal squeezing-out, of value." He calls this the "infusion" that "completes the strong mixture."[48] Here appears the dual movement which I have emphasized: the initial commitment to life's surface and the subsequent enhancement provided by subjectivity. James, then, repeats the Conradian trope sketched above: the shift from the merely visible to the valuable.

There should be no misunderstanding. Neither Conrad nor James advocates an abandonment of the visible surface; they rather hold that such a surface is insufficient, and that the completed aesthetic gesture resides in the relation of event to subject. "I confess," writes James in the preface to *The Princess Casamasssima*, "I never see the *leading* interest of any human hazard but in a consciousness (on the part of the moved and moving creature) subject to fine intensification and wide enlargement."[49] And later: "This in fact I have ever found rather terribly the point – that the figures in any picture, the agents in any drama, are interesting only in proportion as they feel their respective situations; since the consciousness, on their part, of the complication exhibited forms for us their link of connexion with it."[50] At issue is the establishment of a "psychologistic" theory of literary meaning which insists on the primacy of consciousness and the muteness of the mere event. Quite obviously, this is to incline towards subjectivism. But the move is distinct from an idealist's doubt of external reality. The *meaning* of the physical reality, not its independent existence, is called into question. There is not so much a question of *esse est percipi* (to be is to be perceived) as *significare est percipi* (to mean is to be perceived).

In this regard, the choice of metaphors is instructive. James, in defending the claims of the mind, calls it a "reflecting and colouring medium," a phrase which recalls Conrad's "light of a sincere mood" or his notion of "the moral, the emotional atmosphere."[51] Where the realm of fact is inert, dim and lifeless – "mere bald facts," writes Conrad in *Under Western Eyes*[52] – consciousness is a medium of illumination. Literary meaning, that is, can no longer exist simply through what James calls "the tangle of human relations";[53] the requirement of "intelligibility" demands that incidents and relations become available to a supervening light-giving consciousness.

In another and especially suggestive image, James speaks of Conrad's method as "a prolonged hovering flight of the subjective over the outstretched ground of the case exposed."[54] The spatial figure captures the point nicely, confirming as it does the dualism. The plane of incident and plot, the "case," remains a static expanse, while deeper literary interest lies on another plane altogether – in the movement of a subjectivity that has disengaged itself from two dimensions. By implication, subjectivity stands in opposition to ordinary objective processes – in terms of the metaphor, its prolonged flight violates the laws of gravitational attraction. Plainly, such defiance of the objective represents a positive achievement for James, an overcoming of inhibiting constraint, an emancipation into a loftier and more expansive aesthetic space. "Hovering" is apt. For in James' two-level image, subjectivity does not stand in a fixed correspondence to objectivity; it does not occupy a simple determinate place in a two-term relation. It possesses rather a free play of movement, hovering where it will, while the "ground" of the "case" remains immobile. The image then provides a convenient closing formulation for the development I have been tracing: the disintegration of stable balanced relations between subject and object and the consequent enshrining of consciousness as the repository of meaning and value.

CHAPTER 2

Authority

Arnold and Babbitt: the best self and the new humanism

"The end of art," wrote Yeats in *The Cutting of an Agate*, "is the ecstasy awakened by the presence before an ever-changing mind of what is permanent in the world, or by the arousing of that mind itself into the very delicate and fastidious mood habitual with it when it is seeking those permanent and recurring things."[1] T. S. Eliot, reviewing the book in 1919, cites the remark and then asks: "Why introduce the mind? why not say – the recognition of the permanent in the changing . . ."[2] Yeats' insistent intrusion of the mental is for Eliot a lapse of some magnitude. He makes it the basis for a severe criticism of Yeats in particular, Irish literature more generally. Both tend towards egoism, and the difficulty with egoism is that it blurs the poetic object; "Mr. Yeats's dream is identified with Mr. Yeats's reality." In Joyce, egoism is exploited "to the point of greatness," but in Yeats' portraits "we do not seem to get the men themselves before us, but feelings of Mr. Yeats projected."[3] Yeats would no doubt happily concur. In *The Cutting of an Agate*, he directs the artist to "think less of what he sees and more of his own attitude towards it . . ."[4]

All of this should establish Yeats' relation to the subjectivist tradition, but that is not the principal lesson to be drawn from the episode. More important is Eliot's hostility, and the shape it assumes. For what we have traced until now is the progressive centrality of self as a register of meanings, literary and otherwise, and the dependence on consciousness as the repository of value. Eliot rejects just this point – "Why introduce the mind?" – and, in so rejecting it, he commits himself to a contending literary perspective. The review of Yeats preceded

23

"Tradition and the Individual Talent" by only two months, and quite plainly the attack on egoism prefigures the later talk of "impersonality" and "objectivity." But this did not begin with Eliot, though Eliot brought the ideas renown.

Our present task will be to trace the development of this "objective" tendency explicitly opposed to subjectivism, to indicate its early appearance in the movement and its early consequences, and to begin by briefly returning to Arnold. At first sight, this may appear curious. Arnold was without question committed to the values of mind, no one more so. His apology for culture, his pursuit of disinterestedness, his Hellenism, all move in this direction. They are a sustained appeal for a consciousness which might exceed and enhance utilitarian "machinery." As such, they conform to the tendency in his religious thought already described: the demand for a religious consciousness rather than the sanctions of dogma as the decisive factor in any religious doctrine. "Wherever the free play of our consciousness leads us," Arnold once wrote, "we shall follow."[5]

But Arnold was susceptible to a range of intellectual pressures. Since the pressures often opposed one another, his thought was not free from ambiguity, or even contradiction. As Eliot saw, Arnold was in many ways responsible for the later cultivation of impression and sensation. If he did not spawn Pater, he at least made Pater plausible. But that development, we should recognize, was a matter of as much concern to Arnold as it would later be to Eliot. And this side of Arnold's thought now becomes of interest: the reaction against egoism, sensation and anarchy. The point is well expressed in an early letter to Clough:

As Browning is a man with a moderate gift passionately desiring movement and fulness, and obtaining but a confused multitudinousness, so Keats with a very high gift, is yet also consumed by this desire: and cannot produce the truly living and moving, as his conscience keeps telling him. They will not be patient neither understand that they must begin with an Idea of the world in order not to be prevailed over by the world's multitudinousness.[6]

This would become a standard Arnoldian demand: the need for a principle of organization to offset the drift towards sensuousness and disorder. He would later complain of the "premature" character of English romanticism, its failure to "know enough," its inattention to the "critical effort" – a neglect which made "Byron so empty of matter, Shelley so incoherent, Wordsworth even, profound as he is, yet so wanting in completeness and variety." In the face of these hazards, Arnold came to plead for a controlling critical authority which might restrain the excesses of private indulgence.[7]

Nowhere is the appeal more direct than in the essay on "The Literary Influence of Academies," a reflection "upon the absence, in our own country, of any institution like the French Academy, upon the probable causes of this absence, and upon its results."[8] The essay is a careful, prodding analysis of the limits of the English literary character, its extravagance, its lack of conscience, lack of balance, lack of critical standards – all of which Arnold associates with the absence of an academy. English literature, he concedes, has had supreme and indisputable successes, but in the absence of a "recognized authority," it has revealed its "note of provinciality," which has led to disproportion and imprecision. Against these native deficiencies, he sets the example of the French, whose academy has made possible a measured precision of style, which, according to Arnold, accounts for the superiority of French to English prose. He praises, for instance, the style of Thiers, whose virtues he attributes to "being formed in a good school, with severe traditions, wholesome restraining influences." English prose has no such characteristic virtues, because "the less a literature has felt the influence of a supposed centre of correct information, correct judgment, correct taste, the more we shall find in it this note of provinciality." Correctness is the virtue which the English sorely miss. Arnold goes on to juxtapose specimens of French and English prose, working to this conclusion: "where there is no centre like an academy, if you have genius and powerful ideas, you are apt not to have the best style going; if you have precision of style and not genius, you are apt not to have the best ideas going." But having drawn this conclusion, having insisted on the "provincial spirit" of the English intellectual, he hesitates to recommend an academy. Nations "have their own modes of acting, and these modes are not easily changed"; the English will never have an academy like the French, though they may have academies "with a limited, special, scientific scope."[9] Arnold's pursuit of authority stops short of its object.

The hesitation is revealing and reveals still more when set in the context of Arnold's thought. In the "Doing as One Likes" chapter of *Culture and Anarchy*, he addresses a similar problem described now in political terms: "the anarchical tendency of our worship of freedom in and for itself." The prevailing notion – "that it is a most happy and important thing for a man merely to be able to do as he likes" – has led to "random and ill-regulated action," which goes unchecked in "a system which stops and paralyses any power in interfering with the free action of individuals." The situation has been so aggravated – Arnold is thinking of the riots in Hyde Park – that the nation is "in danger of drifting towards anarchy." What is needed is a principle of order, a vision of the nation "in its collective and corporate character."[10] "But how," asks Arnold, "to organize this authority, or to what hands to entrust the wielding of it?" "And here," he continues, "I think I see my enemies waiting for me with a hungry joy in their eyes. But I shall elude them."[11]

The remark has been cited as an example of Arnoldian urbanity. It is that, but it is also an example of Arnoldian ambiguity. For his eluding is curious. Arnold proceeds to investigate the claims of each class as a satisfactory source of authority. Each is found wanting. Each is bound by endemic defects and limitations. But, suggests Arnold, suppose "we rise above the idea of class to the idea of the whole community, the *State*." The idea is rarely considered; the state is not regarded as a working hypothesis. "And why? Because we habitually live in our ordinary selves, which do not carry us beyond the ideas and wishes of the class to which we happen to belong."[12]

But the basis for a "firm State-power" does not lie in any class; it lies "in our *best self*." In our ordinary selves, we affirm individual class interest: "we are separate, personal, at war; we are only safe from one another's tyranny when no one has any power; and this safety, in its turn, cannot save us from anarchy." "But by our *best self*, we are united, impersonal, at harmony"; "our best self inspires faith, and is capable of affording a serious principle of authority." The state is the "organ of our collective best self": "We are in no peril from giving authority to this, because it is the truest friend we all of us can have; and when anarchy is a danger to us, to this authority we may turn with sure trust."[13]

A division at the centre of Victorian ideology stands revealed. In one stroke Arnold has abandoned hope in liberalist laissez-faire and has sought to transcend the class character of capitalist society. He looks to the state as his "principle of authority" which will restrain the individualism of "doing as one likes." And yet, when he comes to establish a basis for the state, he depends on the very individualism he has set out to contest. He does not look to tradition or moral dogma, but to the self, albeit the best self. The check he proposes *for* the self remains *within* the self; the proposal amounts to a voluntarist appeal to better nature. Confronted by the egoistic individualism of liberal philosophy, Arnold tries to contest the egoism while conceding the individualist premise. He perceives the failure of a moral order based on self-interest, but he envisions no solution beyond the self. What he offers is an inner articulation of the self, an authority from within, self-generated, self-imposed.

In *The Use of Poetry and the Use of Criticism*, T. S. Eliot speaks of Arnold as belonging to a "period of stasis." Eliot then amends this to a "period of relative and precarious stability" and finally concludes that it was a period of "false stability."[14] Arnold, he argues, is the representative figure of a false stability. This is a rather peremptory historical judgment: between the false stability of the Victorians and the true instability of the moderns there may be little to choose. Still, there is a rough justice to Eliot's assessment. One can indeed recognize in *Culture and Anarchy* – as in *Literature and Dogma* – the attempt to straddle a contradiction whose extremes were growing rapidly apart. If Arnold's thought ranged widely, it was perhaps because his culture stretched it so far. On the one side, it inclined toward a self-cultivation which ignored restraining influences – this way lay Pater and aestheticism. But in the other direction, it moved toward authority, a willed rejection of the individualizing habit. Sensitive to the problem, Arnold was cautious in his response. It remained for others to be uncompromising and incautious, and here lies the significance of Irving Babbitt. Deeply indebted to Arnold, concerned with the same set of problems, Babbitt happily carries the Arnoldian premises to a more extreme conclusion,

Babbitt's "new humanism" arose from the same political and literary anxiety which had troubled Arnold: the prevailing laxity of intellectual and moral character in an age dominated by liberal democracy and natural science. Set against the general decline, humanism offered a return to standards, and Babbitt was aggressively unsentimental about the depth of the problem. He called for an abandonment of the ideal of progress, a thoroughgoing rejection of democratic and individualist values. These were distortions which only veiled the underlying reality: "what we see on every hand in our modern society, when we get beneath its veneer of scientific progress, is barbaric violation of the law of measure." In the name of "humanitarianism," complains Babbitt, rigour and discipline have been lost, with the result that "ethical values themselves are in danger of being swept away in the everlasting flux." [15] Literary criticism has suffered a similar fate: in the general drift towards flexibility, criticism "has grown so flexible in fact as to become invertebrate." Humanism, on the other hand (he cites Aulus Gellius here), "really implies doctrine and discipline, and is applicable not to men in general but only to a select few, – it is, in short, aristocratic and not democratic in its implication." [16]

The development is a notable one. Arnold had acknowledged certain historical inevitabilities. As a "liberal of the future," he accepted, even professed to welcome, the move towards democracy, experimental science, and the "general expansion" of culture. If he pressed the claims of authority, it was an authority always considered provisional, in line with Joubert's maxim: "Force till right is ready." Arnold looked to a mitigating of utilitarian vulgarity, an extension of culture comparable to the extension of the suffrage. He hoped for a gradual overcoming of English provincialism, an accommodation between criticism and spontaneity, Hellenism and Hebraism, French prose and English poetry. He studiously avoided partisanship; he aimed always to achieve a calculated poising between extremes.[17]

Babbitt abandons the poise. Liberal democracy, which he habitually refers to as "Rousseauist democracy" or "pseudo-democracy," is an aberration, not a necessity. He derides the attempt to extend culture; far from a solution, this has aggravated the problem. What Arnold had taken to be historical necessities, Babbitt considers unfortunate romantic deviations. Babbitt offered such views throughout his career, but for our present purposes *Masters of Modern French Criticism*, which appeared in 1912, is his crucial publication. The book's ostensible subject is a history of nineteenth-century French criticism (he cites Arnold to validate the subject's importance), but the argument is inspired by contemporary issues. Indeed, Babbitt justifies the study as an attempt to provide background "for the proper understanding of the ideas of our own day." The concluding chapter largely deserts the French in order to oppose Goethe and Emerson as a way of confronting "the chief problem of criticism, namely, the search for standards to oppose to individual caprice."[18]

"With the progress of democracy," he writes, "one man's opinion in literature has come to be as good as another's." The result has been the untempered assertion of individual judgment, which from Babbitt's standpoint has proved fatal to the critical enterprise. As its most unhappy consequence, it has led to the ascendancy of Impressionist criticism, in which "present sensations and impressions are to be made the measure of all things." The Impressionist, complains Babbitt, "is interested in a book only as it relates itself to his sensibility . . ."[19] A quotation from Anatole France characterizes the position: "All of us judge everything by our own measure. How could we do otherwise, since to judge is to compare, and we have only one measure, which is ourselves; and this measure is constantly changing? We are all of us the sport and playthings of mobile appearances."[20]

The sentiment is close to Pater, as Babbitt himself points out, but its suggestions go further. The remark stands as an effective statement of central subjectivist propositions: that there is no reality beyond the reality that appears, that we are therefore confined to private vision and that in consequence "we have only one measure which is ourselves." Such a critical attitude is for Babbitt a cultural catastrophe: "With the spread of impressionism literature has lost standards and discipline, and at the same time virility and seriousness; it has fallen into the hands of aesthetes and dilettantes, the last effete representatives of romanticism, who have proved utterly unequal to the task of maintaining its great traditions against the scientific positivists."[21] This issue continually preoccupies Babbitt, the sense of a general decline uncontradicted by any existing cultural force. Science is as guilty as democracy; both conspire to undermine principles of restraint, measure and authority. Both have had deeply unfortunate consequences for literary and cultural standards. If democracy, in making literature generally available, has produced Impressionist individualism, scientific materialism has led to scientific criticism; and between the two there is for Babbitt little to choose, since both schools converge in the "doctrine of relativity."

If the impressionist is asked to rise above his sensibility and judge by a more impersonal standard, he answers that there is no such impersonal element in art, but only "suggestiveness." . . . If the scientific critic in turn is urged to get behind the phenomena and rate a book with reference to a scale of absolute values, he absconds into his theory of the "unknowable."[22]

What Babbitt insists upon, and what determines his importance for the later modernist argument, is the coherence behind an array of ostensibly disparate problems. Romanticism and Impressionism are only the most immediate antagonists; seen from the proper angle, they are part of a vast intellectual development which includes the parallel movement of "sentimental humanitarianism," "unselective naturalism," and "the nightmare of an unselective democracy," all of which, according to Babbitt, uphold the supremacy of the autonomous individual and lead therefore to a weakening of authority – political, moral and literary. Babbitt regards the antagonist, then, as a single *Weltanschauung*, and against it he poses an equally comprehensive system of values. In order to preserve authority, to maintain "a feeling for absolute values," he is willing to overturn the intellectual assumptions of empiricism, liberalism and romanticism.[23]

Babbitt's problem is conceived in Arnoldian terms, and Arnold appears throughout the text. Given a chaos of competing individualities, how can one secure an organizing centre? But, as is plain, in his solution Babbitt seeks far more than Arnold's invigorated liberalism. He presses the claims of authority farther. His humanism abandons an "unselective democracy" in favour of the "keen-sighted few." It stands relativism, Rousseau, originality, democracy and science on one side, and against them it positions tradition, authority, and an aristocracy of the intellect. Humanism assaults the primacy of sensation and sensibility and insists on "discipline," "standards," "virility" and "seriousness."

Conrad: physis *and* psyche

This brings us back to Conrad and to *The Nigger of the "Narcissus,"* for Conrad too – nothing is clearer – defends discipline and standards, virility and seriousness. As a political meditation – and we ought not to be misled by the fact that in Conrad the *polis* floats – the novel stands firmly within the tradition of Arnold and Babbitt. Conrad, too, makes a plea for order, community, "solidarity." He, too, regrets the "modernizing habits" of individualism and class antagonism. In this respect, the near mutiny aboard the "Narcissus" occupies within the novel much the place that the Hyde Park riot occupies in Arnold's work. It is the dramatic centre of a cautionary tale, designed to remind us of the danger, in Arnold's phrase, of "random and ill-regulated action," the worship of an individual's right "to do as he likes": "to march where he likes, meet where he likes, enter where he likes, hoot as he likes, threaten as he likes, smash as he likes."[24]

On the "Narcissus" the marching, smashing, hooting figure is, of course, Donkin, who first appears as "The sympathetic and deserving creature that knows all about his rights, but knows nothing of courage, of endurance, and of the unexpressed faith, of the unspoken loyalty that knits together a ship's company."[25] Loyalty is "unspoken" and faith "unexpressed." To know one's rights, on the other hand, is to be, like Donkin and Wait, noisy, insistent, even mutinous. The association is important – to lay claim to personal rights is not only to threaten group solidarity; it is to violate an ethic of self-effacing silence and to drift into voluble self-assertion. Here Conrad is not alone. Through much of the late nineteenth century, the sound of reform seems to have been as disquieting as its political consequences. It is the *noise* of social agitation which is often the great prod to the imagery of reaction. The crowd "hoots" and "jeers" in Arnold, "groans" and "hisses" in George Eliot, "hums" and "buzzes" in Carlyle. All through Conrad's novel, the challenge to "unspoken loyalty" is anarchic speech. This culminates during the failed uprising, when "A raging voice sobbed out a torrent of filthy language."[26]

But what is telling in Conrad is the way that speech becomes a figure for consciousness. The emerging antithesis between Donkin and Singleton is not only an opposition between modern anarchy and what Arnold calls the "strong feudal habits of subordination and deference,"[27] not only between garrulous insubordination and silent fidelity, but also, and crucially, an opposition between consciousness and unconsciousness. Indeed the crisis in the solidarity of the "Narcissus" is in large measure the result of a too keen consciousness, an undue susceptibility to doubt and a consequent weakening of social bonds. This revolves, of course, around the figure of Wait – the "centre," as Conrad called him, of the ship's "collective psychology." Wait's illness, his pose, his self-deception provoke the self-reflection of the crew. Issues are raised that would better remain submerged, not only issues of human suffering and mortality, but questions of responsibility and duty, of individual claims in opposition to collective needs. Acute consciousness individualizes: that was the lesson of Pater. The more intently self-aware one becomes, the more social obligation loses its reality and its hold. The result on the "Narcissus" is an oversophistication among the men, a fall from primitive unreflective obedience into conscious duplicity. Towards Wait, says the narrator, "We were inexpressibly vile and very much pleased with ourselves. We lied to him with gravity . . . as if performing some moral trick with a view to an eternal reward."

Through him we were becoming highly humanised, tender, complex, excessively decadent: we understood the subtlety of his fear, sympathised

32

with all his repulsions, shrinkings, evasions, delusions – as though we had been over-civilised, and rotten, and without any knowledge of the meaning of life.[28]

To understand Wait, to sympathize with him, is to lapse into decadence. Understanding here leads not toward but away from "knowledge of the meaning of life." This is because for Conrad knowledge of life's meaning does not imply a full and comprehensive consciousness, an intimate awareness with all human capacities, an ability to identify with any human manifestation. Indeed, in some sense, the most satisfactory knowledge implies a willed *inability* to understand certain matters; as the French Lieutenant in *Lord Jim* will say of life without honour: "I can offer no opinion – because – monsieur – I know nothing of it."[29] Knowledge becomes a qualified good; everything depends on what one knows. In a moment of self-disgust, the narrator asks, "What kind of men were we – with our thoughts?"[30]

Singleton, ceaselessly loyal, is a man without thoughts, "meditative and unthinking." He "seemed to know nothing, to understand nothing." Conrad calls him "profound and unconscious," but the suggestion is inescapable.[31] He is profound *because* unconscious. Shortly after the publication of the novel, R. Cunninghame Graham wrote to Conrad, admiring the portrait of Singleton, while suggesting that he would make a more impressive model if he had an education. Conrad is blunt in his reply. A Singleton with education is impossible. And what would an education serve? Singleton is already "in perfect accord with his life." Conrad goes on to ask Graham,

Would you seriously, of malice prepense cultivate in that unconscious man the power to think. Then he would become conscious – and much smaller – and very unhappy. Now he is simple and great like an elemental force. Nothing can touch him but the curse of decay – the eternal decree that will extinguish the sun, the stars one by one, and in another instant shall spread a frozen darkness over the whole universe. Nothing else can touch him – he does not think.

Would you seriously wish to tell such a man: "Know thyself." Understand that thou art nothing, less than a shadow, more insignificant than a drop of water in the ocean, more fleeting than the illusion of a dream. Would you?[32]

Consciousness, then, enfeebles. As long as Singleton remains unconscious, "Nothing can touch him." Conrad's use of the phrase, his repetition of it, is interesting; he will repeat it many times in *Lord Jim*, using it to designate an ideal of perfect safety which is encouraged by submission to duty and jeopardized by the extension of awareness. Duty is an antidote to consciousness. Thus Marlow, in *Heart of Darkness*, avoids the temptation of atavism, not by invoking "fine sentiments," but by applying himself to work.

Fine sentiments, be hanged! I had no time. I had to mess about with white-lead and strips of woolen blanket helping to put bandages on those leaky steampipes – I tell you. I had to watch the steering, and circumvent those snags, and get the tin-pot along by hook or by crook. There was surface-truth enough in these things to save a wiser man.[33]

But the example of Marlow should serve as a caution. For whatever his *avowed* attitude, Marlow plainly represents the virtues of consciousness – no one more so. As a narrator he is curious, brooding and reflective, unwilling to record an event without submitting it to exacting consideration. He exemplifies the claims of consciousness, even if he hesitates to defend them. And this returns us to the issue raised earlier: namely, the tension between thematic representation and narrative form. The thematic sympathies of *The Nigger of the "Narcissus"* are plainly on the side of duty, obedience, authority and silence, and against individualism, consciousness and loquacity. But through the person of the narrator, as I have earlier shown, there is an implied commitment to the values of a registering consciousness. Singleton's "unexpressed faith" may be the supreme virtue endorsed in the novel, but it is the narrator who gives expression to that claim.

The novel then – and this is the reason for paying it such close attention – reveals an emergent crisis. Conrad dramatizes the same threat that Arnold and Babbitt had recognized: the assertion of individual will as the only criterion of judgment. Against this challenge, he, too, makes an appeal to authority and hierarchy, rejecting a liberal ideal in favour of a corporate social order, with honour, obedience and selflessness as the dominant virtues. Conrad, in short, participates in the late-century movement toward the undermining of the sovereign individual subject and toward nostalgia for more traditional pre-capitalist values.

But the sovereign subject has not disappeared; it has only retreated to safer, if more narrow, ground. For if Conrad shares Babbitt's desire for order, he also shares Pater's conviction that consciousness is the source of meaning and value. Indeed, we can see in *The Nigger of the "Narcissus"* an alternation between the values of consciousness (which secure meaning and are exemplified by the narrator) and the values of unconsciousness (which facilitate work and solidarity and are exemplified by Singleton). These values, as I have suggested, do not come into direct thematic collision in the novel, but they reveal the phenomenon I have intended to articulate: the dissociation of fact and subjectivity. As far as any explicit attachment of value is concerned, Conrad's primary sentiments are clearly with Singleton and within the realm of fact. Nonetheless, and crucially, there remains an implicit attachment to conscious subjectivity as a source of literary meaning. *The Nigger of the "Narcissus"* occupies an interesting place in Conrad's development, and in the development of modernism, when the defence of work and solidarity must begin to accommodate the claims of consciousness.

We first approached these issues by way of the novel's preface, to which we may now return, so that this prolegomenon may conclude what it began. In the preface Conrad pursued literary definition in divergent directions: he inclined, on the one hand, toward life's "visible surface," and on the other toward an inner artistic descent and a dependence on "temperament." We may now associate this tension with the more general conflict between authority and consciousness. Conrad's desire for descriptive rigour might itself be seen as a flight from subjectivity and individual idiosyncrasy; devotion to fact, to the world as it is, becomes a principle of order and control. Fidelity to the visible universe is in this sense a principle of authority, a principle of restraint which limits potential lapses into personal sentiment or personal taste. Conrad, one might say, submits to the physical world, in much the way Singleton submits to duty. But a second line of argument in the preface asserts the constitutive role of consciousness, and Conrad's attitude recalls Pater's defence of "sense of fact" against "fact." Precise description is only one aspect of the programme. At some point, a registering, witnessing consciousness becomes necessary, a consciousness which "endows passing events with their true meaning."

These two aims – the registering of fact and the recording of consciousness, *physis* and *psyche* – have invited contradictory interpretations of Impressionism; it has been characterized as both a precise rendering of objects and an unrepentant subjectivizing. The struggle between them is submerged, though revealing, in *The Nigger of the "Narcissus,"* but in Conrad's work over the next several years – and principally through the introduction of Marlow – it will become conspicuous. The impulses will then collide, profoundly and importantly, but *The Nigger of the "Narcissus"* represents a poise between them, when they stood in a certain complementarity. Still, the *agon* of modernism has already begun to emerge: its ideological crisis, the struggle between its values and its forms, the instability in the forms themselves.

CHAPTER 3

Dating Hulme / parsing modernism

"Dating Hulme" is a modest and manageable way of setting the problem. "Parsing modernism" puts the matter more contentiously and indicates the lines of a larger project: to identify within modernist thought certain root constituents – values, concepts, attitudes, beliefs – and to establish relations between them: relations of priority, mutual dependence, incompatibility, contradiction. "Dating," of course, is an historical procedure. "Parsing" is what we may call structural or functional. And yet I want to parse modernism, or to *begin* parsing modernism, by dating Hulme.

The present focus is English modernism within the period 1908–14. That is a brief period and has generally been considered in one piece. But as a single piece, it is ragged, rough-edged and discontinuous. Not surprisingly, its theoretical developments have been seen on the model of a "welter" or a "seething cauldron." Its leading figures – Hulme, Pound, Lewis, Ford – have been regarded as inconsistent, even incoherent. The idea here is that coherence has been unnecessarily lost, and this through one particular lapse: the neglect of any temporal or historical dimension, the tendency to regard the period as a simultaneous critical moment. In fact, the critical concepts were not generated simultaneously; they do not all belong together. Although the time was short, changes were rapid. If the ideas of 1915 are assimilated to those of 1912, or the ideas of 1912 to those of 1908, the intelligibility of each is lost. That is why dating is necessary to parsing. If the temporal dimension collapses, then the structure disappears, much as a musical structure would disappear if all notes were struck at once.

Such a project obviously extends beyond T. E. Hulme, but

Hulme makes a useful start. His career is closely bound to the period. He was present at one of the movement's earliest manifestations, the Poets' Club of 1908–09; he wrote essays on the modernist position through its formative years and until his death in 1917; and in 1924 his work was collected, at a time when the movement was acquiring its literary identity.

The posthumous publication of *Speculations* (1924)[1] had its intended results: the rescuing of Hulme's work from obscurity, and the return of his thought, if not to the modernist foreground, at least to its looming background. Almost as soon as the volume appeared, it won its author the comfortable status of an acknowledged precedent. Eliot, reviewing the work in the *Criterion*, praised Hulme as a "solitary figure . . . the forerunner of a new attitude of mind, which should be the twentieth-century mind, if the twentieth century is to have a mind of its own."[2] This is the place which has since been Hulme's, the valued predecessor, the cherished forerunner of modernism. It is no meagre role; other forerunners have fared worse; and *Speculations* is in large measure responsible for the reputation. It remains the work through which he is known.

But while *Speculations* has gained Hulme a certain prominence, it has done so at increasing expense. Herbert Read, who assembled the volume, drew on published, unpublished and unfinished writings, early, late and undated – presumably, in order to show the range of Hulme's attitudes and interests. But the result has been that Hulme has the appearance of a wildly inconsistent enthusiast, a follower of Bergson, Nietzsche and Sorel, and as if that were an insufficiently heterogeneous lot, an equally fervent admirer of Husserl, G. E. Moore and Charles Maurras. In recent years this has begun to undermine Hulme's standing – to the extent that Herbert Schneidau can write that "it is now generally recognized that Hulme was not an original or serious thinker, nor even a literary critic."[3]

That he was not "even" a literary critic seems to me the least telling of the charges. It is a point happily conceded. Nor is it necessary to insist on Hulme's originality. It may be true, as a biographer has held, that "there is scarcely an argument or instance in Hulme's writing" that does not derive from someone else.[4] But that does not diminish Hulme's interest. Indeed, he turns out to be interesting just insofar as he is derivative, just insofar as he submitted himself to a range of influences not previously conjoined. "T. E. Hulme" might be seen merely as the name of an intellectual site, a place where intellectual currents converged.[5] If that does not make him a "serious thinker," it at least makes him worth treating seriously.

That Hulme is eclectic is evident. But he was by no means as capricious, as indiscriminate, as intellectually fitful, as it may appear. The intention here is to restore some of the lost coherence, and thereby the seriousness, of his thought. This would be a limited exercise were it not that Hulme's intellectual development was so closely bound to the vicissitudes of early modernism.

Much of the interpretive confusion has derived from a single, apparently trivial, editorial lapse: Read's failure to fix correct chronology for the texts. The essays in *Speculations*, thus appearing together, gave an air of simultaneity to Hulme's opinions. Certainly, if he had held all those opinions all at once, then the persistent complaints of paradox and contradiction would be fair and telling.[6] In fact, he did not, though this has escaped critical attention. What have appeared as contradictions were almost without exception changes of mind. His thought passed through a number of distinct and irreconcilable phases, and in separating what has been too casually agglomerated, it will become possible to see Hulme's career, and early modernism more generally, as something more than a welter of passionate opinion.

Hulme's biography remains sketchy, but what is necessary is known. He attended Cambridge and was sent down in 1904 in somewhat embarrassing and unclear circumstances.[7] He lived in London, travelled briefly to Canada, returned, studied on the Continent, and by 1907 had read, listened to, and become acquainted with Henri Bergson. For the moment this takes us as far as we need to go. Hulme quickly assumed Bergson's standpoint; it was as a Bergsonian that he returned to England and made his first appearance in modernist literary circles.

Not atypically, Hulme had passed his early intellectual life preoccupied with the growth of science and its moral and religious consequences. The issue was for him, in William James' phrase, "living," "forced," and "momentous."[8] Hulme seems to have been unable to turn elsewhere until he had discovered a satisfactory position on the subject. Nor was he evasive or sentimental about the matter. He took the materialist position seriously and addressed it in its extreme form, often identifying it by means of this remark from Munsterberg:

Science is to me not a mass of disconnected information, but the certainty that there is no change in the universe, no motion of an atom, and no sensation of a consciousness which does not come and go absolutely in accordance with natural laws; the certainty that nothing can exist outside the gigantic mechanism of causes and effects; necessity moves the emotions in my mind.[9]

Hulme found this kind of claim completely unsettling. If it were accepted, it would threaten not only religious belief but the possibility of any moral realm at all: "it is impossible, if mechanism be a true account of the world, for us to believe in any preservation of values." Within the materialist perspective, "the word 'value' has clearly no meaning. There cannot be any good or bad in such a turmoil of atoms."[10]

Against this background Hulme discovered the work of Bergson, which seems to have produced a miraculous cure. Reading Bergson "put an end to an intolerable state"; "I had been released from a nightmare which had long troubled my mind"; it was "an almost physical sense of exhilaration, a sudden expansion, a kind of mental explosion."[11] The important step was simple. It involved Bergson's attack on materialist explanation on the grounds that it neglects or distorts crucial aspects of conscious experience. Materialism introduces into consciousness factors only appropriate to the external world – quantity, causality – and attempts to make the inner and "intensive" realm continuous with the outer and "extensive" sphere.[12] But, according to Bergson, no such continuity obtains. He does not dispute the soundness of science within its own boundaries; the error of materialist explanation is that it mistakes this part of reality for the whole. Hulme describes the "general idea" behind Bergson's work as the "endeavor to prove that we seem inevitably to arrive at the mechanistic theory simply because the intellect, in dealing with a certain aspect of reality, distorts it in that direction. It can deal with matter but it is absolutely incapable of understanding life."[13]

In Bergson's terminology, the error is a result of our habitual thinking "in terms of space,"[14] our penchant for analysing reality into discrete spatial entities. The way to contest materialism is to show the existence of phenomena not susceptible to such "spatial" analysis – that is, to prove the reality of "intensive manifolds." Bergson submits consciousness and freedom to consideration and concludes that they resist scientific analysis. Properly conceived, therefore, materialism poses no threat, because it applies to an altogether different realm. He concludes his *Time and Free Will* by announcing that the "problem of freedom has thus sprung from a misunderstanding: it has been to the moderns what the paradoxes of the Eleatics were to the ancients, and, like these paradoxes, it has its origin in the illusion through which we confuse succession and simultaneity, duration and extensity, quality and quantity."[15] It is the illusion, in short, through which the characteristics of the subject are confused with those of the mechanical world. Bergson is willing to concede that, at the level of the superficial self, actions are analysable, automatic, spatial and causal; but for the "deeper" self (*le moi profond*) such categories cease to apply.

This line of argument is by now familiar. But I take time to repeat it because Hulme repeated it so tirelessly. It represented for him a solution to a consuming anxiety – and also an opportunity. Half a jump ahead of the Bergsonian fashion, he took great pains to maintain his advantage. Between 1909 and 1912, he wrote over a dozen essays on Bergson. His translation of the *Introduction to Metaphysics* was published in 1913.[16]

Bergson's refutation of materialism was the first issue to seize Hulme's attention, but the implications of the argument went further, and Hulme willingly accepted them. If reason was "inevitably" distorting, then the project of a comprehensive rational understanding of the world was pointless and naive. Such an attitude led quickly to an anti-intellectualism, which Bergson accepted with equanimity and Hulme with enthusiasm. On its basis Hulme constructed a general Anglo-Bergsonian perspective: a scepticism towards the claims of traditional metaphysics, and a rejection of the rationalist belief in historical and social progress. Attending meetings of the Aristotelian Society in London, he appears to have sat in uncharacteristic silence and more characteristic contempt. In 1911, he travelled to Bologna for an international philosophic conference, and sent his impressions to the *New Age*. They typify his attitudes of the time.

Hulme asserts his "rather sceptical opinion of philosophy," which he considers "not a science but an art," and he indicates his contempt for the rationalist pursuit of the "one Truth, one Good." "I am a pluralist," insists Hulme. "There is no Unity, no Truth, but forces which have different aims . . ." To the rationalist, "this is an absolutely horrible position."[17] The essay becomes a carping satire of the naive ambitions of philosophers. Hulme himself, he tells us, would rather watch a parade in the street than attend the opening conference on "Reality," since "they would be certain to talk inside of progress, while the only progress I can stand is the progress of princes and troops, for they, though they move, make no pretence of moving 'upward.'"[18]

Hulme's career as a poet ended in 1912. His oeuvre comprised six published poems, none of them more than nine lines. In his lifetime he published no essay specifically devoted to literature or literary theory. His importance for the modern movement came from a few telling contributions that appeared at opportune moments. As early as 1908, he belonged to the Poets' Club, and served as its honorary secretary. He left the club the following year but continued in a literary discussion group, of which, according to F. S. Flint, he was the "ringleader."[19] During this period, he published two poems, delivered "A Lecture on Modern Poetry," and contributed an essay on Haldane to the *New Age*. These are among his earliest surviving texts, and they contain the outline of a distinct literary posture.

The lecture, presumably delivered to The Poets' Club, provides the most extensive formulation, and deserves the most attention. It is an effort to establish a large-scale historical context within which modern poetry can be understood. As will become his habit, Hulme passes casually over vast intellectual epochs in the pursuit of even vaster generalizations. According to his scheme, the "ancients" had attempted to evade the fluidity and instability of the world by constructing "things of permanence which would stand fast in this universal flux which frightened them." In their poetry, for instance, they wished "to embody in a few lines a perfection of thought . . . hence the fixity of the form of a poem and the elaborate rules of regular metre." The same desire manifested itself in the building of the pyramids, and the "hypostatized ideas of Plato." The claim, in brief, is this: "Living in a dynamic world they wished to create a static fixity where their souls might rest."[20] Purity of form became a refuge. But with the advent of "modernity" (the date of which is left unspecified) a thorough change in perspective occurred. "The whole trend of the modern spirit" is away from "absolute duty" and "absolute truth": "we no longer believe in perfection, either in verse or in thought, we frankly acknowledge the relative."[21] In Hulme's scheme, the history of thought, most broadly conceived, is from Platonic fixity to Bergsonian fluidity. With this shift in *Weltanschauung*, Hulme associates a corresponding change in literary forms. Since poets will "no longer strive to attain the absolutely perfect form in poetry," the predominance of "metre and a regular number of syllables" disappears. From the perspective of the new "impressionist poetry," regular metre is "cramping, jangling, meaningless, and out of place," a remnant that has become constraining. Hulme betrays no nostalgia for the fading past: "Each age must have its own special form of expression, and any period that deliberately goes out of it is an age of insincerity."[22]

Poetic subject-matter undergoes a similar shift. Traditional poetry treated "big things," "epic subjects," and thus fit easily into metrical regularity. But such grand poetic statements have become obsolete. Even the lyrical perfection of Shelley, Keats and Tennyson is outmoded. The modern poet remains "tentative and half-shy." Whistler's paintings are a paradigm; what has "found expression in painting as Impressionism will soon find expression in poetry as free verse." Modern poetry, in short, "has become definitely and finally introspective and deals with

43

expression and communication of momentary phases in the poet's mind."[23] "We are no longer concerned that stanzas shall be shaped and polished like gems, but rather that some vague mood shall be communicated. In all the arts, we seek for the maximum of individual and personal expression, rather than for the attainment of any absolute beauty."[24]

That is one movement in the lecture, and in Hulme's thought generally: the confining of poetry to the restricted sphere of personal expression. It corresponds to the negative aspect of Bergson's philosophy: the rejection of any large-scale metaphysical system, or of any comprehensive intellectual schema. But there is a second movement, no less Bergsonian, no less crucial. It is best described as the attempt to escape the bounds of the ordinary, the conventional, the commonplace. The attitude appears most clearly in Hulme's antagonism to prose.

Prose, insists Hulme, represents language in a stage of decline; it uses "images that have died and become figures of speech." He compares it to a "reflex action" such as the lacing of one's boots, an action accomplished with an "economy of effort" and "almost without thinking." That is how prose treats language: "we get words divorced from any real vision,"[25] words used as mere "counters" in order "to pass to conclusions without thinking." The aim of poetry is precisely to resist such a tendency: "It always endeavors to arrest you, and to make you continuously see a physical thing, to prevent you gliding through an abstract process."[26] Where prose is indirect and conventional, poetry is vivid, physical, direct. Condensed to an aphorism: "Prose is in fact the museum where the dead images of verse are preserved."[27]

This second emphasis, then, leads Hulme to large claims on behalf of poetry – poetry as "the advance guard of language"[28] – even while his other emphasis insists on restricting the poet's range. As we shall see, this is a characteristic modern strategy: to narrow the domain of the literary, even as the claims for literature increase. In Hulme's case, the dual movement reflects still more general aims, which derive from his Bergsonian perspective: first, to abandon any obsolete metaphysical or epic pretensions; and second, to escape the constraints of ordinary and prosaic reality in order to see a deeper truth.

For Bergson, and consequently for Hulme, the two great

dangers coincide, as do their solutions. Both systematic philosophy and ordinary thought are subject to the same distortion, since both depend on the constructs of reason and the conventions of language. The pressing need is to recognize the reality which exceeds these rational conventions, because "by intellect one can construct approximate models, by intuition one can identify oneself with the flux."[29] The transcendence which "intuition" provides in Bergson's philosophy is furnished by the "image" in Hulme's literary theory.

The concept is best approached through example. Hulme's poem "Autumn" appeared in the first volume of Poets' Club verse (1909):

> A touch of cold in the Autumn night –
> I walked abroad,
> And saw the ruddy moon lean over a hedge
> Like a red-faced farmer.
> I did not stop to speak, but nodded,
> And round about were the wistful stars
> With white faces like town children.[30]

Two characteristics of the poem will lead us to the point. First is its self-conscious restraint, the deliberate avoidance of the grand scale. The scene is slight, the tone conversational, the diction homely; there is only a "touch" of cold; the narrator's activities are reduced to the most commonplace: "walked," "saw," "nodded." "I did not stop to speak, but nodded," – that puts the issue nicely. There is no pause for speech, no lyric flight, no pantheistic interchange with nature, only a terse acknowledgement: a nod. The second point concerns the use of metaphoric image. Take, for instance, the poem's fourth line. The moon/farmer simile is introduced with a sudden deflation of rhythm; the image occupies the whole line and ends the poem's first sentence. The effect is to foreground the comparison and to make it bear considerable poetic weight. The same technique occurs in the metaphor and simile which end the poem: "With white faces like town children." Again the comparison obtrudes, this time as the conclusion of the poem, and again the result is to bestow privileged attention on the trope.

Of importance here is the relation between these two, fairly obvious, characteristics. For just to the extent that the poetic subject remains muted and slight does the role of the image become predominant. In the absence of any narrative, any development of ideas, any articulation of character, the images themselves come to attract the poetic regard. Further, in being so stressed, they stand against the triviality of the poetic scene.

What is enacted in the poetry is enacted in the theory. On the one hand, Hulme sees the image as part of the modern retreat from "epic subjects," "heroic action," "big things." It is an expression of the new "tentative and half-shy" temperament, whose poetry has abandoned "absolute beauty" in favour of "personal expression." The image is to be visual and concrete, replacing large-scale philosophic vision, emotional effusion, the declamatory impulse. Instead of momentous sentiments unfolding in regular verse, the modern method is simply to be the "piling-up and juxtaposition of distinct images in different lines."[31] The image reflects the modesty of modernism.

On the other hand, the image, though perhaps modest, is by no means shy. Images are "the very essence of an intuitive language,"[32] because they disrupt the habitual patterns of thought, producing what Hulme calls the "other-world through-the-glass effect,"[33] the sense of strangeness which makes possible a deeper and more intuitive vision. "Ordinary language communicates nothing of the individuality and freshness of things" – only poetry can produce the "exhilaration" of "direct and unusual communication."[34] Thus the importance of the image: it allows poetry to avoid literary excess without succumbing to the commonplace.

The insistence on the primacy of the image is the specific literary point that has been Hulme's most influential. But what should by now be clear is that for Hulme the image was not a matter of merely formal poetic concern. It was part of the attempt, indeed a considerable part, to find a satisfactory definition for modern poetry. In this regard Hulme makes three points which are central to his literary position: that poetry is to avoid pursuit of the epic, the absolute and the permanent; that it is likewise to avoid the prosaic and conventional; that a poetry of images is therefore the appropriate literary method. There is a fourth point, which has so far been submerged but which will come into increasing prominence: namely that the poetic strategy is to be founded on a radical literary individualism.

46

Throughout, Hulme depends on notions such as "sincerity," "feeling," "personality," "introspection," "expression." These are the qualities which characterize the new poetry, which, indeed, distinguish modern from ancient and poetry from prose. And Hulme's particular formal enthusiasms – for free verse and the image – are consistently defended in terms of the drive toward the "maximum of individual and personal expression." Free verse makes it possible to communicate "some vague mood"; the arrangement of images allows the poet "to suggest and to evoke the state he feels." [35]

In trying to establish a literary position that is at once anti-metaphysical and nontrivial, anti-herioc and yet not commonplace, Hulme takes emotional subtlety as the basis for modern poetry. In this he remains a faithful Bergsonian. As metaphysics becomes untenable, it is the intuiting subject which becomes pre-eminent. Similarly, as the epic aspiration disappears from literature, personal expression takes its place. The struggle of modern poetry becomes the struggle of *le moi profond*: against language, against convention, against habit, against the seductions of metaphysics, in order to achieve satisfactory expression. All of this should give pause. For what it means is that one of the decisive notions of literary modernism, the image, was first elaborated from a point of view opposed to the developed modernist perspective, as well as to Hulme's later attitudes.

The image was not justified in terms of tradition, objectivity, reason or authority – not even at first in terms of precision or clarity. It was rather defended as anti-traditional, individualist, intuitive, expressive. The issue leads us from Hulme to a point of wider consequence, namely the distinctive character of early modernist doctrine. For I now want to show that Hulme's attitudes were not personal idiosyncrasy, that they were embedded in the doctrinal orientation of those years, that early modernism, in short, stood against the later orthodoxy.

As far as the particular matter of dating Hulme is concerned, I have so far made only a modest point: namely the continuity of his opinions in the years 1908–11. But this provides a frame in which to consider the more difficult question of his later thought. To this I will return presently. Dating takes time.

CHAPTER 4

Ford: the passing of great figures

The Victorian sage in retirement

There are difficulties in approaching Ford. When he argued that art should correspond to the incoherence, the tenuousness and the "odd vibration"[1] of life, he was no doubt thinking of his own life. Self-dramatizing and self-parodying, he was not systematic, precise or rigorous. His distortions of fact were legion and confessed; his acts of memory were occasions to correct reality. He is nevertheless indispensable. His relation to Pound would itself justify including him here. But my claim is larger: I want to set him with Hulme as an exemplar of the early development of modernism.

Ford had the virtues of defects. If he was not theoretically-minded, he was at least concrete, wide-ranging, direct, unconstrained. There was scarcely an issue of popular controversy – from the Irish question to the investiture of American cardinals[2] – that didn't provoke his comment. And though his thought wandered, it wandered within discernible limits. For all of his vagaries, Ford had a recognizable point of view which came to be identified with a general literary attitude; what is more, he had an acute susceptibility to the movements of the age. He thus achieves the status of a "representative figure."

What he represents most particularly is the extension of a literary tradition. Self-consciously, almost wilfully, he placed himself in the line of Flaubert, Maupassant, Turgenev – a group he once called "the first really conscious writers";[3] more immediately, he identified his descent from Conrad and James. As will become obvious, he transformed the tradition as he extended it. Nevertheless, it was Ford who carried its standard into the pre-war critical arena. At a moment when a distinct literary tradition was being recognized as such, he became its current embodiment – in Pound's phrase, "the shepherd of English Impressionist writers."[4]

Though Ford at this time had yet to publish the novels on which his reputation now depends, he stood in a position of some literary prominence. The *Fifth Queen* trilogy, completed in 1908, was well received. His poetry was highly regarded among the young: Richard Aldington called "On Heaven" (1914) "the greatest poem written in this century – at least in English,"[5] and Pound described it as the "most important poem in the modern manner."[6] From 1907 to 1915 Ford was an active literary journalist, often producing several essays weekly, and as editor of the *English Review* (1908–09) he had positioned himself as a link between two generations, publishing work by established writers such as Hardy, James and Conrad, and younger writers such as Pound, Lewis and Lawrence, to whom he remained an active source of encouragement.

But it was in his critical doctrine that Ford was of most consequence in this period. In the intensified literary struggles of the pre-war period, he became the acknowledged representative of Impressionism. If he was not its most distinguished practitioner – a laurel Ford himself would variously bestow on Conrad, James or Maupassant – he was without question its most enthusiastic and visible proponent. Where Conrad skirted identification with the term, Ford, having for long enough been called an Impressionist, came to call himself by that name. And once committed to the name, he assumed the task of explaining what it meant. This would make him the target of the anti-Impressionist reaction, but it also meant that the Impressionist influence on pre-war literary activity was transmitted almost entirely through Ford's interpretation of the method.

Ford developed his notions slowly and with hesitation. During the years before the war, he was consistently involved in immediate, topical, journalistic debate – on matters social as well as literary. These are some of the most neglected of his writings, but it was out of this daily and mundane context that he developed the literary position with which he is associated. His aesthetics took shape in reaction to his politics. Ford set out to retrieve literary value from social degradation.

"Could anything be more depressing than the present state of public affairs?"[7] Ford was fond of beginning the new year with a portentous remark. This one was his opening utterance of 1910 and struck a note that became increasingly pronounced in his work up to the war: a sense of the decline and disarray of the present, which he regarded as a precipitous fall from Victorian innocence. *Ancient Lights* (1911), for instance, began as a reminiscence of the pre-Raphaelites, with Ford drawing on his early personal memories and his facility for anecdote. But it concludes far from where it began, as a lengthy reflection on the peculiarities of the present. In the last chapters Ford virtually deserts the pre-Raphaelites in order to brood over the changes since his childhood. Towards the book's end, he feels obliged to acknowledge the vehemence of his opinions. "Upon reconsidering these pages," he writes, "I find that I have written a jeremiad. Yet nothing could have been further from my thoughts when I sat down to this book."[8]

"Jeremiad" is excessive. But continually, in this period, Ford interrupted his literary reflections in order to engage in critical comment on the contemporary scene, to account somehow for modern conditions, in which the scale of art and life seemed so markedly diminished. In a typically casual and intermittent way, he arrived over time at passionate opinions on some pressing social questions. If they existed in isolation, they would be of little interest. But they do not. They are closely bound to Ford's literary struggles, and, moreover, reveal attitudes and anxieties one would not have expected to see revealed. This is the great advantage of Ford in a study such as this. His origins are available; he was too garrulous to suppress them.

The moral of the age, insisted Ford in *Ancient Lights*, is that "we are standardizing ourselves and we are doing away with everything that is outstanding."[9] That became his perpetual pre-war complaint. He attributed the change to the spread of democracy, mass education and mass culture. A stratified social order has been obliterated, and in its place there stands a democracy of "amiable mediocrity," "comparative cleanliness," "comparative light."[10] We have "reduced everything in scale." "We are the democracy, the stuff to fill graveyards, and our day has dawned."[11]

The age has a second moral: the rise of science has destroyed simplicity. It has generated such intricacy and sophistication that once manageable questions have become "exceedingly complicated";[12] life is "much more bewildered than it has ever been since the Dark Ages."[13] "Practical politics have become so much a matter of sheer figures that the average man, dreading mathematics almost as much as he dreads an open mind, is reduced, nevertheless, to a state of mind so open that he has abandoned thinking – that he has abandoned even feeling about any public matter at all."[14] These two tendencies, towards standardization on the one side and complexity on the other, became Ford's great social preoccupations. They marked for him a thorough break with the Victorian era, the consequences of which he saw everywhere: in the extension of the underground railway, in the decline of good restaurants. But the most notable and disturbing change was intellectual: the disappearance of any coherent attitude towards the range of social and cultural facts. Nowadays, he writes, "any connected thought is almost an impossibility"; there is a "disease of thoughtlessness."[15]

In 1909 Ford published an essay called "The Passing of the Great Figure," and the phrase became his shorthand characterization of the recent historical developments. Carlyle, Ruskin, Mill, Newman, Arnold, Tennyson, George Eliot – these were Ford's great figures, "the last of the priests,"[16] who represented in his eyes social stability, moral consensus and intellectual reflection, and whose passing signalled a fundamental transformation in English culture. In their place stood the new technical specialists – economists, scientists, bureaucrats – and the daily press. The specialist brought an end to generalizing thought, and the popular press vulgarized whatever thought remained: "An immense reading public has come into existence and the desire of those who cater for it is not to promote thought but to keep it entertained."[17] The great figure, on the contrary, "commanded respect – he insisted upon it – not because he was going to give pleasure by the beauty of his words or the music of his periods, but because he was a sort of moral alchemist. He cared comparatively little whether or not he was going to give pleasure; he was going to solve the riddle of the universe"; now "with each cheapening of the modes of production the public has seemed to read rottener and rottener books."[18]

The "passing of the great figure" is by no means a refined notion; but if it leaves history largely unexplained, it goes some distance towards explaining Ford. It places him. What in fact has passed, and what is now unavailable to Ford, is precisely the moral and political conviction of the Victorian sage. The hostility towards the established order remains. The sense of crisis remains. Indeed, much of Ford's critical antagonism derives from these same Victorian predecessors. He attacks the vulgarization of art, the self-interested pursuit of profit, the adulteration of manufactured goods, the decline of excellence. There are strains of Carlyle and Ruskin. But Ford, as he himself is acutely aware, stands at a further stage of intellectual disaffection. He shares the antagonism without the command- ing ideological perspective. He possesses no comprehensive vision, no moral authority, no proposals for reform. The great Victorian figure implied the possibility of a coherent and encompassing point of view – not the partial glimpse of the specialist, but the wide and comprehensive vision of a moral prophet. In a democratic and technological society, argued Ford, such figures were obsolete and unwanted; democracy would not tolerate their privileged status; science suppressed their urge to generalize. Where Arnold could enjoin his readers to "see life steadily and to see it whole," Ford laments that "we may contemplate life steadily enough to-day; it is impossible to see it whole."[19]

We stand to-day, in the matter of political theories, naked to the wind and blind to the sunlight. We have a sort of vague uneasy feeling that the old feudalism and the old union of Christendom beneath a spiritual headship may in the end be infinitely better than anything that was ever devised by the Mother of Parliaments in England, the Constituent Assemblies in France, or all the Rules of the Constitution of the United States.[20]

The remark is perfectly characteristic. Ford abandons theory, attacks democracy and expresses nostalgia for the feudal church. In his casual and unsystematic way, he provides as good a measure as any of the extent to which the nineteenth-century progressive consensus has come undone. And this will shortly prove to be a point of consequence: the association of a declining liberalism with the rise of literary modernism.

In *Culture and Anarchy*, Arnold had addressed an issue which would preoccupy Ford four decades later, the disarray which results from an expanding and irresponsible press. Arnold introduced the case of a Nonconformist spokesman who tried to counter the editorial opinion of the *Saturday Review* by citing the intellectually suspect *British Banner*, as though one were equivalent to the other. This was for Arnold a mockery: "The speaker had evidently no notion that there was a scale of value for judgments on these topics." [21] Arnold used the incident to dramatize the difficulties of rational discourse, arguing the need for an "authoritative center" [22] to combat such confusion.

In 1909, Ford contemplates an analogous case. He imagines a contemporary Gladstone trying to rally opposition to "misrule in Macedonia," only to discover that there no longer existed any moral consensus upon which he could depend. His views would receive no greater hearing than any other opinion on the subject. Gladstone, suggests Ford, might find an outright hostility, or "and this is still more likely – he might find that the public mind was utterly unable to make the effort to interest itself at all in the matter of Macedonia." [23] No matter how passionate the advocacy, there will be equally passionate counter-advocates, and no way of deciding between the competing positions: "Divergent views find to-day such an easy expression that the mind at all inquiring is perpetually driven now in one direction, now in another . . . And this produces in the public mind a weariness, a confusion that leads in the end to something amounting almost to indifference." [24]

The contrast should help locate Ford within a tradition. Arnold recognizes an increasing distortion but never doubts that there is indeed a "scale of value," however obscured beneath the prevailing cultural chaos. He depends still on the authority of the *Saturday Review*. Ford, on the other hand, has no confidence in such persisting values. Where Arnold's point is that right reason must be redeemed from vulgarity, Ford suggests that right reason has lapsed altogether, leaving the modern world in a state of "social agnosticism": "We know so much, we know so many little things that we are beginning to realise how much there is in the world to know, and how little of all that there is, is the much that we know. Thus there is an end of generalisations."[25]

On these grounds he defends James against the charge of evading the great political subjects of the day: "I suppose that it is a sufficient answer . . . to say that Mr. James knows nothing of Politics, War, or the Lower Classes. Nobody does. Nowadays all these things are so much in the melting-pot of conflicting theories."[26] Ford thus accedes to scepticism. As an intellectual stance, it is not elaborate, sophisticated or unique; it conforms in large measure to the prevailing response to the pre-war social crisis: suffragette and working-class militancy, the Irish question, the uncomfortable alliance between the Liberal and Labour parties, the provocations of the Tories in Northern Ireland. Part of the reason I take the time to elaborate his historical outlook is that it provides an articulate measure of the declining assurance and conviction of the intellectual class.

Little moderns

But for the purposes of this study, the greater reason is the relation between Ford's historical and literary sense. It is not what one might expect, and it is the more interesting for that, because the very same factors which Ford sees as a cause of intellectual confusion and social mediocrity represent for him a distinct literary *opportunity*. The heterogeneity and complexity of modern life, the decline of excellence, the rise of specialists and the daily press, the passing of great figures – that is, just those conditions which prompt his social "jeremiad" – have the beneficial effect of freeing the artist from entangling involvements. The world has become too chaotic, and issues too complex, for any moral pontificating. This makes possible a restriction of attention to art, and a release from extra-artistic responsibilities.

According to Ford, the chief characteristic of Victorian art was its aspiration towards moral pre-eminence, which he consistently interprets as antagonistic to the artistic process. The same moral prophets who symbolized social harmony were in literature the causes of stultification. Here, for instance, is his characterization of George Eliot:

George Eliot was, in fact, a great figure. She was great enough to impose herself upon her day; she probably never sought, though she certainly found, the popularity of sensationalism. Taking herself with an enormous seriousness, she dilated upon sin and its results, and so found the easy success of the popular preacher who deals in horrors. She desired that is to say, to be an influence: she cared in her heart very little whether or no she would be considered an artist.[27]

Moral influence and art thus become opposed considerations. Victorian stability, hierarchy and social consensus had permitted a link between literature and prophecy which invited the moralizing of art, and which was therefore a substantial danger to literature. On the other hand, the disintegration of a unified social order and the complication of modern life have allowed, even obliged, the artist to substitute private expression for public declamation. This, for Ford, is a considerable benefit. In the essay on "Modern Poetry" (1909) he expresses delight in "the abolition of the moral standpoint as a factor in modern verse." The poet "no longer takes himself with a seriousness altogether preposterous" and has become therefore "more sincere."[28] He writes, that is to say, "along the lines of his own personality and his own personal experience. He does very much less generalising from the work of contemporary Scientists, Divines, and Social Reformers."[29] Ford denies that this marks a decline in the quality of poetry. It simply represents the end to an obsolete ambition; and "upon the whole there is, nowadays, more good poetry written in the course of a year than there was when the great figure flourished in Victorian days":[30]

Instead, that is to say, of making the acquaintance of two or three enormous poets like Tennyson or Rossetti, whom one suspected always of posing, of forcing the poetic note, of giving not so much what they intimately liked as what they regarded as appropriate for a poet to like – instead of these few great figures we have made the acquaintance of a number – of a whole circle – of smaller, more delicate, and more exquisite beings.[31]

With the history of the novel he makes a similar case and is even more sweeping in his critique: "the whole of the fiction of England from the days of Beowulf to those of Meredith is – as art – almost entirely negligible."[32] In particular, he derides the "peaks" of the novel, dismissing Thackeray, Scott and Fielding with "their sentimentality, their sensationalism, their snuffy moralisings, their pitiable valuation of life, their slipshod writing, their general and defiant amateurishness."[33] He finds Dickens only slightly less contemptible. Richardson, almost alone, escapes attack. Indeed, in trying to account for the vicissitudes of the novel's development, Ford describes Richardson's influence as having "passed over the water" through the enthusiasm of Diderot, where it matured in the hands of Chateaubriand, Flaubert, Maupassant and Turgenev. Only through the recent efforts of Conrad and James did the novel's artistry return to England. The art of the English novel is therefore just beginning, "having been born to consciousness with the year 1892 or thereabouts . . ."[34]

It was "Profound Moral Purpose"[35] which delayed the event, and in Ford's 1913 appreciation of James what he admires most is James' refusal of profound morality, and any purpose but the strictly artistic. James is a "philosophical anarchist," "a purely non-historic personality," who "couldn't by any possibility be the great writer he is if he had any public aims": "Mr. James alone, it seems to me, in this entire weltering universe, has kept his head, has bestowed his sympathies upon no human being and upon no cause, has remained an observer, passionless and pitiless . . ."[36] This is the opening Ford now sees: the modern age, having discredited the moral aims of art, has freed it to remain itself, and in banishing it from social purpose, has sent it into opportune exile.

Ford addressed the dedication of *Ancient Lights* to his two daughters, making it the occasion for some paternal advice founded on bitter experience. His own childhood, writes Ford, was one of awkwardness and humiliation; "I always considered myself to be the most obscure of obscure persons – a very small, a very sinful, a very stupid child."[37] This dismal situation he attributes to his familiar antagonists, "those terrible and forbidding things – the Victorian great figures":

To me life was simply not worth living because of the existence of Carlyle, of Mr. Ruskin, of Mr. Holman Hunt, of Mr. Browning, or of the gentleman who built the Crystal Palace. These people were perpetually held up to me as standing upon unattainable heights, and at the same time I was perpetually being told that if I could not attain these heights I might just as well not cumber the earth.[38]

Based on this experience Ford gives his children the following advice: "Do not . . . desire to be Ruskins or Carlyles. Do not desire to be great figures. It will crush in you all ambition; it will render you timid; it will foil nearly all your efforts."[39]

The gesture is characteristically Fordian: a refusal of "adult" morality and an embrace of childhood insignificance and irresponsibility. It is a recurrent, though obscured, attitude in Ford's work and binds together apparently disparate elements. It appears, for instance, in his much-repeated praise for the simplicity and ascetic unworldliness of Christina Rossetti; in the creation of a character like John Dowell (in *The Good Soldier*) with his childlike credulity, asexuality and trust; in Ford's praise of contemporary poets as "smaller, more delicate, and more exquisite beings."[40] It appears most prominently and revealingly in Ford's own pose as a *naïf*, his deliberate cultivation of the unserious. He wrote once that he hoped he would never be taken as standing for "sound doctrine and common sense,"[41] and towards the end of *Ancient Lights* he makes a great play of the fact that "to myself I never seemed to have grown up."[42] He dwells on his present fondness for childish pranks, confessing that he still hesitates to enter the kitchen because "lurking at the back of my head, I have always the feeling that I am a little boy who will be either 'spoken to' or spanked by a mysterious *They*."[43]

This opposition between small children and great figures may be a revealing psychological pose, and Ford's reflections on his Victorian childhood deserve more attention than they have received. But my concern is less with psychological origins than with literary effects, with the use of "the artist as child" as a rhetorical stratagem. It puts in stark terms the tendency we have been considering: the shift in attention from large things to small, from public responsibility to private expression, from an "adult" earnestness and self-seriousness to "childlike" intimacy, sincerity, and amoralism. In *The Nigger of the "Narcissus"* Conrad too had relied on the metaphor of a child; Singleton in an important passage is described as "a child of time," "one of the everlasting children of the mysterious sea." The association is central for Conrad. It positions Singleton and his disappearing children against the new "grown-up children of a discontented earth." It emphasizes the historical movement which has replaced heroism by self-interest. But Conrad depends on a set of associations which markedly differ from Ford's. The men of Singleton's era were "impatient and enduring, turbulent and devoted, unruly and faithful."[44] Their "childishness" implied the traditional virtues of innocence, unselfconsciousness, simplicity, naturalness – virtues which made possible a harmonious and effective social order. Ford, on the contrary, defines childhood in opposition to moral and social obligation, as a refuge from any such concerns.

This change of emphasis indicates certain obvious differences in temperament between Ford and Conrad. But it points as well to a general division within Edwardian consciousness which stands revealed in two of its most popular successes: Baden-Powell's Boy Scout movement and J. M. Barrie's *Peter Pan*, two mythologies of childhood vastly more popular than any modernist myth. Both creations managed to capture the public imagination almost immediately; indeed they have not yet released their hold; but plainly they reveal opposing cultural pressures. Scouting reflected the tendency to see childhood as an early adulthood, as a continuing preparation for the assumption of social responsibility. *Peter Pan*, of course, stood in exuberant antagonism to just that tendency. Barrie aimed to preserve a region of innocence as distant as possible from adult morality. Where scouting invited a premature virility, *Peter Pan* (always played by a woman) was childishly epicene. Where Baden-Powell told his recruits that they could learn to shoot, obey orders and grow up quickly, Barrie told his that they could fly, fantasize and refuse to grow up. Peter Pan declined to "learn solemn things."[45] Baden-Powell, on the other hand, intoned:

The nation is showing signs of illness. We can diagnose it as "bad citizenship." We know the kind of remedy to apply, namely, education of the rising generation in "character" . . . It is by such a "snowball" movement that we may hope to take a really useful part in bringing strength, both moral and physical, to our Empire.[46]

The divergence of Barrie and Baden-Powell is obviously profound, but the two may owe their respective successes to the same historical concern, which I have approached through the anxieties of Ford: the sense, following the Boer War, of a newly precarious England, complex, inharmonious and waning in confidence. The value of scouting and Peter Pan as cultural artifacts is that they provided extreme and alternative responses to the situation: on the one side, an appeal to the extension of authority and discipline as safeguards of moral (and imperial) stability; on the other side, a desperate flight from moral complexity and political decline.

Conrad and Ford are not to be assimilated to such a severe opposition. Still, the division within the popular consciousness appeared within the literary movement, and the shift from Conrad to Ford was, among other things, a shift from a style of moral earnestness to one of moral scepticism. Indeed, in early 1914, when the avant-garde began to attract wide attention, Ford offered his support on the basis of a willed hostility to traditional moral standards. It seems pretty certain, he wrote in January 1914, "that we of 1913 are a fairly washed-out lot and that we do desperately need a new formula":[47] "what we want most of all in the literature of to-day is religion, is intolerance, is persecution, and not the mawkish flap-doodle of culture, Fabianism, peace and good will. Real good religion, a violent thing full of hatreds and exclusions!"[48] Such became Ford's standard position. Four months later, reviewing *Des Imagistes*, he writes in a similar vein that "one needs to be reckless nowadays":

One wants it desperately; it is a hunger; it is a thirst. One is too safe, in one's views, in one's house, in one's pantaloons. I should respect myself more if I could burgle a Wesleyan chapel and wear a purple-and-green satin dressing-gown at Rumplemayer's, and, just for once, say what I really think of a few people. But I have not the courage. That is why I admire my young friends – they do that sort of thing.[49]

Beneath the ironic posturing is a serious and increasingly important point – the deliberate flouting of bourgeois conventions and traditions, of proprieties, amenities and responsibilities, and the insistence on an art that has nothing to do with prevailing social norms, indeed with any traditional norms at all.

Continually in this period Ford urges such restriction of artistic attention. Morality and social advocacy are fatal infatuations; the only sound foundation for contemporary art is personality. The "official altruism" of the Victorian age made possible social harmony, the great figure and morally portentous art; it has outlived its historical justification. What remains is an outmoded liberal creed which stands in the way of artistic advance and which Ford attacks with increasing scorn. By 1914, he speaks of it with unmixed contempt: "How can a man, an educated man, a man ex-officio a member of the ruling classes – or any man who can read at all – hold the vast number of contradictory opinions that are necessary to a 'Progressive' of to-day?"[50]

Hulme, Pound and Eliot would ratify this attitude with varying depths of passion. Ford is never so systematic in his reaction. He drifts towards a "sentimental Toryism," but his dominant intellectual tone remains sceptical. For Ford what characterizes the contemporary world are "its confusing currents, its incomprehensible riddles, its ever present but entirely invisible wire pulling, and its overwhelming babble."[51] The modern age is a "terrific, untidy, indifferent empirical age,"[52] with the result that "the accepted truth of to-day is the proven lie of to-morrow."[53] And the artist, unlike the specialist, "has not the power, the energy, or the austerity to state what will be good for to-morrow." The artist's only business can be "to register a truth as he sees it, and no more than Pilate can he, as a rule, see the truth as it is."[54]

In the face of complexity, then, Ford responds by confining artistic vision to the immediacy of personal observation, a matter of particular importance in his later remarks on Impressionism. Like Pater before him, Ford arrives at a severe epistemological scepticism, which devalues not only the moralizing impulse but the very facts to which a morality may pertain. Like Pater, he locates the only sure source of value in the artistic temper. Ford can thus write in "English Literature of To-day" (1909) that the artist deals "not in facts and his value is in his temperament."[55] In *Ancient Lights* (1911) he is more adamant: "I have for facts a most profound contempt. I try to give you what I see to be a spirit of an age, of a town, of a movement. This cannot be done with facts." Unabashedly he concedes, "This book in short is full of inaccuracies as to fact, but its accuracy as to impressions is absolute."[56]

At the moment the point worth reiterating is the *historical* justification which Ford offered for this literary position. Typically in this period he has defended artistic change on the basis of social change. Because modern society has become a fragmented "gnat-dance," modern poets (e.g. de la Mare) are right to be tenuous and vague. And because political issues have become so complicated, novelists (e.g. James) are right to ignore them. In fact, the great complaint Ford makes against his contemporaries is their failure to yield sufficiently to the exigencies of the present, the failure to concede the fragmentation, the fragility, the precariousness, and to write accordingly. The great need, he insists, is for an up-to-date idiom which acknowledges that modern life has become a "dance of midges."[57]

Hulme, too, had provided an historical apology for modern literature, and plainly the two converge. But Ford's vision was by no means as philosophical or as vast. It was rather a gradual and piecemeal adjustment to a rapidly changing situation. And that is its interest. Because Ford was so immediately responsive to change, he reveals – perhaps better than any of his literary contemporaries – the historical and social pressures on the literature of the moment. His retreat to a sceptical individualism was not only a literary retreat – from moralizing, generalizing, rhetoric, sentimentality – but quite confessedly a retreat from mass culture, widening democracy and the political crises of a declining liberalism. In these last two chapters, then, we have established a movement towards literary individualism and the complex of factors encouraging that movement. Philosophically, there has been a flight from an encroaching scientific materialism; politically and socially, a recoiling from mass democracy and technical complexity. In each case, the individual subject became the refuge for threatened values. The process was almost territorial: as traditional values were jeopardized, there was a retreat to the surer, if more modest, zone of the self.

In any event, all of this should situate Ford firmly within the subjectivist tradition that we have traced from Arnold and Mill to Conrad and James, and then to Hulme. Ford extols individual temperament at the expense of public fact. He embraces the relativity of knowledge and abandons hope of transcending a private perspective. The poetic virtues he praises are "sincerity" and "intimacy"; he is suspicious of a public and adult morality. But Ford in these early writings has done more than reaffirm subjectivist attitudes; like Hulme he has radicalized those attitudes – retreating without hesitation to personality, severing moral and political involvements, lapsing towards scepticism to a degree that predecessors such as James and Conrad had resisted. We can now begin to consider the wider consequences of this change.

CHAPTER 5

Egoists and Imagists

"The Ego and His Own"

Max Stirner may seem an unlikely figure to appear in the present context, but he would be unlikely in any context. He was, and has remained, an intellectual oddity, acknowledging no predecessors, belonging to no school, the author of one book of consequence, which appeared without warning, stirred immediate controversy, and then fell into obscurity. That his work has survived at all has been due to the unrestrained enthusiasm of intermittent admirers. And only because one of those periods of enthusiasm coincided with the first stirring of literary modernism, does Stirner obtrude here.

He obtruded upon the world as Johann Kaspar Schmidt in 1806 and was given the sobriquet "Stirner" as a child – apparently because of a long, sloping forehead. Little else of his childhood is known, and not much more of his adult life. At the university he studied philosophy, attending Hegel's lectures, but he received only qualified approval on his examination. This made employment difficult. In 1839 he finally found a teaching position at Madame Gropius' Institute for the Instruction and Cultivation of Young Girls. From all that can be gathered, his personal life was lonely and unhappy. His first wife died in childbirth; his second left him after four years of marriage. In his later years he was sent to prison for debt. His funeral was virtually unattended.

During the early 1840s he attended meetings of *Die Freien*, the young Hegelian group around Bruno and Edgar Bauer, in which setting he could pursue his philosophic interests. He published a few articles of slight interest, including some for the *Rheinische Zeitung*, which Marx edited for a time. His one philosophic work, his only link to posterity, was composed in great privacy and published in 1844 under the title *Der Einzige und sein Eigentum* (translated as *The Ego and His Own*). It caused immediate and vehement controversy, drawing criticism from Hess, Feuerbach and, most notably, Marx and Engels, in *The German Ideology*. Stirner's work, as Sidney Hook put it, "exploded like a bombshell among the ranks of his former comrades-in-arms."[1]

The Ego and His Own was an early and extreme statement of philosophic egoism; indeed no statement of the position could be more extreme. Stirner blithely rejected all previous philosophy, all theology, all intellectual system, all political order. They were chimerical – the only reality was the individual ego, whose needs and desires were their own justification.

I am unique. Hence my wants too are unique, and my deeds; in short, everything about me is unique. And it is only as this unique I that I take everything for my own, as I set myself to work, and develop myself, only as this. I do not develop man, nor as man, but, as I, I develop – myself.[2]

Up to a point Stirner is following Feuerbach, who in *The Essence of Christianity* (1841) pursued a similar anti-metaphysical goal. In his attempt to provide the "solution of the enigma of the Christian religion," Feuerbach had argued that Christianity, like all religion, was based on a sham, the illusion of an independent deity. In fact, religious impulses were only displaced human impulses, "the disuniting of man from himself": "man in relation to God denies his own knowledge, his own thoughts, that he may place them in God." As far as Feuerbach was concerned, this had caused needless human suffering, and his aim therefore was "the realization and humanization of God – the transformation and dissolution of theology into anthropology." Humanity, not divinity, would then become the object of the religious yearning.[3]

Stirner wrote out of the same sceptical and secularizing impulse, but he sought to carry the argument further. From his perspective, "man" (considered as a species) was no more substantial than "divinity." Both were abstractions; both represented the displacement of more fundamental egoistic drives. "*Man*, you see, is not a person, but an ideal, a spook."[4]

64

The ego alone is concrete, and the "religion of Humanity is only the last metamorphosis of the Christian religion."[5] Stirner's aim was to free the ego from any slavish attachment to a "higher" calling, since "Every higher essence above me, be it God, be it man, weakens the feeling of my uniqueness." The egoist recognizes no obligation or authority:

He does not look upon himself as a tool of the idea or a vessel of God, he recognizes no calling, he does not fancy that he exists for the further development of mankind and that he must contribute his mite to it, but he lives himself out, careless of how well or ill humanity may fare thereby.[6]

The egoist philosophy, then, was conceived in deliberate opposition to Feuerbach's altruistic humanism; it was actively anti-social. "The self-willed egoist," writes Stirner, "is necessarily a criminal, and his life is necessarily crime."[7] The Ego and His Own contains an elaborate theory of human development, in which history is conceived as a progress towards a consummate egoism which would at last do away with selflessness, collectivism and abstract moral system. To that end, Stirner advocates a war of "each against all." "Away, then, with every concern that is not altogether my concern! You think at least the 'good cause' must be my concern? What's good, what's bad? Why, I myself am my concern, and I am neither good nor bad. Neither has meaning for me."[8]

The celebrity of The Ego and His Own was intense but short-lived, principally no doubt because the social revolutions of 1848 relegated the question of egoism to a distant background.[9] Stirner's work fell into complete eclipse. "Si jamais auteur, si jamais ouvrage paraissait voué au définitif oubli," wrote a French critic at the turn of the century, "c'est bien Max Stirner, c'est certes l'Unique et sa Propriété."[10] But in 1888, a German poet named John Henry Mackay discovered a reference to Stirner while reading Lange's History of Materialism in the British Museum. He spent the next ten years tracing what could be found and in 1898 published the first critical work on Stirner: Max Stirner: Sein Leben und sein Werk. A spate of Stirneriana followed. In the following ten years, Der Einzige und sein Eigentum was translated into Italian, Russian and, twice, into French. In 1907 the American anarchist Benjamin Tucker sponsored an English translation. Between 1900 and 1929, forty-nine editions of the work appeared.

The available text became the occasion for a Stirner revival, whose most important manifestation in English modernism was the *New Freewoman,* a biweekly journal, which began publication in 1913.[11] Harriet Shaw Weaver was its publisher; Dora Marsden managed the editorial policy; and Steven Byington, Stirner's translator, was a contributor. The feminist movement had been the occasion for the journal's founding, but the editorial policy was feminist only in a greatly strained sense. Marsden had hardly more interest in the suffragette cause than in any other cause, and, as she later explained, the early emphasis on women's issues was "more in the nature of retort than of argument."[12] The *New Freewoman*'s principal and overriding concern was to trumpet Stirnerian egoism, and the rhetoric was deafening. Readers were informed that on crucial issues Stirner had anticipated Bergson by more than half a century and had refuted Marx before Marx began writing. With characteristic hyperbole, *The Ego and His Own* was called "the most powerful work that has ever emerged from a single human mind."[13]

As might be expected, the journal's standpoint was consistently and radically individualist. Abstractions were dismissed as spurious intellectual constructions; concepts such as "equality," "unity," "humanity" and "law" were called the "futile products of men who pursue their own shadow," "delusions of intelligences too feeble to be quite aware of what they speak."[14] On the other hand, "will," "life" and "self" were celebrated as healthy, because egoistic, notions. All political programmes were excoriated, but especially those depending on "humanitarian" or "progressive" opinions. It seems worthwhile, ran an editorial, "to get behind the generality 'Progress' since obviously there exists no such thing."[15] Indeed, as Stirner had taught, there is only one thing, the willing ego. "The egoist stands for nothing: his affair is to see to it that he shall not be compelled to kneel."[16] Selflessness is a phantasm, and "as for goodwill, it has no real existence . . . In a few thousand years, after experimenting with every 'constructive' scheme of government, 'divine' and human, men will begin to understand that the only will existent is Self-will."[17]

Though the Stirnerians inclined to dismiss Nietzsche's work as derivative and popularized, it should be plain that the Nietzschean vogue helped to animate these anti-humanitarian, anti-democratic, anti-metaphysical tendencies. In an essay published in the *New Age*, Remy de Gourmont made the Nietzsche–Stirner connection explicit:

We have learnt from Nietzsche to pull down the old metaphysical structures built upon a basis of abstraction. All the ancient corner-stones are crumbled to dust, and the whole house has become a ruin. What is liberty? A mere word. No more morality, then, save aesthetic or social morality: no absolute system of morals but as many separate systems as there are individual intellects. What is truth? Nothing but what appears true to us, what suits our logic. As Stirner said, there is my truth – and yours, my brother.[18]

This is the extreme expression of attitudes that many had first approached by way of Bergson. Rational intellection is overthrown; will and instinct usurp its place. Systematic philosophy is summarily rejected; traditional patterns of thought are seen as distorting and unsatisfactory. The wilful individual becomes the source of such truth as the world allows. And while the Bergsonians hesitated here, the Stirnerians and Nietzscheans were intent to pursue the point. If the ego was the world's centre and its circumference, then religion, morality, democracy and equality drop from consideration. They are life-denying and intellectually insupportable, and they obscure more central issues.

Stirner conceived the issue in its most severe outlines, and he demands attention for that reason. But though he provided a visible and persuasive formulation, it is worth insisting that the egoist philosophy by no means represented a Continental intrusion into British intellectual life. As should by now be apparent, the ideology of subjectivity was implicit in a prominent tradition of English thought – from Arnold, Mill and Pater to Hulme and Ford. Indeed, the embrace of philosophic egoism in the pre-war years might be seen as simply the deferred conclusion of a few Victorian premises. And though its completed form would no doubt have been antipathetic to both, the egoist position was prepared in Arnold's grounding of religion in "personal experience," and in Pater's willing withdrawal into the "solitary chamber" of solipsistic perception.

Still, the working out of intellectual dynamics is a notoriously erratic process. Conclusions have been known to trail premises by hundreds of years. Why egoism at this moment? It would take us too far afield to undertake a comprehensive account, but it is worth reiterating a suggestion raised in connection with Ford Madox Ford; namely that the coincident pressures of mass culture and technical culture put an unbearable strain on the culture of liberalism. No longer was it plausible to claim, as Mill and Arnold had claimed, that harmony obtained between individual needs and collective aspirations; class conflict was too visible, severe and irremediable. Nor was it reasonable to insist that the lay individual consciousness was capable of expert scientific generalization; evidence to the contrary was too considerable. In the face of working-class militancy, religious and philosophic scepticism, scientific technology and the popular press, there was a tendency – especially among the artists and intellectuals – to withdraw into individual subjectivity as a refuge for threatened values. Among this group, liberalism decomposed into egoism. And where liberal ideology had made the individual the basis on which to construct religion, politics, ethics and aesthetics, egoism abjured the constructive impulse and was content to remain where it began: in the sceptical self.

The point is not, of course, that such a tendency was pervasive or general. I am not trying to characterize the *Zeitgeist* but to isolate a specific strain of thought, the reaction of a group of intellectuals who defined egoism against the dominant traditionalism and progressivism. But it was just this calculated antagonism towards prevailing norms that would make these attitudes so important for modernist literature. What, then, does egoism have to do with literature?

Pound/Upward

In January 1908, at the age of twenty-two, Ezra Pound abandoned his teaching position at Wabash College in Indiana and sailed for Europe. He passed several months in Venice, and while he was there, paid to have his first volume of poems, *A Lume Spento*, published. Pound then departed for London, arriving with no friends, no prospects for employment and almost no money. But from that precarious beginning he took a series of long, quick strides. By the end of 1909, he had met Hulme, Yeats and Ford Madox Hueffer, found a publisher for his poetry and received a lectureship at the Regent Street Polytechnic. He was satirized in *Punch* and reviewed in the *Evening Standard*. *Personae* appeared in 1909, *Exultations* in 1910 and *Canzoni* in 1911.

Then in the spring of 1912 in a scene that has entered modernist legend, Pound turned to Hilda Doolittle and Richard Aldington "in a tea-shop – in the Royal Borough of Kensington" and baptized them "*les imagistes*." The first published use of the term came several months later in Pound's preface to *The Complete Poetical Works of T. E. Hulme*. He referred there to previous groping efforts in 1909, and then proclaimed that "As for the future, *Les Imagistes*, the descendants of the forgotten school of 1909, have that in their keeping." That was the first polemical salvo and represented an important turning. Literary activity was now to be conceived in terms of a movement, even if the movement had as yet only a leader and two followers. Pound had scorned the Parisian tendency to have "eight schools for every dozen of poets,"[19] but his own proportion was as yet scarcely more impressive.

Pound's intentions, of course, were loftier, and to realize them he undertook an active propagandizing function. In his "London Notes" for *Poetry* magazine, he wrote in recognizably strident tones that "The youngest school here that has the nerve to call itself a school is that of the *Imagistes*."[20] He arranged for F. S. Flint to interview him on the subject, and this interview was published in March 1913 alongside Pound's own "A Few Don'ts by an Imagiste." In the latter half of that year the determined effort began to achieve visible results. By that point Pound had managed to bring new, if not always enthusiastic, recruits into the *Imagiste* camp; these included D. H. Lawrence, Amy Lowell and William Carlos Williams, and from their work and the work of others he put together the *Des Imagistes* anthology, which was accepted for publication in the summer of 1913 but did not appear until February of the following year. At the same time he was extending attention to the plastic arts, pursuing new relations with Henri Gaudier-Brzeska and drawing closer to Wyndham Lewis. From Pound's point of view, and it is his point of view that we are for the moment assuming, the efforts of several years were at last achieving noteworthy success. He had arranged to spend the winter with Yeats in Sussex, and he left London with a sense of increased urgency and self-confidence. On December 19, 1913, he wrote excitedly to Williams that "we are getting our little gang after five years of waiting."[21]

Another event which took place in December has the advantage of returning us to the main line of argument. The *New Freewoman* changed its name. The journal had begun publication in June 1913 and in August Pound had assumed control of the literary side. By December his place was secure enough for him to participate in a minor in-house insurrection. With several other contributors, he addressed a letter to Dora Marsden, complaining that the title of the journal was misleading and suggesting that it be changed to one "which will mark the character of your paper as an organ of individualists of both sexes, and the individualist principle in every department of life."[22] Marsden acceded to the request: in January of 1914, the *New Freewoman* became the *Egoist*, the name chosen out of homage to Max Stirner. As the *Egoist* it would achieve literary celebrity, publishing over the next several years Joyce's *Portrait of the Artist as a Young Man* and the early chapters of *Ulysses*, Wyndham Lewis' *Tarr*, the poetry of Pound, Richard Aldington and H. D., and the criticism of T. S. Eliot.

Though the incident is in itself peripheral, it points to more central matters. First, it shows the position of relative power which Pound and his allies had achieved. Their numbers and their celebrity were now sufficient to allow a more aggressive posture. During this same period, for instance, Pound was attempting to bully Harriet Monroe into altering the policy of *Poetry*. He resigned in favour of Ford, who promptly returned the favour, and Pound grudgingly agreed to remain. "I am willing to reconsider my resignation," he wrote to Monroe, "pending a general improvement of the magazine, and I will not have my name associated with it unless it does improve."[23] Quite obviously, Pound was developing an acute consciousness of his own literary importance. In a letter to Amy Lowell, he described himself as the only person in London "with guts enough to turn a proselyte into a disciple."[24]

The second point, and one worth pursuing, concerns Pound's relation to Stirnerian egoism. With the other signatories of the letter, Pound opposed the name of the *New Freewoman* because it failed to reveal the commitment to the "individualist principle in every department of life."[25] If this were a unique avowal, it would be of no importance, but in fact the egoistic leaning was as pronounced in Pound as it was in Hulme and Ford. In Pound's case the most important influence was Allen Upward. Upward is perhaps the most obscure of the early moderns, and the more that is known about his life, the less it coheres. In September of 1913, *Poetry* provided this biographical sketch:

Mr. Allen Upward, born in Worcester in 1863, has had a varied life. A scholar, a barrister, a volunteer soldier who ran the blockade of Crete and invaded Turkey with the Greek army, he is also the author of plays, romances, poems and of *The New Word*, that powerful plea for idealism which aroused England six years ago, and for which Mr. Gerald Stanley Lee, in *Crowds*, demands the Nobel Prize.[26]

One might have added that he was a scoutmaster and the author of several detective stories. Like Ford, Upward was a member of an earlier generation who found himself suddenly immersed in a new movement and allowed it to sweep him along in its enthusiasms. When *les jeunes* were still *jeunes*, he was fifty. Pound happened across his work in *Poetry*, and, as Upward described it, he "rose up and called me an Imagist. (I had no idea what he meant.)"[27] One of Upward's poems was included in the anthology; and for a brief period he frequented the new literary *cénacle*. Then in 1915, when Amy Lowell assumed control of the anthology, Upward found himself excluded, a circumstance which provoked his poem "A Discarded Imagist," and his active involvement in the movement came to an end.

Upward's importance, though, lay not in his literary contribution, but in his intellectual example. Davie has demonstrated in persuasive detail Upward's bearing on Pound's verse style and poetic ideas.[28] One can also find him behind many of Pound's early critical positions. In 1907 Upward published *The*

New Word and in 1913 *The Divine Mystery*. The former was a wide-ranging sardonic meditation on contemporary thought, which took the recent Nobel legacy as its problem text. In bequeathing an annual prize for literature, Alfred Nobel had stipulated that the award be granted to "the person who shall have produced in the field of literature the most outstanding work of an idealistic tendency." Taking advantage of a barrister's training, Upward subjected the clause "idealistic tendency" to a withering analysis which, by the time it was complete, left few modern idols standing. *The Divine Mystery* was a reflection on the origins and development of religion, which provided for Pound what Frazer and Tylor would provide for others: a suggestive comparative reading of religious and mythic beliefs. According to Upward, the Christian gospel ought not be taken as a received dogma but as

an old, old story, retold from generation unto generation. Its words and signs are inherited from a primeval language, a true catholic speech, whose grammar is being recovered in our days from the tombs and dust of prehistoric peoples, from the daily life of savage tribes, and from the tales that are still the bible of the peasant and the child.[29]

The traditional content of religion thus becomes the subject matter of anthropology and psychology.

After discovering Upward's poetry, Pound read *The New Word* and *The Divine Mystery* with enthusiasm, calling the two works "as interesting philosophically as any that have been written in our time."[30] The books now seem amateurish and meandering, but, in their undermining of certain bourgeois conventions, they prepared the way for the more violent and systematic criticism of the modernists. Pound's own enthusiasm would persist. In 1937, he responded to Michael Roberts' inquiries about Hulme by suggesting that Roberts read Upward. Pound offered to lend his own copies of the works, describing himself as the "sole reader of all Upward's books, now surviving."[31]

Several of Upward's notions found their way into Pound's thought, but unquestionably the most important was the urbane, if nonetheless extreme, version of the egoist position. Where Pound kept at a distance from Dora Marsden's more technical polemics, he became a doting admirer of Upward.

Pound was fond of intellectual cataloguing; in 1915, when he compiled a list of the crucial ideas behind the aesthetic renaissance, he associated Upward with the "modern sense of the value of the 'creative, constructive individual,'" which was as "definite a doctrine as the Renaissance attitude *De Dignitate*, Humanism." [32]

By this point, Upward's position will sound familiar. He denies the legitimacy of all abstract and general terms, insisting that reality belongs to particulars alone. "When is the good not the good?" queries Upward, and answers: "When it is an abstract noun." The same, he contends, holds true for people; individuals alone are real, and Upward writes with bitterness of the "absurdity of supposing that man is a species": "When, instead of thinking of men one by one you think of them all at once and call your thought humanity, you have merely added a new word to the dictionary and not a new thing to the contents of the universe." [33]

Pound cites this remark in an essay on Upward in the *New Age*. It is, of course, precisely congruent with Stirner's egoism; indeed at the centre of *The New Word* is an attack on Stirner's *bête noire*, the "religion of humanity." Upward calls "humanity" "a false word," since "it means that there are, or ought to be, no differences between men."

The Religion of Humanity is not the worship of the best man, nor of the best in man. It is the worship of the middling man. It is the consecration of that instinct which causes men to kill to their own loss the best man, to starve the poet and to stone the prophet, to scourge and crucify the Christ. [34]

Pound subscribed to such views enthusiastically, adapting them to his own demands for the pre-eminence of art. Upward's work, he insisted, ratified the belief that a "nation is civilised in so far as it recognises the special faculties of the individual, and makes use thereof." On such grounds the artist and the intellectual are to be ceded a special place within the social order; there is to be a "syndicat of intelligence." [35] As Pound wrote in another essay of this period: "the aristocracy of entail and of title has decayed, the aristocracy of commerce is decaying, the aristocracy of the arts is ready again for its service." [36]

The Pound/Upward connection is worth detailing because it puts in visible and concrete form the general point we have been working towards: namely the presence of a distinct train of thought, a radical egoism, which links the literary attitudes of early Hulme, Ford and Pound and which, as we have now repeatedly seen, was encouraged and confirmed by a complex set of attendant factors. This has been plain enough. What is now at issue is the changing character of that individualism. In Hulme and Ford, it had been a largely passive response to a complex historical situation, a sceptical withdrawal to the self. But in early 1914, the movement began to gain a sudden and considerable strength. Experiments in poetry and the fine arts won new adherents, and alliances between the arts were struck. Outlets for the work were increasingly available; patrons provided new sources of funds, and the press began to take notice (the pages of *The Observer* became the arena for an angry exchange of manifestos). In short, the London avant-garde attained a certain institutional strength: it now had numbers, an audience and a financial base. And as its material position became more secure, it became more inclined to attack than to flee.

Poets rampant

As late as the autumn of 1913, in "The Serious Artist," Pound had displayed a certain restraint in his apology for art, offering a defence of poetry on grounds of social utility. "It is obvious," he wrote, "that ethics are based on the nature of man." And it is equally obvious "that the good of the greatest number cannot be attained until we know in some sort of what that good must consist." The function of art is to provide such knowledge. The arts, that is, "give us our best data for determining what sort of creature man is"; they are a science, just as chemistry is, but where chemistry deals with the composition of matter, the subject of the arts is "man, mankind and the individual." Good art reflects that subject accurately; it "bears true witness." On the other hand, "bad art is inaccurate art." And if the artist lies, his offence "is of the same nature as the physician's and according to his position and the nature of his lie he is responsible for future oppressions and for future misconceptions."[37]

Such attitudes find a place within the humanist tradition, and Pound himself connects the essay to Sidney's *Defence of Poesy*. He conceives of art as fundamental and consequential, and he willingly acknowledges the social obligation of any such serious endeavour. But over the next several months, Pound's attitudes suffered dramatic change, and his was only part of a more general transformation. In the first week of 1914, Ford made the remark (already quoted) that "we of 1913 are a fairly washed-out lot," and that what contemporary literature most needs "is religion, is intolerance, is persecution, and not the mawkish flap-doodle of culture, Fabianism, peace and good will." Two weeks later Lewis published "The Cubist Room" in the *Egoist*, a passionate defence of the new art. And on January 22, Lewis, Pound and Hulme delivered lectures at the Quest Society, with Hulme presenting his "Modern Art and Its Philosophy," in which he announced the "break-up of the Renaissance human-istic attitude." In each of these cases there was a strident new assault on the prevailing state of culture, but perhaps the best instance of the emerging point of view was an essay of Pound's, "The New Sculpture," published in the *Egoist* on February 16.

It began as a summary of the recent Quest Society lectures, but from there Pound launched into a bitter harangue against artistic involvement in the social realm. "So long a humanist," the artist has fed humanity "out of his hand and the arts have grown dull and complacent, like a slightly uxorious spouse." Pound derides such pursuit of respectability. "We are sick to death," he wrote, "of the assorted panaceas, of the general acquiescence of artists, of their agreement to have perfect manners, and to mention absolutely nothing unpleasant." What is needed is manifest hostility to the social order, and now "the artist has at last been aroused to the fact that the war between him and the world is a war without truce. That his only remedy is slaughter." The new artist "recognises his life in the terms of the Tahiytian savage"; he "must live by craft and violence." "The artist has been at peace with his oppressors for long enough. He has dabbled in democracy and he is now done with that folly." And Pound concludes with undiminished contempt:

"Modern civilisation has bred a race with brains like those of rabbits and we who are the heirs of the witch-doctor and the voodoo, we artists who have been so long the despised are about to take over control . . . And the public will do well to resent these 'new' kinds of art."[38]

Pound thus comes to a position as anti-democratic and as anti-humanitarian as that of Stirner, Nietzsche or Upward. The social justification for art, as found in "The Serious Artist," has disappeared. Social amenities and social responsibilities are not only irrelevant to artistic process; they are obstacles. The pressing need is for an aesthetic individualism that recognizes its antagonistic relation to the social whole.

In July of 1914, the Vorticist journal *Blast* made its first appearance, and it included the most vehement and programmatic statement of this attitude. Vorticism appealed "TO THE INDIVIDUAL"; it was a popular art but has "nothing to do with 'The People'"; on the contrary, in the Vorticist conception of art, popular art "means the art of the individuals." Art allows of no involvement with schemes of social reform, nor does it depend on fidelity to nature: "We want to leave Nature and Men alone"; "We believe in no perfectibility except our own." Moral constraints thus drop away: "There is one truth, ourselves, and everything is permitted."[39] The fundamental and recurrent principle was the self-sufficiency of the artist. Pursued to an extreme, this led not only to antagonism between art and society but also to opposition between art and tradition.

This latter point was the particular preoccupation of Italian Futurism, which was at that time the dominant avant-garde sect. Under Marinetti's leadership, the group had dedicated itself to the pursuit of a "new beauty" deriving strictly from contemporaneity: "power under control, speed, intense light, happy precision . . . the conciseness of effort, the molecular cohesion of metals in the infinity of speeds, the simultaneous concurrence of diverse rhythms . . ." all of which implied a complete break with previous art. Indeed the only precursors Marinetti allowed were "the gymnasts, the tight-rope walkers, and the clowns."[40]

Futurism was highly visible on the London scene from 1912 to 1914, with lectures and performances attracting crowds and the attention of the press. Eager to extend his cultural sway, Marinetti attempted to recruit London artists to his position. He was insistent, unscrupulous and singularly unsuccessful. Far from producing the desired Futurist conversion, Marinetti managed to unify English artists in opposition. Hulme, Lewis, Pound and Gaudier-Brzeska (among others) converged on the need to combat Futurism. They rejected the cult of technology, speed and machinery, the wilful lawlessness of Futurist pictorial composition and the poetic principle of "words at liberty." Futurism, as we shall see, became an important polemical adversary, and much of English modernist doctrine was defined in opposition to its principles.

On one point, however, there was important agreement: the need for decisive literary rupture. Thus, in the midst of a violent repudiation of Marinetti, Lewis conceded that since in England "Futurist" implied only that a painter was "occupying himself with questions of a renovation of art, and showing a tendency to rebellion against the domination of the Past, it is not necessary to correct it."[41] And Pound, even while opposing Futurist methods and Futurist preoccupations, acknowledged the force of Apollinaire's remark that "on ne peut pas porter *partout* avec soi le cadavre de son père." To that extent, he wrote, "we are all Futurists."[42]

And so they were. Both Imagists and Vorticists shared the hostility to an established and constraining tradition and its entrenched dogmas, in particular the notion that certain forms have a validity sanctioned by long use. In Remy de Gourmont's phrase: "What we need is less models and more of the free light of life which you hide from us."[43] When an angry letter writer took Pound to task for inattention to classical norms, he rejoined: "The modern renaissance, or awakening, is very largely due to the fact that we have ceased to regard a work of art as good or bad in accordance with whether it approaches or recedes from the 'Antique,' the 'classical' models."[44]

Épater l'académie became a persistent impulse, leading to deliberate confrontation with established reputations. Richard Aldington, especially vigorous in this regard, claimed that "the artist has to deny and disprove principles erected by his ancestors in order to keep intact their great common principle of freedom."[45] Aldington began by attacking Shelley and Tennyson, who would become familiar targets, and went on to suggest – nothing could be more heretical – that Milton might have benefited from the use of free verse. In a similar vein Hulme had written that he was "in favor of the complete destruction of all verse more than twenty years old."[46] And Ford advised an aspiring poet to forget "about Piers Plowman, forget about Shakespeare, Keats, Yeats, Morris, the English Bible and remember only that you live in our terrific, untidy, indifferent empirical age, where not one single problem is solved and not one single Accepted Idea from the past has any more magic."[47] It is well to note how far this is from Eliot's formula. As far as the early moderns were concerned, tradition constrained the individual talent.

Again *Blast* gave consummate expression to the attitudes. "We stand for the Reality of the Present," it announced, "not for the sentimental Future, or the sacripant [*sic*] Past."[48] Traditional values, then, were explicitly and insistently rejected, but not, as with the Futurists, out of an attachment to modern technology: Marinetti's "automobilism" was bitterly satirized. The Vorticist argument was more epistemological than technological. It was founded on the same premise that we have uncovered in Hulme, Ford, Sturner and Upward: the primacy of immediate individual perception. The present contains all that is immediately available to the creating artist. "Life is the Past and the Future," wrote Lewis. "The Present is Art." The Future and the Past were distant "and therefore sentimental." Indeed: "Everything absent, remote, requiring projection in the veiled weakness of the mind, is sentimental." "The new vortex," accordingly, "plunges to the heart of the Present."[49]

I have been insisting on two things; the depth of the opposition to traditional and social norms and the way such opposition depended on an aggressive individualism. That is to say, it was just to the extent that the individual was invested with pre-eminence that tradition and society could be so thoroughly dismissed. Since "our only measure of truth is our own perception of truth," then allegiance to external standards disappears; what is rather needed is withdrawal from life (and tradition), and revolution within art. As Lewis put it, "Reality is in the artist, the image only in life . . ."[50]

"Reality is in the artist" – this marks a completion of the individualizing process traced from Arnold to Ford. The single criterion of judgment has become the autonomous artistic agent who acknowledges no extra-individual standard and who stands against the concatenated bogey of humanism, democracy, society and tradition. Art, in brief, is an apotheosis of individualism, a detachment from class, context, history and nature. As the *Blast* manifesto says, "The moment a man feels or realizes himself as an artist, he ceases to belong to any milieu or time."[51]

In his study of the period, Stanley Coffman identifies the prevailing literary sensibility as anti-romantic and remarks that the Vorticists were "concerned with deprecating the significance of the individual."[52] This has become something of a critical commonplace, but what has been said above should sufficiently undermine the plausibility of the view. Pound's comment of September 1914 is representative. "The vorticist movement," he wrote, "is a movement of individuals, for individuals, for the protection of individuality."[53] Coffman, however, is not committing a simple blunder; the blunders in this area are rarely simple. If he reads the movement as anti-individualist, it is no doubt because the movement would go on to read itself that way. I have been trying to show at some length the inadequacy of that reading, to point out that modernism was individualist before it was anti-individualist, anti-traditional before it was traditional, inclined to anarchism before it was inclined to authoritarianism. It remains to account for the change.

CHAPTER 6

Hulme: the progress of reaction

The classical phase

In the last several pages we have advanced as far forward as 1914 and have seen the increasing vehemence of aesthetic egoism in the months before the war. T. E. Hulme introduced the subject. Under Bergson's influence he provided an early justification of modern poetry as a retreat from epic sweep to emotional intimacy, from metrical rigidity to a "vague mood," from absolute beauty to "personal expression." Although Hulme saw these principles as revolutionary, later observers have quite reasonably pointed to their continuity with established literary traditions. Kermode, for instance, sees him as "informed by *l'âme romantique*" and writes that Hulme "hands over to the English tradition a modernised, but essentially traditional, aesthetic of Symbolism."[1] Despite Hulme's protestations to the contrary, runs the claim, he should be assimilated to the earlier movement, and furthermore, "once it is granted that Hulme was trying to do much the same thing as Mallarmé, it becomes evident that he did not do it very well."[2]

This is an important but partial truth. Its force depends on reducing Hulme's volatility, on confining attention to his early works, on seeing Hulme, in short, as irredeemably Bergsonian. Kermode restricts attention to "the image" and then proceeds to argue that its metaphysical justification was "borrowed from Bergson."[3] Donald Davie pursues a similar line: "It is probably due to Hulme that much modern criticism is Bergsonian, perhaps without knowing it."[4] And Davie writes further that "later writers have abandoned the Bergsonian element in Hulme's vocabulary, while often retaining, tacitly or unconsciously, his Bergsonian assumptions."[5]

The influence of Bergson cannot be in any dispute. It was decisive early in Hulme's development; it was indeed crucial for his theory of the image; and it affected almost all of his specifically literary writings. The temptation to assimilate Hulme to Bergson is therefore overwhelming. But it is to be resisted. It distorts Hulme and obscures crucial developments in modernist theory. Such, at any rate, is what I now intend to show. In particular, my point will be that Hulme moved far from his early beliefs, that his later thought stood deeply (and not just implicitly) opposed to Bergson, and that his developed position represents an alternative strain in modernist doctrine.

Bergson's philosophy was for Hulme a way not only of challenging the orthodoxies of science but of validating new anti-romantic literary impulses. For in Hulme's presentation of the position, its principal emphasis was sceptical. From his point of view, both romantics and rationalists were guilty of naive over-reaching. Set against both, modernity was to be modest, tentative, impressionistic, abandoning the attempt to construct any epic vision, whether literary, philosophic or scientific – as distant from Shelley as it was from Huxley.

Still, though this was what Hulme most valued in Bergsonism, both the doctrine and its followers tended in another direction. Irving Babbitt, for one, was quick to recognize the continuity between Bergson and earlier romantic thought. In *Masters of Modern French Criticism* (1912), he praised the reaction against scientific positivism as "highly laudable" but suggested that it would be preferable to "effect our escape from intellectualism not by sinking below it, after the fashion of the Bergsonians and pragmatists, but by rising above it."[6] He criticized Bergson in particular for seeing no escape from "frenzied intellectualism" but "an equally frenzied romanticism."[7]

Whether Bergson's philosophy was "frenzied" is a question we can leave to one side. But whether it is a *romanticism* is of more importance. And without struggling against the inadequacies of the term, it can be asserted with little hesitation, as others have insisted before,[8] that Bergson indeed shared certain conventionally romantic attitudes and predilections. He resisted the intrusions of intellect, devalued science, emphasized will and spontaneity, and made intuition the cornerstone of his philosophy. Hulme had originally looked to Bergson as an ally in the contest between freedom and mechanistic determinism, and he had apparently not yet considered the romantic implications which would shortly disturb him. The crucial impetus came from Action Française, a group with which, like Eliot after him, he would come into close sympathy.[9] Specifically, the source was Pierre Lasserre's *Le Romantisme français*, which had been published in 1907. In an interpretation which has become familiar, even standard, Lasserre contended that late nineteenth-century intellectual decadence was the product of a romanticism whose principal tenets – optimism, individualism, sentimentality – derived from Rousseau. As far as Lasserre was concerned, the consequence was a grotesquely distorted vision of the human situation:

Le Romantisme (sentiments) polarisait les aspirations et les espérances de l'âme individuelle sur un chimérique idéal de félicité. Le Romantisme (idées) affirmait comme possible, comme prochain, un ordre social qui, abolissant la dureté naturelle des conditions de la vie, annulant l'égoisme humain, ferait régner le bonheur pour tous. Ces deux rêves creux, généralisations monstrueuses de l'idée de volupté passive, n'ont aucun sens intrinsèque; mais ils portent le témoignage le plus intéressant de la décadence de l'énergie vitale et de la corruption de l'humeur chez les esprits qui les enfantent ou s'en nourrissent.[10]

Against this unfortunate influence, Lasserre advocated the restraint of classicism, and it was this that brought him into sympathy with the political position of Charles Maurras. The anti-romantic and the anti-liberal married happily. In the decade after the Dreyfus affair Action Française emerged as the most outspoken partisan of extreme political reaction, and in 1908, when its daily newspaper was founded, Lasserre became the literary critic. He led the assault on the romantic sensibility – in literature, in philosophy and in university education – while Maurras and others pressed for a revival of French nationalism and the restoration of the monarchy.

Hulme and Babbitt were the two figures most responsible for introducing Lasserre to the English-speaking world. Indeed, the two were so faithful in representing his position that Lasserre himself has almost dropped from historical notice.

Babbitt read *Le Romantisme français* shortly after it appeared, and his preoccupation with romantic decadence, a preoccupation he would teach T. S. Elliot to share, probably stems from his early reading of that work; much of *Rousseau and Romanticism* traces closely the lines Lasserre had drawn fifteen years before. But, though Babbitt is deeply indebted to the French example, he remains hesitant about extending cultural analysis into the political realm. In the preface to *The New Laokoon* (1910) he commends Lasserre's "brilliant and virulent" attack on romanticism but goes on to mention his unhappiness at discovering *Le Romantisme français* in a bookshop specializing in works of political reaction. Babbitt expressed regret that "a legitimate protest against certain tendencies of nineteenth-century life and literature should be thus mixed up with what we may very well deem an impossible political and religious reaction."[11]

Hulme, however, found the confluence of literature, politics and religion very much to the point. And by no means did he find the project impossible or regrettable. He embraced the programme of reaction almost as soon as he discovered it. That Hulme does not share the hesitations of Babbitt is more than an accident of temperament. It is a measure of rapidly changing attitudes on an issue we have neglected for some time. Babbitt first occupied our attention as a zealous defender of cultural order and political authority, as an heir of Arnold, who inherited the suspicion of individuality and "doing as one likes" without inheriting Arnold's attachment to liberalism and democracy. He extends the claims of authority. And yet he, too, can extend them only so far. After his long and insistent appeal for "standards" in *Masters of Modern French Criticism*, Babbitt in the final pages makes a telling concession: "Nowadays if we have standards they must be inner standards . . ."[12] Like Arnold before him, Babbitt, though intent to contest individualism, struggles within the bounds of its assumptions. Hulme, on the other hand, learned from Action Française to disregard those bounds, to reject the inevitability of the individualist premise and, in so doing, to make ever more severe demands on behalf of order and authority.

Hulme's first acquaintance with the Action Française group probably occurred in 1911. The following year he published "A

Tory Philosophy" in the *Cambridge Magazine*, one of the earliest of Hulme's works to show marks of Lasserre's influence. The essay is still constrained by a lingering scepticism, with Hulme going to great lengths to acknowledge that what he has to say is only personal opinion. He cites Nietzsche's remark that "Philosophy is autobiography" and quotes Renan: "Philosophies and theories of politics are nothing in the last resort, when they are analysed out, but the affirmation of a temperament."[13] But having offered this disclaimer, Hulme proceeds to a highly partisan attack on the romantic worldview; and together with the more celebrated "Romanticism and Classicism," "A Tory Philosophy" provides an early version of a familiar modernist distinction.

Following Lasserre, Hulme associates romanticism with the belief that humanity is "something rather wonderful" whose capacities have only been inhibited by the "restrictions of order and discipline." From Rousseau, argues Hulme, "one is carried on to the conception that anything that increases man's freedom will be to his benefit."[14] "Here is the root of all romanticism: that man, the individual, is an infinite reservoir of possibilities; and if you can so rearrange society by the destruction of oppressive order then these possibilities will have a chance and you will get Progress."[15] Since the outset of his career, Hulme had attacked naive convictions of inevitable progress. But from the Bergsonian perspective, he had nothing to counterpose, beyond the sceptical rejection of rationality, unity, science. And precisely those aspects of Bergson's thought which Hulme had celebrated as antagonistic to science – intuition, freedom, consciousness – invited, as Lasserre and Babbitt pointed out,[16] a return to romantic and individualist principles.

The classicism of Maurras and Lasserre had the advantage of offering an explicit and well-defined alternative; Hulme can thus define the classical view as the "exact opposite" of the romantic: "Man is an extraordinarily fixed and limited animal whose nature is absolutely constant. It is only by tradition and organisation that anything decent can be got out of him." Humanity is "incapable of anything extraordinary." This is so, because "either by nature, as the result of original sin, or the result of evolution, he encloses within him certain antinomies."

Within the human temperament inheres a "war of instincts" which ensures that the future human condition "will always be one of struggle and limitation." The classicist then has no faith in progress, and believes in the need for a discipline which can introduce order into this "internal anarchy." "Nothing is bad in itself except disorder; all that is put in order in a hierarchy is good."[17]

The vicissitudes of the romantic/classical distinction will emerge later. For the moment the notable point is the incompatibility between the embrace of "classicism" and the Bergsonism which Hulme had so passionately articulated. It appears as though this occurred only gradually to Hulme, who in his initial enthusiasm had attempted to make the doctrines converge.[18] When he learned of the Action Française hostility to Bergson, he was sufficiently disconcerted to visit Lasserre in order to discuss the antagonism. Lasserre's personal response to Hulme is unavailable, but his opinion of Bergson was conveniently published elsewhere. In "La Philosophie de Bergson" published in L'Action Française in 1911, Lasserre pointed out that, although in principle Action Française advocated only a political programme – viz. the restoration of the monarchy – in practice it had wide implications: "la réforme politique implique une réforme intellectuelle générale."[19] The continuity between the political and cultural programmes depends on their common method: "à prendre pour fondements et pour guides de la théorie et de la pratique les rapports naturels et nécessaires des choses, les lois de la réalité."[20]

On just this issue did Bergson's incompatibility become evident. The Bergsonians denied the validity of such a method; they insisted on the incommensurability of past and future, holding in Lasserre's description that, "tout ce qui est, est unique en son genre."[21] "A ce que nous jugeons et prononçons au nom de la raison interprète de l'expérience, les bergsoniens opposent ce qu'ils appellent 'la vie' – la vie qui se moque des arrêts et limitations de la raison et dont le propre est d'inventer toujours des expériences nouvelles."[22] To reason, the Bergsonians oppose intuition; to classical discipline and constancy, they oppose the élan vital and evolutionary progress. To tradition they oppose novelty. The Bergsonian philosophy, concluded Lasserre, "est la justification métaphysique du réfus de penser." [23]

Hulme did not abandon his attachment to Bergson at once. Into 1912, he continued to write expository articles, and his translation of Bergson's *Introduction to Metaphysics* appeared in 1913. But his philosophic emphasis was rapidly and dramatically shifting, and this had important consequences for his attitudes towards the new art. Once Hulme accepted Lasserre's definition of romanticism, he was obliged to reorient his critical bearings. No longer could the move from "ancient" to "modern" be considered a natural and desired development, an emancipation from outmoded beliefs. On the contrary, the "liberation" was now seen as simply a new form of romantic decadence. What was needed was not an art which mirrors the modernizing tendencies but one which contests them: a "classical revival." [24]

In the lecture on modern poetry, Hulme had challenged the legitimacy of rules and conventions; he had seen them as constraining the possibilities for self-expression. But by 1912 he scornfully defined the romantic as one who "imagines that everything is accomplished by the breaking of rules." [25] The classical artist, on the other hand, believes "that there are certain rules which one must obey," [26] and vehemently rejects dependence on "personal inspiration." Instead of demanding verse which will be "tentative" and "vague," Hulme now calls for "a period of dry, hard, classical verse." [27] It is a noteworthy shift, representing the entrance into the modernist polemic of a new and divergent strain of thought which will become increasingly pronounced. Already, it ought to be obvious that Hulme's classicism stands not only against his own Bergsonism but also against the general individualist perspective which embraced freedom and self-expression and which rejected any limits imposed by tradition or convention. The initial terms of a decisive literary opposition begin to emerge. On the one side, the key concepts are order, discipline and restraint; on the other, they are freedom, expression, individualism. This was a promised consequence of dating Hulme: an undermining of the homogeneity of modernist doctrine, the recognition of conflicting currents.

The process is not complete. Although the opposition between romantic and classical is widely considered Hulme's most important contribution to modernism, and although it is certainly the issue which has figured most prominently in appreciations of his work, it is worth intimating here what will shortly become obvious: that this, like the Bergsonism, represented only a provisional phase in his thought and that he would move to a further stage, in which he rejected the romantic/classical distinction.

This is not the way the distinction has been treated. The essay "Romanticism and Classicism" in particular has assumed a privileged status in Hulme's *corpus*. The essay was unpublished at the time of Hulme's death, and when it appeared in *Speculations* its date was unspecified. It has been regarded as the most mature statement of Hulme's opinions – partly, no doubt, because of T. S. Eliot's later embrace of the classical position. In any case, Read gave support to this view by hypothesizing that Hulme, at the time of his death, was intending to publish the essay in a series of pamphlets, implying that it represented the furthest development of his thought.

But though left undated, "Romanticism and Classicism" is datable. Early in the text, in emphasizing the exuberance of the classical revival, Hulme refers to an incident in Paris: "About a year ago, a man whose name I think was Fauchois gave a lecture at the Odéon on Racine, in the course of which he made some disparaging remarks about his dullness, lack of invention and the rest of it."[28] Hulme goes on to describe the riot which the lecture provoked and draws the conclusion that "these people interrupted because the classical ideal is a living thing to them and Racine is the great classic."[29] The man's name was indeed Fauchois. He was scheduled to give his lecture before a performance of *Iphigénie en Aulide*. But, as he began to speak, several members of Action Française leapt onto the stage. There were twelve arrests, including that of Jean Graveline, a physician, who led the Camelots du Roi, the militant youth arm of the movement. The incident took place on November 3, 1910, and was duly noted in the December issue of *L'Action Française*. "A l'Odéon manifestation contre le conférencier

Fauchois, contempteur de Racine: arrestation du Dr. Graveline et de nombreux Camelots du Roi."[30]

The important detail, of course, is the date. Hulme's "about a year ago" would put "Romanticism and Classicism" sometime in late 1911 or early 1912. In either case, it is clear that the essay belongs to the period of "A Tory Philosophy" (May 1912), his only other extended consideration of the romantic/classical opposition, and not to the last phase of his thought (circa 1916), where Read places it. The matter would be trivial, if it did not bear so closely on larger issues. But the hasty acceptance of Hulme's "classicism" implies more than a local and scholarly confusion. Not only does it confuse Hulme's career; it obscures a distinction of considerable importance in modernist ideology. Drawing that distinction is the next step.

Husserl, Frege, Moore

What follows is best approached through one further textual mishap. It concerns the essay which begins *Speculations*, "Humanism and the Religious Attitude," Hulme's longest, most comprehensive and most considered piece of writing. I refer to the essay as "Humanism and the Religious Attitude," but that is already misleading: for what is most striking about the text as it appears under that title is what is absent. In late 1915 and early 1916, Hulme published a series of essays in the *New Age* which he called "A Notebook." With one significant exception these became the long *Speculations* essay; the exception was the opening of the series. Herbert Read, when he came to compile *Speculations*, seems to have been unaware of the *New Age* contributions. In any case he never refers to the missing instalment, which is unfortunate because it does much to clarify ostensible contradictions in Hulme's thought.

Hulme there is unusually frank about his changing attitudes. He begins by discussing the great intellectual obstacle of the current day, the difficulty of escaping scepticism: "Living in a sceptical atmosphere, you are in an unnatural attitude which prevents you seeing objective truth." Such, he acknowledges, was the difficulty which impeded his own development. "I at one time thought that the pragmatists, relativists, and human-

ists were right, and that all the 'ideal' sciences, logic, mathematics, ethics, etc., could all have meaning and validity only, in
reference to the human mind . . ." [31]

The allusion here is to the 1908–1912 phase of his thought,
when Hulme had habitually attacked the illusions of rationalist
objectivity and had insisted, following Nietzsche, that philo
sophy was only autobiography – the period, in short, that he
now describes as "tainted" with subjectivism.[32] This remark
alone should undermine Alun Jones' casual claim that
"Hulme's metaphysical position remained virtually unaltered
throughout the eight years of his life as a writer."[33] On the
contrary, the change was avowed and thoroughgoing. Hulme
now assails scepticism, relativism and individualism, and
announces his new belief that truth and reality are independent
and objective, not relative and personal. Put in the philosophic
terms which Hulme favours, the literary importance of the shift
is not immediately apparent. Nevertheless, the philosophy is
worth pursuing. It raises issues neglected in the history of
modernism; it puts in austere form certain matters which tend to
blur easily; and it leads naturally into central aesthetic problems.
This ought to justify the following excursus.

In 1894, the Danish logician Gottlob Frege published a review
of Edmund Husserl's first substantial text, *The Philosophy of
Arithmetic*. Frege is the most prominent forebear of twentieth-
century analytic philosophy, Husserl the founder of phenomenology. The two traditions have since pursued their aims in
mutual disregard, and for this reason the brief convergence
between Frege and Husserl has been prized by historians of
philosophy. I mention it here because its implications for
literature, though less immediate, are no less interesting.

The Philosophy of Arithmetic was the first of two projected
volumes, whose aim was "a radical analysis of the 'psychological origin' of the basic mathematical concepts."[34] The idea
was to elucidate certain fundamental arithmetic notions –
number, totality, multiplicity – in terms of mental faculties and
mental operations. Such investigations had become increasingly
popular during this period, when it appeared that the successes
of scientific psychology would make possible a general re-

interpretation of traditional bodies of thought. Husserl's project was in line with the empiricist inspiration we have considered in Arnold and Mill. Just as Arnold, for instance, had wanted to secure religion on the bedrock of "experience," Husserl intended to submit mathematics to a psychological reading.

Frege in his review took this perspective severely to task. He described Husserl's work as "the result of a widespread philosophical disease," part of the "devastation caused by the influx of psychology into logic." In his passion for "scientific justification" Husserl had attempted to cleanse arithmetic in the "psychological wash-tub," and "the mixture of psychology and logic that is now so popular provides good suds for this purpose." According to Frege, however, such a "mixture" leads to fundamental errors. When "everything is shunted off into the subjective," the objective character of mathematical truth is lost, and this makes nonsense of the endeavour.

The confusion of the subjective with the objective, the fact that no clear distinction is ever made between expressions like "Moon" and "presentation of the moon," all this diffuses such an impenetrable fog that the attempt to achieve clarity becomes hopeless . . . In reading this book, I have been able to see how very difficult it is for the sun of truth to penetrate the fog which arises out of the confusion of psychology and logic.[35]

Although psychological activity is no doubt present whenever we are engaged in mathematics, such activity, says Frege, is not to be identified with mathematics itself. Mathematics is self-subsistent and objective, and can only be understood as such. Its truths have nothing to do with what, or how, we think of them. "If a geographer were to read a work on oceanography in which the origin of the seas were explained psychologically, he would undoubtedly receive the impression that the very point at issue had been missed in a very peculiar way. I have the same impression of the present work."[36]

Frege would insist upon this point throughout his career, always with the same passion. It is not, however, Frege's intellectual development that is interesting here, but Husserl's. For after the appearance of Frege's review, Husserl's philosophy underwent a dramatic shift. The second volume of the mathematical study was abandoned, and when his next book,

the *Logical Investigations* (1900), appeared, Husserl had joined
Frege as a vehement opponent of the psychological perspective.
The *Logical Investigations* is the founding text of phenomenology, and, in outlining the phenomenological method,
Husserl defines it precisely against the fallacy of "psychologism." The first volume of the work was a sustained attempt "to
show that the exclusively psychological grounding of logic, to
which our age ascribes so great a value, rests on a confusion of
essentially distinct classes of problems, on presuppositions
erroneous in principle concerning the character and the goals of
the two sciences which are involved here – empirical psychology and pure logic."[37]

That, of course, is just the position which Frege urged, and,
once committed to the new attitude, Husserl was outspoken and
untiring in its defence. (Perhaps somewhat abashed at the
violence of his recanting, he cites Goethe in his preface: "There
is nothing to which one is more severe than the errors that one
has just abandoned.") He speaks with scorn of "our psychologically obsessed age" and protests against the intermingling of
"a vague empirical generalization with an absolutely exact,
purely conceptual law." Put most concisely: "What is not
psychological is not accessible to psychological illumination."[38]
J. S. Mill had held of logic that "as far as it is a science at all, its
theoretic grounds are wholly borrowed from psychology."[39]
Formerly sympathetic to this position, Husserl now contests it
bitterly. Logic, in his view, borrows nothing from anything.
"We deny," he writes, "that the theoretical discipline of pure
logic, in the independent separateness proper to it, has any
concern with mental facts, or with laws that might be styled
'psychological.'" On the contrary, it is pure, ideal and objective
and to be elucidated as such.[40]

This bears directly on the *New Age* essay of December 1915.
Hulme spoke there of overcoming his belief that "logic,
mathematics, ethics, etc., could all have meaning and validity
only, in reference to the human mind."[41] Several paragraphs
later, he confirmed his debt to Husserl's *Logical Investigations*,
and through the rest of "A Notebook" he uses the phenomenological view of logic to support his claims for a break with "the
Renaissance tradition." Logic, he writes at one point, deals

"with these quite *objective* sentences. In this way the anthropo-morphism which underlies certain views of logic is got rid of."[42]

The "getting rid of" anthropomorphism became Hulme's chief intellectual endeavour, and, while Husserl provided the logical arguments, G. E. Moore furnished the ethical. *Principia Ethica*, first published in 1903, has been most often linked to literature through the enthusiasms of Bloomsbury, for whom Moore's most important contention was that only the love of people and beautiful objects was good in itself. But Moore had another, more direct (though less visible and well-known) influence on modernist thought – this, as one may gather, through the person of Hulme.

For at the centre of *Principia Ethica* was the attempt to prove the non-psychological, non-naturalist, non-subjective character of ethical value. The argument placed Moore in direct dispute with Mill's utilitarianism and with Spencer's evolutionary ethics – indeed with any effort to identify moral good with some set of physical or psychological conditions, such as "pleasure" (in Mill's scheme) or "more evolved" (in Spencer's). According to Moore, such attempts committed what in a famous phrase he called "the naturalist fallacy," the idea that good can be defined in terms of natural properties.[43] In fact, contends Moore, "Good" cannot be defined at all. "If I am asked 'What is good?' my answer is that good is good, and that is the end of the matter." Naturalism, in short "offers no reason at all, far less any valid reason, for any ethical principle whatever." "Good" is a property of things, but it is a "non-natural" property, and it cannot be translated into any other terms.[44]

The analogies with the Husserlian attack on psychologism in logic are striking – and they struck Hulme forcibly. Just as Husserl denies that logic can be reduced to psychology, Moore denies that ethical value can be identified with anything outside of the ethical sphere. Both of them, in short, contest the scientizing impulse, which would assimilate their subjects to some more fundamental realm. Logic and ethics are to be autonomous disciplines not susceptible to any reduction. On this issue, Moore and Husserl position themselves as far as possible from the empiricist proclivities of the previous century.

Hulme enthusiastically endorses their attitude: it provides for him the sought-after escape from the confines of the human personality. Husserl's phenomenology and Moore's ethics supplied a philosophical justification of the objective character of meaning and value. Given this standpoint of objectivity, Hulme could purge the last vestiges of humanism from his thought. Now he would insist that questions of ultimate value had nothing to do with subjectivity.

Moore employs another example which helps underscore the point. The utilitarian philosopher Henry Sidgwick had attempted to prove that the only things that we value are those things which stand in "relation to human existence, or at least to some consciousness or feeling." To dramatize his argument, Sidgwick had adduced the fact that "no one would consider it rational to aim at the production of beauty in external nature, apart from any possible contemplation of it by human beings."[45] "Well," responds Moore, having cited the case, "I may say at once, that I, for one, do consider this rational . . ." He asks the reader to imagine two worlds. One is to be as beautiful as can be conceived, full of "mountains, rivers, the sea; trees, and sunsets, stars and moon." The other is to be the ugliest imaginable: "simply one heap of filth, containing everything that is most disgusting to us, for whatever reason, and the whole, as far as may be, without one redeeming feature." Now, asks Moore, even if we agree that no human being would see either world, "still, is it irrational to hold that it is better that the beautiful world should exist, than the one which is ugly?" Moore contends that it is by no means irrational, and accordingly concludes that our values are not exclusively determined by reference to human existence. We favour certain things, events, states of affairs, whether or not they are connected to humanity.[46]

This takes us back both to art and to Hulme. For, as we shall now see, it would become essential to Hulme's aesthetic that art, like ethics and logic, be emancipated from the anthropomorphic, its value not to be derived from its "humanity," "vitality" or "realism." The argument which Moore made against Sidgwick Hulme will make against the reigning critical establishment. He will come to advocate an aesthetic attitude which derives "not from a delight in life but from a feeling for certain absolute values, which are entirely independent of vital things."[47] From the time of his acceptance of the romantic/classical distinction (1911 or 1912) Hulme had been committed to the struggle against artistic individualism; what I want now to show is that, in pursuing the critique, he came to a position more extreme than the classical, and which is identified with classicism only on pain of much confusion.

The making of an anti-humanist

By the middle of 1912 Pound had announced the formation of the Imagist movement and set out to persuade others of its existence. Wyndham Lewis, after a period of struggle, had begun to abandon representational art; his *Kermesse* was painted that year.[48] Ford was beginning to formulate his theories of Impressionism. These antagonists had not yet come into collision, but the stage was set. Late in that year Hulme left London for Berlin, where he spent the next nine months. The departure marks a transition in his career, for it brought to an end his direct involvement in literature. The five poems comprising *The Complete Poetical Works of T. E. Hulme* were published in the *New Age* in January 1912; he would publish no more poetry. Nor would he contribute to literary theory. During his nine-month stay in Germany, he developed the opinions of his last phase of thought. It was probably during this period that he became acquainted with the work of Husserl (and returned to Moore with new sympathy). It was certainly then that he made acquaintance with the work of Wilhelm Worringer.

In 1908 Worringer had published his doctoral dissertation under the title *Abstraktion und Einfühlung*. Its success was immediate. "I cannot help being aware," wrote Worringer later, "of how much the publication of this doctorate thesis of a young and unknown student influenced many personal lives and the spiritual life of a whole era."[49] Whether the book affected as many lives as the Austrian annexation of Bosnia and Herzegovina that same year is questionable, but for Hulme in particular the work was indeed momentous – not so much for its treatment of specific art-historical issues but in the implications of Worringer's basic conceptual aim: a critique of the theory of empathy (*Einfühlung*).

This theory, most closely associated with the work of Theodor Lipps, was at that time dominant in German aesthetics. Its fundamental premise, in Worringer's concise paraphrase, was that "Aesthetic enjoyment is objectified self-enjoyment. To enjoy aesthetically means to enjoy myself in a sensuous object diverse from myself, to empathize myself into it."[50] The art work, that is to say, achieves success by reflecting the impulses of its audience, and, writes Lipps, "Only in so far as this empathy exists, are forms beautiful. Their beauty is . . . the ideal freedom with which I live myself out in them."[51] Such a view, rejoins Worringer, applies only to the "narrow framework of Graeco-Roman and modern Occidental art." For other periods and other styles – for instance, Egyptian or Byzantine art – a different principle of explanation is needed. To that end, Worringer elaborates a "counter-pole" to the urge to empathy: the urge to abstraction (*Abstraktionsdrang*), which does not aim to mirror human impulses but seeks instead to construct the art-object as something distinct and autonomous. The two artistic tendencies, suggests Worringer, reflect two fundamental attitudes toward the world. Empathy is the product of a "happy pantheistic relationship of confidence between man and the phenomena of the outside world." It inclines toward the "truths of organic life, that is toward naturalism in the higher sense." Abstraction, on the other hand, is the product of a "great inner unrest inspired in man by the phenomena of the outside world." "Just as the urge to empathy as a pre-assumption of aesthetic experience finds its gratification in the beauty of the organic, so the urge to abstraction finds its beauty in the life-denying inorganic, in the crystalline or, in general terms, in all abstract law and necessity."[52] Only in the context of this distinction, insists Worringer, can we understand primitive, Egyptian and Byzantine art: he proceeds to a detailed investigation of their historical character.

Lipps had intended his theory of empathy not only as an aesthetic postulate but as a general philosophic and psychological principle which aimed to account for our ability to perceive objects and other individuals. This is worth mentioning because Lipps also appeared in Husserl's *Logical Investigations*, where he is criticized as a proponent of psychologism. Indeed Worringer's argument against Lipps and on behalf of abstraction bears notable similarities to Husserl's defence of "pure logic," and, though I know no evidence of any contact or influence, the theories of the two figures met in Hulme's enthusiastic embrace.

Hulme was not interested in the historical details of *Abstraction and Empathy*, only in the theoretical insights which provided him with a new polemical apparatus. He had conversations with Worringer at the Berlin Congress of Aesthetics in 1913, and though he had at one point called Lipps "the greatest writer on aesthetics," he now settled on abstraction at the expense of empathy.[53] Returning to England later in the year, he began a brief but impassioned career as an art critic.

Jacob Epstein had recently given a show of sculpture and drawings which had met with an unsympathetic critical response. Hulme, a friend of Epstein's, rallied to his defence in an essay, "Mr. Epstein and the Critics," printed in the *New Age* in December. Hulme set himself the task of "attempting to protect the spectator from certain prejudices." And here he unveils his most recent theoretical ordnance. He argues that there has been a "certain general state of mind which has lasted from the Renaissance"[54] but has now finally entered a period of disintegration. Epstein's work is seen as part of a new sensibility contesting the traditional Renaissance *Weltanschauung*: Hulme cites with derision one critic who had accused Epstein's sculptures of "rude savagery . . . as distant from modern feeling as the loves of the Martians." To this Hulme replies, "Modern feeling be damned! As if it was not the business of every honest man at the present moment to clean the world of these sloppy dregs of the Renaissance."[55]

Over the next several months Hulme continued his defence of the new art, championing the work of Epstein, Gaudier-Brzeska and David Bomberg and, with some reservation, the paintings of Lewis and Wadsworth. He saw in their work an expression of the "geometric" attitude which abjures realism and vital form in favour of abstraction. He distinguished three tendencies within the modern movement in the fine arts: Post-

Impressionism, analytical Cubism and this "new constructive geometrical art," which he so aggressively defended and so eagerly explained, regarding it as "the only one containing possibilities of development."[56]

On January 22, 1914 he gave a lecture to the Quest Society on "Modern Art and Its Philosophy," in which he expressed his new point of view in a series of three theses:

> (1) There are two kinds of art, geometrical and vital, absolutely distinct in kind from one another . . .
> (2) Each of these arts springs from and corresponds to a certain general attitude towards the world . . .
> (3) – this is really the point I am making for – that the re-emergence of geometrical art may be the precursor of the re-emergence of the corresponding attitude towards the world, and so, of the break up of the Renaissance humanistic attitude . . .[57]

About this formulation there are several points to be made. First – and this is something both Hynes and Jones have observed – it indicates the partisan turning which Hulme gave to Worringer's scholarly classification.[58] In Hulme's hands *Abstraktionsdrang* was not simply a heuristic concept but a weapon in the critical debate, a way of justifying radical *contemporary* experiments. Against theorists of naturalism, Worringer provided a legitimizing counterweight.

The second issue concerns the development of Hulme's opinions. In five years he has renounced virtually every major proposition to which he had given assent. In his Poets' Club phase of 1908 and 1909, he had justified modern art as subjective, tentative and relativist; modern poetry was to imitate Impressionist painting; art was to avoid the pursuit of formal perfection in favour of the "maximum of individual and personal expression."[59] By 1914, Hulme was the severest critic of such attitudes, which he now identified as part of the Renaissance and romantic legacy.

This reversal has been suggested in the contrast between Hulme's Bergsonism and the classicism he adopted from Action Française, an opposition which will prove central in the later developments of modernist theory. But the terms of the opposition are not exhaustive; and again Hulme furnishes a way of making a distinction. For his classicism, as should begin to be

clear, was no final stopping place. After his return from Berlin –
and primarily under the influence of Worringer and Husserl – he
moved to a new attitude which found classicism as unsatisfactory as romanticism; the goal became not a classical, but
an anti-humanist and geometric, art.

This last shift has been completely, though by this time we
cannot say surprisingly, neglected. Hulme's classicism has been
blithely assimilated to his later enthusiasms, as though these
were simply different names for the same attitude. Cork, for
instance, writes that Hulme "saw the opposition between
geometrical and 'vital' art as identical with the opposition he
had already formulated between religious and humanist,
classical and romantic."[60] And Raymond Williams writes that
Hulme "sees romanticism as the extreme development of
humanism, and is concerned to reject it, and to prepare for a
radical transformation of society, according to different principles which he calls classical."[61] Williams, that is, identifies
Hulme's *classicism* with his *attack on humanism*; others make the
same assumption. The failure to distinguish clearly between
classicism and anti-humanism not only confuses Hulme's
thought – which would be a relatively minor confusion, for
which Hulme is in some measure responsible – it obscures an
important distinction in the modernist perspective. The
romantic/classical opposition is simply not identical with the
humanist/anti-humanist opposition – not in ordinary use, not in
Hulme's use. Once Hulme saw *humanism* as the root of the
problem, he ceased to regard the romantic/classical division as
fundamental.

I have said that the value of dating Hulme is that it lets us escape
from the false homogeneity of *Speculations*; it enables us to see a
succession of attitudes instead of a confused mass of opinion. We
can now fix Hulme's classicism in the period 1911–12 and it
becomes possible to make good sense of certain remarks which
have been ignored.

For instance, in January of 1914, in one of his first essays on
the "new constructive geometric art," written shortly after his
return from Berlin, Hulme insists that geometric art alone
provides the genuine alternative to "slop and romanticism," an
alternative "*which has quite mistakenly sought refuge in the conception*

of a classical revival" – this from a man who some two years earlier had made a "classical revival" the centre of his programme.[62] In his lecture at the Quest Society that same month, he goes to great lengths to distinguish between classical and geometric sensibilities; the former is representational, vital and human-centred, the latter anti-representational, anti-vital and anti-human. He criticizes the tendency to "erect the classical and our own conception of art into an absolute and look on all art before the classical as imperfect strivings towards it, and all after as decadence from it."[63] The criticism is made more direct in "Humanism and the Religious Attitude" in a section called "Partial Reactions": "There are people who, disgusted with romanticism, wish for us to go back to the classical period, or who, like Nietzsche, wish us to admire the Renaissance. But such partial reactions will always fail, for they are only half measures – it is no good returning to humanism, for that will itself degenerate into romanticism."[64]

Classicism, then, is abandoned as insufficiently radical. Where it had once seemed the saving alternative to romanticism, it is now regarded as a precursor of romantic decline. Such a change is thoroughly consistent with the broader movements of Hulme's thought. Given his commitment to an "untainted" anti-subjectivist aesthetic, classicism was indeed a "half measure." Husserl and Moore had persuaded him that truth, meaning and value were independent of the individual, and Worringer made plain that the pursuit of vital human form was only one aim in the history of art, not an essential attribute of art as such. If the aesthetic goal becomes an anti-vital abstraction – "a desire for austerity and bareness, a striving towards structure and away from the messiness and confusion of nature and natural things" – then classical art provides an inappropriate refuge.[65] The opposition between romanticism and classicism (which Hulme had once considered fundamental) collapses: both are phases of the wider organicist and humanist Occidental tradition. Certainly, this is the logic of Worringer's own argument. *Abstraction and Empathy* concludes with an appendix which discusses the need to escape the parochialism of the Western tradition. Hulme himself sounds this theme repeatedly in the last two years of his life. Against classical humanism, he posits what he calls the "religious attitude," which "is not *life* at its intensest," which "contains in a way an almost *anti-vital* element," which embraces dogma, which denies human perfectibility, and whose aesthetic expression involves geometric abstraction: "the searching after an austerity, a monumental stability and permanence, a perfection and rigidity, which vital things can never have . . ." [66]

Hulme's justification for abandoning classicism should be clear. The only possible standpoint for contesting a decadent romantic tradition is to discard the tradition altogether, its humanist origins along with its romantic deliquescence. The embrace of aesthetic abstraction, of philosophic objectivism, of the "religious attitude," represents the positioning of his theory at the furthest remove from an anthropomorphic perspective. The "geometric" replaces the "classical" as the only possible salvation, and Hulme's references are now habitually to Byzantine and Egyptian art rather than to the definitive work of Shakespeare and Racine.

There remains a further, and interesting, consequence of Hulme's changing attitudes. In his pursuit of an extreme anti-individualist perspective, he has been obliged to revise his sense of the history of art. His early subjectivist poetic ("A Lecture on Modern Poetry") fell within a conventional model of linear change. The historical movement of thought was from absolutism to relativism, from permanence to fluidity, from epic grandeur to lyric modesty. The twentieth century represented the culmination of the process, and modern art, argued Hulme, ought to adopt the impressionistic individualism appropriate to its age.

Under Lasserre's influence, the scheme suffered its first dramatic transformation. The modern individualizing tendency was no longer conceived as the furthest stage of development but as the decadent conclusion of a romantic phase. History should move forward by glancing backward. The way towards cultural health was a rejection, not an embrace, of those individualizing habits and a return to classicism. The onset of decline was dated "Rousseau"; the aim, therefore, was a reassertion of those pre-Rousseauist aspirations associated with dignity, restraint and modesty.

But Hulme's next perception – legitimized by Husserl, Moore and especially Worringer – was that romanticism was only a symptom, an aggravated consequence of the Renaissance humanist outlook:

the change which Copernicus is supposed to have brought about is the exact contrary of the fact. Before Copernicus, man was not the centre of the world; after Copernicus he was. You get a change from a certain profundity and intensity to that flat and insipid optimism which, passing through its first stage of decay in Rousseau, has finally culminated in the state of slush in which we have the misfortune to live.[67]

Romanticism is only the proximate target; the really pressing need is for an overcoming of Renaissance categories of thought. And here, as Hulme learned from Worringer, the classical period provides no solution, since it, too, was bound to a humanistic and vitalist perspective. The fundamental distinction, according to Worringer, falls between Oriental and Occidental, and *Abstraction and Empathy* concludes by insisting that art history must recognize this distinction, if "it is to pass beyond a narrowly European outlook."[68] Hulme arrives at the same conclusion. Not only has he relinquished a linear view of history in favour of a cyclical theory, but the cycles have been steadily enlarged. "Romanticism" is no longer the name of the dying phase, nor is "Renaissance." It is Western humanism, from its classical origins to its present decline. Any effective alternative must come from outside the European tradition.

Through Hulme I have meant to retrieve a distinction that has been lost in the rapidity of literary change, a distinction between classicism on the one hand and anti-humanism on the other – attitudes profoundly divergent though habitually conflated. Once they have been separated, it becomes possible to recognize the importance of certain aesthetic aims that do not fall easily under the rubric of classicism – for instance primitivism and abstraction. This has immediate benefits, as we will see in the next chapter.

Hulme, as I have pointed out, abandoned literature after 1912. He wrote no more poems, no more literary essays. His artistic emphasis settled firmly on the fine arts. And this shift corresponds to a changing focus within the English modern movement generally. Through 1913, the literary polemic was pursued in literary terms. Conrad, James, Ford and Yeats defined the bounds of the controversy. But in 1914 the emphasis shifted; this resulted not only in a new attention to painting and sculpture, but in a revision of the literary perspective.

The significance of Hulme's last essays lies precisely in his articulation of these new artistic demands. What his developed position represented, and what would prove to be of such great consequence, was a distinct artistic valorization, one which sought to purge the human, the organic, the subjective, the mental, the vital, and insisted instead on the independence and objectivity of form, value and meaning. This view stands as far as possible from both Stirnerian egoism and Fordian Impressionism. But though opposing, it was no less successful, and in 1914 the competing perspectives converged.

CHAPTER 7

Symbol, impression, image, vortex

"*Imagisme* is not symbolism . . . On the other hand, *Imagisme* is not Impressionism . . ."

(Pound, "Vorticism")

The problem with Imagism

We have traversed the pre-war literary ground repeatedly. This is the last time. Until now, the attempt has been to trace the separate development of two broad perspectives, considered separately because they developed without notable mutual influence. But in 1914 these tendencies – egoist and abstractionist, realist and formalist – met. The convergence brought together conflicting aesthetic demands, as in the quotation above: Pound defining *Imagisme* against Impressionism and symbolism, and doing so in an essay on Vorticism.

It will be useful to recall some chronology. In 1908–09, the Imagist movement had early avatars in two literary groups, the Poets' Club and its unnamed successor, whose preoccupations, according to F. S. Flint, were free verse, French literature, and "the Image," and whose central figure was T. E. Hulme.[1] Pound joined the group in 1909 not long after his arrival in London, and literary discussion continued in more informal fashion, with Hulme, Flint and Pound as regular participants. In 1912 Pound named Richard Aldington and Hilda Doolittle "Imagistes" and in October he used the term in print for the first time (in connection with Hulme's poetry). Polemic and recruitment intensified. Late in the following year the anthology *Des Imagistes* was accepted for publication, and it appeared in February 1914, containing poems by Aldington, Pound, H. D., Ford, Joyce, Lowell and Upward.[2] Then, several months later, in a dispute over the future of the movement, Pound and Amy Lowell quarrelled, and a split ensued. Subsequent Imagist anthologies were published with Lowell's sponsorship, while Pound turned his attention elsewhere.

So much is generally agreed. But beyond the level of documentary record, there has been little but controversy. In 1961, Alun R. Jones, a biographer of Hulme, wrote a short essay in which he claimed that Ford Madox Ford had unjustifiably occupied a predominant place in the history of Imagism. In fact, argued Jones, Ford misunderstood the tenets of the doctrine, was unacquainted with the poets involved, and in general "shows himself to be hopelessly out of touch" with the period. Jones argues that Hulme was the decisive moving force and that Pound "owes the ideas behind the imagist movement to Hulme."[3] This view fits well with Flint's early version of events and with the two full-scale histories of the movement.[4] It tallies with Kermode's assertion that Imagist principles were "all Hulmian," with Hynes' remark that "the originator of Imagism was clearly Hulme," and with Hughes' judgment that Hulme was the "father of imagism."[5]

But shortly after Jones' essay, Frank MacShane, Ford's biographer, wrote a response in which he took extreme issue with the earlier analysis. He pointed out that Ford was indeed acquainted with the Imagist poets and argued that Ford crucially anticipated aspects of the doctrine.[6] This corresponds with Ford's own sense of events, and with Pound's claim in "This Hulme Business" that the critical light "shone not from Hulme but from Ford . . ."[7] More recently, Herbert Schneidau has made the case for Ford, calling Hulme's role in Imagism a "myth."[8]

I, too, find it useful to construct an opposition between Ford and Hulme, but not because I am in search of a father for Imagism. The task of genealogy, the task I have set myself, is not so much a search for ultimate origins as for relative contributions. Ford and Hulme became plausible rival claimants, because English modernism divided between Fordian and Hulmean principles.[9] The personal claims, of course, are less interesting than the conflict of principle, and the aim here is to account for that developing conflict in the period just before the war. If I choose to elucidate it from the standpoint of Pound, that is because when egoism converged with abstraction, when Ford converged with Hulme, they converged upon him. We can roughly circumscribe our attention within the year between the acceptance of the Imagist anthology, in the summer of 1913, and the outbreak of war the following summer.

Impressionism and the prose tradition

Of Ford, Pound wrote in 1914: "I find him significant and revolutionary because of his insistence upon clarity and precision, upon the prose tradition; in brief, upon efficient writing – even in verse."[10] He frequently returned to this point. Ford was the one who defended "direct speech and vivid impression," who believed that "poetry should be written at least as well as prose," who insisted upon "the importance of good writing as opposed to the opalescent word, the rhetorical tradition."[11] These are attitudes that quickly became part of Pound's literary faith; the debt is highly visible and many times acknowledged. In the thirties Pound added a footnote to one of his published letters: "It should be realized that Ford Madox Ford had been hammering this point of view [the praise of objectivity] into me from the time I first met him (1908 or 1909) and that I owe him anything that I don't owe myself for having saved me from the academic influences then raging in London."[12]

Pound did not respond to Ford's salutary advice immediately. By the time he arrived in London in 1908, he had spent several years pursuing the study of Provençal poetry, and his own early work bears the weight of those researches. It is stylized and over-embellished, the sort of poetry which Ford described as dealing "in a derivative manner with mediaeval emotions."[13] Pound himself would later refer to the *A Lume Spento* volume as "a collection of stale creampuffs."[14] The poem "To the Dawn: Defiance" illustrates that point in six lines:

> Ye blood-red spears-men of the dawn's array
> That drive my dusk-clad knights of dream away,
> Hold! For I will not yield.
> My moated soul shall dream in your despite
> A refuge for the unvanquished hosts of night
> That *can* not yield.

With "blood-red," "dusk-clad" and "moated," it is clear that Pound is not yet an enemy of the adjective, the ornament or the unnecessary word.

In 1911, Pound followed Ford to Giessen in Germany, in order to solicit an opinion on his third volume of verse, *Canzoni*. He recalls the incident in his obituary for Ford. Ford, writes Pound, "felt the errors of contemporary style to the point of rolling (physically, and if you look at it as mere superficial snob, ridiculously) on the floor . . ." The roll "saved me at least two years, perhaps more. It sent me back to my own proper effort, namely, toward using the living tongue . . ."[15]

No doubt the actual conversion was not so abrupt or kinetic. But by 1912–13 Pound had adopted a vehemently anti-rhetorical critical perspective, and Ford rises sharply in his pantheon. In "Status Rerum" of 1913, he wrote that he "would rather talk about poetry with Ford Madox Hueffer than with any man in London." He elaborates the point as follows:

Mr. Hueffer's beliefs about the art may be best explained by saying that they are in diametric opposition to those of Mr. Yeats.

Mr. Yeats has been subjective; believes in the glamour and associations which hang near the words. "Works of art beget works of art." He has much in common with the French symbolists. Mr. Hueffer believes in an exact rendering of things. He would strip words of all "association" for the sake of getting a precise meaning. He professes to prefer prose to verse. You would find his origins in Gautier or in Flaubert. He is objective.[16]

In Pound's view, then, Ford is to be conceived as an opponent of rhetoric and a defender of the prose tradition – a precise objectivist in an age of subjectivists. That view would be sufficiently intelligible, were it not for an array of related facts.

First – there is a curious dissociation in Pound's critical judgment. Concurrent with his praise of Ford is a severe criticism of Impressionism, although Impressionism was Ford's acknowledged literary doctrine. In *Poetry* magazine of June 1914, Pound was calling Ford "significant and revolutionary," while in *Blast*, which appeared almost simultaneously, he was defending Vorticism at the expense of Impressionism: "Impressionism, Futurism, which is only an accelerated sort of impressionism, DENY the vortex. They are the CORPSES of VORTICES."[17]

Second – although Pound described Ford as an opponent of the subjective, Ford himself characterized his Impressionist method as a frank recognition "that all art must be the expression of an ego, and that if Impressionism is to do anything, it must, as the phrase is, go the whole hog." The Impressionist novelist "gives you, as a rule, the fruits of his own observations and the fruits of his own observations alone," and his art therefore is a "frank expression of personality." [18]

This hardly qualifies as the self-description of an objectivist. Still, the contradiction would be less consequential if it stopped here, where it might be dismissed as simply Pound's misreading of Ford's intentions. But if there is misreading, it extends to Ford himself. In reminiscences of the pre-war literary conflicts, he would write in 1919 that the various new sects united in the belief that "the artist should express by his work his own personality," and this, says Ford, accounted for their *hostility* to Impressionism. Whereas Ford was calling for the "frank expression of personality" in 1914, five years later he described the leading Impressionist tenet as the belief that "the artist must aim at the absolute suppression of himself in his rendering of his subject." [19]

There is a deep confusion here which is not to be evaded with talk of Pound's inconsistency or Ford's unreliability. It is a confusion which ushered in the movement of 1914, and which continues to distort present estimates of the period. Its most direct consequence is the continuing debate over whether Impressionism is "subjective" or "objective," but its implications extend much further.

Ford's notions of Impressionism were developed over time, but the most important work was produced between 1912 and 1914 in statements such as "On Impressionism," "The Poet's Eye" and the preface to the *Collected Poems* of 1914. Through his later career he would return to elaborate and amplify the method – and I will draw on these subsequent clarifications – but the fundamental principles were conceived in the essays written shortly before the war.

Impressionism is a realism. Ford made this point early and with increasing insistence. The root axiom was simple – "the general effect of a novel must be the general effect that life makes on mankind" – and that principle became the basis for a range of specific and characteristic Impressionist techniques.[20] Speeches were to be short, because it would be implausible for a narrator to recall long speeches; characters were not to answer one another directly, because in life that almost never happened. The withholding of information, the prominence of a narrator, the abrupt juxtapositions, all were defended on such grounds. In general, argues Ford, the aim is to produce the "illusion of reality," and to the question, "Why try to produce an illusion?" Ford's reply is: "Why then write?"[21] He praises Pound and the Imagists who belong to the "category of realists," recognizing that the supreme literary goal is "the rendering of the material facts of life, without comment and in exact language . . ."[22]

"For a quarter of a century," wrote Ford in 1911, "I have kept before me one unflinching aim – to register my own times in terms of my own time . . ."[23] Those who were not so unflinching became targets of critical attack. Here, for instance, is Ford on Yeats in the essay "Modern Poetry" of 1909:

It is a charming thing, it is a very lovely thing, it is a restful thing, to lose ourselves in meditations upon the Isles of the Blessed, and very sweet songs may be sung about them. But to do nothing else implies a want of courage. We live in our day, we live in our time, and he is not a proper man who will not look in the face his day and his time.[24]

Let us take this attitude as a first strain in Fordian Impressionism, and let us refer to it as a *civic realism*, in which the artist assumes, as it were, the responsibilities of citizenship in the modern world, and according to which the artist's goal is to reflect contemporaneity, or – in Ford's credo of that period – "to register his own times in terms of his own times." Because Yeats registered other times in other terms, he provoked Ford's jeer. Pound never jeered at Yeats, but, like Ford, he took pains to express his differences.

Yeats' *Responsibilities* was published in early 1914 almost concurrently with *Des Imagistes*. The volume created a certain amount of confusion at the time, representing as it did a change in Yeats' verse: toward the more austere style of his later phase. In May Pound reviewed the new volume, raising the question as to whether this new Yeats – "gaunter, seeking greater hardness of outline" – had become an *"Imagiste."* His answer was unequivocal: "No, Mr. Yeats is a symboliste," though Pound went on to concede that Yeats from time to time wrote *"des images."* [25] The review is of some interest, because it appeared in the midst of a crucial period of self-definition. Imagism had gained a set of adherents, some provisional principles and a name; what followed was an attempt to establish coherence. The opposition to symbolism became a way of locating the distinctive Imagist perspective.

A decade earlier, in the essay "Magic," Yeats had affirmed three principles:

> (1) That the borders of our minds are ever shifting, and that many minds can flow into one another, as it were, and create or reveal a single mind, a single energy.
> (2) That the borders of our memories are as shifting, and that our memories are a part of one great memory, the memory of Nature herself.
> (3) That this great mind and great memory can be evoked by symbols. [26]

Though far from any religious orthodoxy, such attitudes obviously serve a religious function in Yeats' thought, a point he himself recognized: "deprived by Huxley and Tyndall, whom I detested, of the simple-minded religion of my childhood, I had made a new religion . . ." If so, Arthur Symons was its high priest. In *The Symbolist Movement in Literature*, he presented literature as a votive offering.

> Here, then, in this revolt against exteriority, against rhetoric, against a materialistic tradition; in this endeavour to disengage the ultimate essence, the soul, of whatever exists and can be realized by the consciousness; in this dutiful waiting upon every symbol by which the soul of things can be made visible; literature, bowed down by so many burdens, may at last attain liberty, and its authentic speech. In attaining this liberty, it accepts a heavier burden; for in speaking to us so intimately, so solemnly, as only religion had hitherto spoken to us, it becomes itself a kind of religion, with all the duties and responsibilities of the sacred ritual. [27]

Yeats, like Symons, positioned himself against the hegemony of scientific explanation and continued to insist on the possibility of transcendence (via symbols) to a unified spiritual realm. Symbolist literature represented an attempted overcoming of the materialist spectre, and against the tendency of scientific literature (by which he referred to literary naturalism) "to lose itself in externalities of all kinds," Yeats urged a return to "suggestion" and "evocation." A symbol, he writes, "is indeed the only possible expression of some invisible essence, a transparent lamp about a spiritual flame," and the symbolist work of art points past itself and past the physical world to "something that moves beyond the senses." [28]

Whatever it was that moved beyond the senses, Ford and Pound took no interest in it; indeed on this issue the two stood closer to Yeats' antagonist Huxley. Fordian Impressionism was "scientific" because it represented, faithfully and rigorously, the artist's impressions, and Ford criticized the poetry of Yeats because it forsook immediate perception in favour of imaginative wanderings through mystical arcana. Pound, too, liked to compare art to science (the "arts, literature, poesy, are a science just as chemistry is a science") and in one of his early manifestos he insisted that "the natural object is always the *adequate* symbol." [29] The pursuit of transcendence is thus summarily abandoned. Pound is proposing a strict confinement of art to the physically and psychologically given; there is no superior realm to which this is inferior; the first tenet of Imagism was "Direct treatment of the 'thing', whether subjective or objective." [30] This shift represents a *naturalizing* of the poetic sign; the sign still points, but to this world rather than to any other. [31]

If modern poetry was to be "scientific," it must therefore be loyal to its "data," the data of immediate perception. Ford, in his essay on "Modern Poetry," appealed to poets to look the contemporary world "in the face," and on this point the younger generation was still more adamant. Pound commended Fletcher for an art "that dares to go to the dust-bin for its subjects." And Lewis would write in *Blast* that "A man could make just as fine an art in discords, and with nothing but 'ugly' trivial and terrible materials, as any classic artist did with only 'beautiful' and pleasant means." [32] Since there was no aesthetic interest in what lay *behind* immediate reality – in, for instance, Yeats' "great mind" and "great memory" – then the success of a poem did not depend on "suggestion" or "evocation," but rather on "direct treatment." Whereas Mallarmé had written that "To *name* the object is to destroy three-quarters of the enjoyment of the poem . . ." Pound would bluntly remark that, "when words cease to cling close to things, kingdoms fall, empires wane and diminish . . ."[33] Refusing to strain after the ineffable, Pound, under the influence of Ford, conceived Imagism as a setting of limits – in Schneidau's phrase, Imagism as discipline.[34]

Discipline is what qualified Ford as "defender of the prose tradition." For "prose," in Ford's use and Pound's appropriation, indicated not simply a category of linguistic expression, but a habit of mind, a temperament more than a mode. Prose is the pleasure taken in "exact, formal and austere phrases," the pursuit of limpidity and modesty, the refusal of artificial literary conventions. Ford deliberately confounds the standard distinction between prose and poetry, suggesting that the poets "should have insisted on capturing prose for themselves at the start," and contending that prior to 1912 the only poetry he came across was to be found in prose. On the other hand, on the rare occasion when he was in sympathy with a poet – as with Christina Rossetti, Walter de la Mare, or Robert Browning – it was "the prose qualities of those passages" to which he attached importance.[35] Such attitudes led Ford to set rigorous boundaries to permissible literary expression. Outside of those boundaries lay rhetoric, moralizing, authorial intrusion, obsolete word choice. Literature is pared to its essentials, in conformity with the principle that "that art is the greatest which most economises in its means."[36] In large measure, then, the cult of "prose" like the cult of "realism" is a negative enterprise, the banishing of everything beyond the prosy real.

Against Yeats' drift into a Rosicrucian haze, Ford had situated art firmly within the immediately visible present. Indeed, he insisted on a present so visible and so immediate that it served to exclude any wider moral, political or metaphysical excursus. Life was a sequence of impressions; there was to be no superfluity, no bombast, only "a quiet voice," "just quietly saying things." As for poetic diction, the poet should use "such language as he ordinarily uses."[37]

The point which Pound considered most fundamental, and from which he derived a set of aesthetic corollaries, was the Fordian insistence on presentation without elaboration – in one of Ford's slogans, "Never comment: state."[38] In Pound's view, this was the great lesson which poetry could learn from prose (he would later say that "*Imagisme* of '12 to '14 set out 'to bring poetry up to the level of prose'").[39] And in one of the "Approaches to Paris" series, he explained more fully.

I think this sort of clear presentation is of the noblest traditions of our craft. It is surely the scourge of fools. It is what may be called the "prose tradition" of poetry, and by this I mean that it is a practice of speech common to good prose and to good verse alike. It is to modern verse what the method of Flaubert is to modern prose, and by that I do not mean that it is not equally common to the best work of the ancients. It means constatation of fact. It presents. It does not comment. It is irrefutable because it does not present a personal predilection for any particular fraction of the truth . . . It is not a criticism of life, I mean it does not deal in opinion. It washes its hands of theories. It does not attempt to justify anybody's ways to anybody or anything else.[40]

These are Pound's words, but if there were a Fordian orthodoxy, it would be expressed in this way. "Constatation of fact" is as far as possible from the symbolist "expression of an invisible essence," and to oppose the two phrases is to emphasize the extent of Pound's commitment to a natural rather than a transcendent basis for poetry. This is the "scientific" and "realist" aspect of the new literary programme, on which both Ford and Pound so fiercely insisted.

Shortly after Pound's review of *Responsibilities*, Ford published his own set of comments in the *Outlook*. He began by recalling his former attitude towards Yeats: "I didn't like his confounded point of view. I hated, and do still hate, people who poke about among legends and insist on the charms of remote islands."[41] He refers the reader to Yeats' poem "The Lake Isle of Innisfree" and then offers his "prose-impressionist" preference for a poem which would begin like this:

> At Innisfree there is a public-house;
> They board you well for ten and six a week.
> The mutton is not good, but you can eat
> Their honey. I am going there to take
> A week or so of holiday to-morrow.

If these lines seem only a grotesque parody, it is worth recalling some lines from the poem "On Heaven," in which Ford's heaven turns out to be "a little town near Lyons":

> There's a paper shop
> Painted all blue, a shipping agency,
> Three or four cafés; dank, dark colonnades
> Of an eighteen-forty *Maîrie*.

The contrast in poetic aspirations is, of course, severe. Yeats' aim is to evoke a realm which exists in opposition to immediate reality, which exists only in the poetic imagination and which stands as a pastoral refuge from the "roadway" and "pavements grey." The vision of Innisfree, then, partakes of the urge to transcendence, the desire to pass beyond the visible, the immediate and the close at hand. The island remains an imaginative ideal, whose ideality is enforced through a carefully poeticized language.

Ford, on the other hand, has forcibly restored Innisfree to recognizable reality. He has abandoned pastoral, and abandoned rhetorical effect in favour of precise descriptive detail, making the island real by making it ordinary. All that remains of transcendence is a "holiday." Even in "On Heaven," a poem which would surely seem to involve transcendence – what more transcendent than heaven? – Ford never oversteps human limits to pass into the supernatural, since

> one is English,
> Though one be ever so much of a ghost;
> And if most of your life has been spent in the
>   craze to relinquish
> What you want most,
> You will go on relinquishing,
> You will go on vanquishing
> Human longings, even
> In Heaven.[42]

And God appears in the poem as

> A man of great stature,
> In a great cloak,
> With a great stride,
> And a little joke
> For all and sundry, coming down with a hound
>   at his side.

Ford enjoyed the gentle debunking of spirituality, finding it "amusing and touching to think of the Blessed Virgin as human and concerned and overworked."[43] The studied naturalizing is a result of Ford's realist criterion, which required literature to enact only those situations which were to be found in contemporary life. That criterion had been the basis of his antipathy toward Yeats, whom he accused of evading literary responsibility by retreating into the shadowy past of Celtic legend. But in the June essay, after mentioning his hostility and proposing his revision of the "Innisfree" poem, Ford announces a change in his opinion. It "began to occur to me that his Celtism might be genuine, or might be a pose, but that in any case it did not matter very much beside the importance of the personality." And he concludes the essay by writing that he wished he "had the faculty of expressing more ungrudgingly my admiration for this great personality and fine poet."

Ford himself is never embarrassed by such inconsistency, but it is something of an embarrassment to his critical position. He is offering what amounts to an alternative literary justification, a new line of critical defence, to which I alluded early in the chapter: namely, Impressionism as a "frank expression of personality," an "egotism." "I do not," he writes, "see how Impressionism can be anything else." He contrasts the Impressionist artist to the average English reviewer, claiming that the chief difference between the two is that the correspondent is obliged "to sacrifice his personality, and the greater part of his readability."[44] Impressionism, on the contrary, makes possible the presentation not of facts alone but of a personal point of view, and the justification of any artistic method, Ford insists, "the measure of its success, will be just the measure of its suitability for rendering the personality of the artist," because personality is "the chief thing in a work of art."[45]

Although Ford had praised the Imagists as "realists," he defended their method of *vers libre* on grounds of personal expression. "Verse which is cut to a pattern," he wrote, "must sacrifice a certain amount . . . of the personality of the writer." On the other hand,

the justification for vers libre is this: It allows a freer play for self-expression than even narrative prose; at the same time it calls for an even greater precision in that self-expression . . . the unit of vers libre is really the conversational sentence of the author. As such it is the most intimate of means of expression.[46]

Here appears the confusion. Ford alternately offers *realism* and *self-expression* as the basis for his literary programme: Impressionism as precise description, Impressionism as egoism. This divergence was not a question of different opinions voiced at different moments in a career. Ford insisted on realism and self-expression concurrently. He moved easily between the two positions, offering no reconciliation, conceding no need for one. Very reasonably, this has troubled his critics, and it seems responsible for the ambiguities in Pound's attitude toward Ford, and in Ford's self-descriptions.

Ford himself provides a way to resolve the ambiguity, without acknowledging it as a resolution – Ford, after all, never acknowledged a problem. In any case, his changing attitudes towards Yeats provide a key. In the 1913 essay "The Poet's Eye," and again in the preface to his *Collected Poems*, Ford restates the civic realist dictum: "to register my own times in terms of my own time"; and then he goes on to express his growing admiration for Yeats' work, whose general effect he compares to "a grey, thin mist over a green landscape, the mist here and there being pierced by a sparkle of dew, by the light shot from a gem in a green cap." "It will at first sight appear that here is a contradicting of the words with which we set out – the statement that it is the duty of the poet to reflect his own day. But there is no contradiction. It is the duty of the poet to reflect his own day as it appears to him, as it has impressed itself upon him." [47]

Civic realism thus collapses into an egoism which no longer attempts to establish shared norms of reality. The literary goal which Ford pursues: "that is one good thing"; and the literary goal which Yeats pursues: "that is another good thing." As Ford puts it in the essay "English Literature of To-day," the artist is unable to "see the truth as it is"; his business, therefore, is "to register a truth as he sees it." [48] Ford, it is clear, depends on two Impressionist criteria: a civic realism and a radical subjectivism. Yeats failed on the basis of one, only to be rehabilitated on the basis of the other.

It is worth following the implications of this subjectivism, which becomes increasingly dominant in Ford's thought. If the artist's obligation is not to represent the world as it is, only the world as it appears, then there is no need to satisfy public and shared norms. The artist is free to present the most idiosyncratic vision as long as it is "truly rendered." Though Ford maintains a standard of "realism," it comes to have a distinctly personal meaning. And it should now be clear how such a "realism" can be compatible with self expression. For the Impressionist, in Ford's view, is entitled, even obliged, to be personal in the presentation of reality, since there must be no pretence of a neutral body of knowledge. To render reality then *is* to manifest individuality. Since they are necessarily personal, perceptions of the real are expressions of the self.

Ford liked to present the tenets of Impressionism as "a certain number of maxims gained mostly in conversation with Mr. Conrad." And when he was not acknowledging Conrad, he was acknowledging James. But it ought to be apparent that on this issue Ford goes beyond his chosen antecedents. Both James and Conrad depended heavily on a conscious subjectivity – nothing could be clearer. But in both writers there remained a crucial *separation* between consciousness and the objective world. It is worth repeating James' well-known description of Conrad's method: namely that it was "a prolonged hovering flight of the subjective over the outstretched ground of the case exposed." In Ford, the "hovering" relation breaks down: objectivity collapses into subjectivity, reality into personality. Realism and egoism thus converge, because Ford identifies realism with a sequence of private perceptions.

In the development of modernism generally we have identified a series of large and related intellectual *displacements*: first, the shift from spiritual transcendence to a naturalist or humanist standpoint; second, the displacement from humanism and naturalism towards subjectivism. Both shifts have been well charted and well described. My own interest is simply to point out that these displacements are linked by a commitment to *immediacy* – that is, the same principle of experimental immediacy which leads to the dismissal of spiritual reality in favour of "this world," leads from "this world" to "my world." Plainly enough, the development of Ford's Impressionist attitudes reveals a similar intellectual pressure. If I have been describing a movement from civic realism to radical subjectivism, I can now suggest a logic to that movement, the logic of immediacy which commits the artist to a directly present reality. What changes in Ford's thought, then, is the notion of what is directly present.

It has not finished changing. Ford, that casual extremist, goes further. And here the well-known passage concerning Mr Slack is worth quoting:

Life does not say to you: In 1914 my next door neighbour, Mr. Slack, erected a greenhouse and painted it with Cox's green aluminium paint . . . If you think about the matter you will remember in various unordered pictures, how one day Mr. Slack appeared in his garden and contemplated the wall of his house. You will then try to remember the year of that occurrence and you will fix it as August 1914 because having had the foresight to bear the municipal stock of the city of Liège you were able to afford a first-class season ticket for the first time in your life. You will remember Mr. Slack – then much thinner because it was before he found out where to buy that cheap Burgundy . . .[49]

And so on. And since "the general effect of a novel must be the general effect that life makes on mankind," Impressionist fiction refuses to impose linear chronology and remains committed instead to the sequence of perceptions and memories. Artistic fidelity is not owed to the event as such, but to the apprehension of the event.

In his memoir of Conrad, Ford writes that he and Conrad came to accept the name "Impressionist" because they "saw that Life did not narrate, but made impressions on our brains."[50] "I see only spots," the painter Pissarro had insisted, and Ford's point is analogous: however ordered and organized the world may appear, this is only a *construction* out of a more fundamental disorganization. Our notions of reality are based on a random array of stimuli – Ford's "various unordered pictures" – which stand in no logical or chronological sequence and assume no natural order. Traditional conventions of representation are rejected as specious and untenable. Ford cites this stanza from Tennyson:

> And bats went round in fragrant skies,
> And wheeled or lit the filmy shape
> That haunt the dusk with ermine capes
> And woolly breasts and beady eyes.

That, says Ford, might be "good natural history," but it is not

Impressionism, "since no one watching a bat at dusk could see the ermine, the wool or the beadiness of the eyes."[51] These facts depend on information not contained in the moment of perception, and Tennyson's passage therefore violates Impressionist tenets. Impressionism confines itself to the "impression of a moment" and not to a "sort of rounded, annotated record of a set of circumstances."[52]

Our first inclination will be to see this as part of the subjectivizing tendency we have been describing. But consider what has become of subjectivity. It appears only through its "unordered pictures," the impressions "of the moment," the impressions "on our brains." The logic of immediacy has not halted at the boundaries of the coherent individual subject; the forces driving to the self lead past the self, to the momentary perceptions, emotions and sensations which exist prior to any sense of integral subjectivity. This amounts to a *third displacement* in Ford's thought, from subjectivism to what we may call a strict Impressionism, in which the instantaneous impression becomes the foundation of his aesthetic position. It is a position close to that of David Hume, that by no means casual extremist, who dramatized the implications of immediacy for personal identity. Hume described the human personality as

a bundle or collection of different perceptions, which succeed each other with an inconceivable rapidity, and are in a perpetual flux and movement. Our eyes cannot turn in their sockets without varying our perceptions. Our thought is still more variable than our sight; and all our other senses and faculties contribute to this change; nor is there any single power of the soul, which remains unalterably the same, perhaps for one moment. The mind is a kind of theatre, where several perceptions successively make their appearance, pass, re-pass, glide away, and mingle in an infinite variety of postures and situations.[53]

Ford, too, moves from a notion of the coherent self, the "frank" ego, towards "a bundle or collection of different perceptions." "The main thing," writes Ford, "is the genuine love and the faithful rendering of the received impression." "Impressionism," he writes elsewhere, "is a thing altogether momentary," and it ought to be plain how this latest movement – towards "strict Impressionism" – questions the stability of the self itself.

Though we may seem to be as far as possible from Pound's assessment of Ford's "objectivity," in fact we have never been closer. Nothing, of course, is plainer by now than Ford's commitment to a subjectivist aesthetic: the insistence on personality as the chief thing in art, the relativism, the scepticism, the tendency towards solipsism, the assertion that art is an egoism. That is not only subjectivism; it is an extreme version of the position. Indeed it is precisely the extremism that accounts for the confusion. Ford is so intent on limiting art to immediacy that the attitudes and sentiments of the artist are refined away; no trace of the artistic self remains; there is only what the self perceives. Nonetheless, as Ford continually insists, the work remains an individual and personal expression – simply in virtue of its constituting a distinct point of view, a single egoistic perspective. Ford's Impressionism, then, is a *subjectivity in which the subject has disappeared*. In the essay "On Impressionism," Ford makes the point as directly as possible: "The Impressionist author is sedulous to avoid letting his personality appear in the course of his book. On the other hand, his whole book, his whole poem is merely an expression of his personality."[54] Plainly, then, Ford makes no attempt to escape the bounds of the personal. But within those bounds, there is to be no *avowal* of personality, and none of the trappings which personality usually involves: opinion, sentimentality, self-indulgence, rhetoric. There is simply to be rendering without comment. This is what Pound calls "objectivity," but if it is so, it is not to be opposed to subjectivity. It is not opposed to the utmost degree of individuality, even idiosyncrasy. Objectivity, in this perspective, is merely a phase of the subjective – namely, that phase where the subject discreetly withdraws, leaving the immediate, uncorrected impression, the "impression as hard and definite as a tin-tack."

Ford was most attractive to Pound for his technical stipulations: the opposition to moralizing, the embrace of contemporary speech, the clarity in presentation. But until 1914 Pound was prepared to accept the further commitments, the realism and the egoism. "The Serious Artist" of October–December 1913 is not only the definitive statement of Pound's early poetic; it is virtually a catechetical rendering of

Ford's literary principles. The essay suggests that "poets should acquire the graces of prose"; it calls for an art that contains "precise psychology." Most importantly, it defends a representational and realist position. Good art is art that "bears true witness," "art that is most precise," And bad art is "inaccurate art. It is all that makes false reports." But like Ford, Pound does not depend on any public or impersonal notion of truth. The stipulated accuracy is accuracy to one's own perceptions. "The serious artist is scientific in that he presents the image of his desire, of his hate, of his indifference as precisely that, as precisely the image of his own desire, hate or indifference."[55] Though subjective, then, the serious artist is scientific in his subjectivity and the "more precise his record the more lasting and unassailable his work of art."[56] Thus to symbolist "evocation," Imagism opposed precision, hardness, clarity of outline. To symbolist transcendence, Imagism opposed the natural world. These attitudes are perfectly congruent with Ford's view of things, and we may consider the period to the beginning of 1914 as the Impressionist phase of Imagism, or at least the Fordian phase. If this were the end of the matter, there would be no difficulty, and there would have been no controversy.

In search of a primary pigment

In an earlier chapter I drew a contrast between "The Serious Artist" and a slightly later essay of Pound's, "The New Sculpture" of February 1914. The point there was how quickly Pound had shifted from a social justification for art to a view of art as a willed assault on society. The two essays will again provide a contrast – this time with a different, though complementary, implication. For if we have just considered Pound's acceptance of realism in "The Serious Artist," less than five months later, in "The New Sculpture," there is violent opposition: "Realism in literature has had its run. For thirty or more years we have had in deluge, the analyses of the fatty degeneration of life. A generation has been content to analyse. They were necessary . . . We have heard all that the 'realists' have to say."[57] In trying to account for such a sudden and extravagant change of view, we would do well to consider the occasion of the essay. Pound's subject, after all, is the new sculpture, which he approaches by recapitulating the views of Hulme and Lewis on the fine arts. He then enters into a discussion of Jacob Epstein's work, which, in its indifference to recording or analysing the world, he regards as emblematic of the new aesthetic. Only at this point does he make his remark about literary realism, and he then returns to sculpture. I mention this because I think it points to a fact of considerable importance, namely the dominant role which the fine arts begin to assume in discussions of art generally. This is especially marked in Pound's work from the beginning of 1914. Until that time he had defined his literary position in literary terms; Yeats, Ford, Tagore, the troubadours and the Imagists had been his customary points of reference. But from the time of "The New Sculpture" he formulated his poetic position with an eye to plastic arts. Kenner has suggested that Pound abandoned his literary allies because he recognized the greater ability of those such as Lewis and Gaudier-Brzeska.[58] This is certainly plausible. We can concede that Gaudier-Brzeska, for instance, was a more interesting artist than Richard Aldington, and that he and Lewis were more temperamentally suited to Pound. Still, if we want to explain the sudden importance for Pound of certain painters and sculptors, we need more reason than their talent, though we certainly need their talent. Let me suggest two further reasons: the recent successes of avant-garde movements in the plastic arts and the advantage of their aesthetic theories.

Beginning with Roger Fry's first Post-Impressionist show in 1910, a series of exhibitions had been staged in London, provoking great controversy in the press and drawing curious attention from the general public. Controversy and curiosity increased in late 1913.[59] A Post-Impressionist and Futurist exhibition was held in October; Marinetti returned to London in November; and in December Jacob Epstein gave a one-man show of sculpture and drawing. This last, we have seen, was the cause of especially vehement debate. A critic named Ludovici reviewed the show in the *New Age*, describing Epstein's work as having "no interest whatsoever, save for cranks and people who have some reason of their own in abetting or supporting

purposeless individualism à outrance. To these the particular
angle of vision of a minor personality has some value – to me it
has none."[60] Hulme, recently returned from Berlin and
passionately enthusiastic about Worringer's new theories,
rallied to Epstein's defence. I have already described some of his
more theoretical arguments. Here the personal hostility is more
to the point. Hulme describes Ludovici as a "charlatan," a
"nuisance" and a "little bantam," compares his writing on
Nietzsche to "a child of four in a theatre watching a tragedy
based on adultery" and calls his criticism of Epstein "disgusting." "The most appropriate means of dealing with him,"
writes Hulme, "would be a little personal violence. By that
method one removes a nuisance without drawing more attention to it than its insignificance deserves."[61]

Apparently startled ("It is the most difficult thing imaginable
to know what to do when one is attacked as Mr. Hulme attacked
me")[62] Ludovici published a response, "An Open Letter to My
Friends," a long paragraph of which is worth quoting as an
indication of how deep and abiding was the hostility to the
avant-garde and how seriously the issue was taken:

The anarchy of the Futurists, because it is an anarchy of art, may seem to some
less noxious and less threatening than that which finds its vent in the open
streets, by means of dynamite and nitro-glycerine. But let me remind all those
who think in this way that art is always prophetic, and that this anarchy in
painting and sculpture is only a forecast of what the most disintegrating and
most dissolvent influences of modern times are accomplishing and will
ultimately try to achieve in every other department of life. Let me warn them,
therefore, that it behoves all those who, like myself, realise this condition as a
danger, to do everything in their power to stand firm, and to resist the attack,
which one day will be general, upon all the most valued institutions of orderly
life; and to be prepared to survive that attack not only with strength, but with
that quality which always wards off every other kind of disease or infection – I
speak of health.[63]

Not surprisingly, the exchange provoked indignant criticism
largely directed at Hulme. For several weeks letters on the
subject appeared in the *New Age*, with one respondent
suggesting that Hulme "ought, were he consistent, to be
squatting naked in Easter Island surrounded by the pre-historic
Art he admires, and dieting himself on roots and toadstools
after the manner of savages."[64] Early in the controversy

Wyndham Lewis came to Hulme's aid, writing a letter to the *New Age* in which he called Ludovici a "cowardly and shifty individual," "a fool," "like some queer insect in terror when attacked." "His dismal shoddy rubbish is not even amusingly ridiculous."[65]

The incident ought to indicate the intensely aggressive character of the polemic. But it is worth pointing out that such hostility was not restricted to avant-garde confrontation with a senescent establishment. Just as pronounced was the antagonism between the avant-garde sects themselves. In October 1913 Lewis and several others had broken with Roger Fry and his Omega Workshop in great bitterness. They sent Fry a denunciation in which they complained that in Fry's group the "Idol is still Prettiness, with its mid-Victorian languish of the neck, and its skin is still 'greenery-yallery' . . ."[66] Hulme picked up the cue. In an essay on Fry's Grafton Group (January 1914), he wrote that "the departure of Mr. Wyndham Lewis, Mr. Etchells, Mr. Nevinson and several others has left concentrated in a purer form all the worked-out and dead elements in the movement." Fry and his group "are nothing but a kind of backwater." Fry himself "accomplishes the extraordinary feat of adapting the austere Cézanne into something quite fitted for chocolate boxes" and the work of the group in general has "a typically Cambridge sort of atmosphere," "a sort of aesthetic playing about."[67]

In the spring Marinetti stepped up his proselytizing campaign and this ignited a fresh sectarian row. On June 7, *The Observer* ran a Futurist manifesto called "Vital English Art" in which Marinetti (assisted by his English ally Nevinson) announced his desire "to cure English art of that most grave of all maladies – passéism." With characteristic sweep he attacked "sentimentality," "sham revolutionaries," "the indifference of the King," "the worship of tradition," "the conservatism of English artists," and the "effeminacy of their art." He gave a Futurist cheer: "HURRAH for motors! HURRAH for speed! HURRAY for draughts! HURRAH for lightning!" and then called upon the English public "to support, defend and glorify" Futurist tendencies in the culture and the "advance-forces of vital English art."[68] He concluded by listing those he meant, among whom were Wyndham Lewis, Edward Wadsworth, David Bomberg and Jacob Epstein.

The objects of Marinetti's praise were not pleased; they took the public endorsement as presumptuous in the extreme. Several of them, joined also by Pound and Aldington, sent a letter to *The Observer*, dissociating themselves from the Futurist movement. Nevinson was expelled from the Rebel Art Centre for using its stationery to propound Futurist opinions. On June 12, Lewis led a group which included Pound, Gaudier-Brzeska and Epstein in disrupting one of Marinetti's lectures. Indeed, Richard Cork has persuasively argued that it was the Futurist intrusion which finally unified Vorticism as a movement. The early press notices for *Blast* nowhere described it as a Vorticist journal, and Cork suggests that the manifestos were added after the latest dispute with Marinetti.[69]

As compared for instance to Ford's casual and undemonstrative exposition of Impressionism (or the quiet revolution Yeats was working in his verse) the activity in the plastic arts was tumultuous and, to those who aspired to tumult, impressive. Since the 1912 inception of *Imagisme*, the literary experiments had won promising but limited gains, which paled before the successes of the plastic arts. Pound was keenly sensitive to the benefits of popular attention and, on grounds of visibility alone, it was natural for him, like Hulme earlier, to turn toward the brighter sun.

But these were not the only grounds. The advances in painting and sculpture brought with them a new aesthetic justification which offered advantages for the evolving literary perspective. Until late 1913, we have seen, Pound had depended heavily on attitudes derived from Ford. Impressionism had offered the possibility of an anti-academic, anti-rhetorical and anti-conventional art. It emphasized the importance of *le mot juste*; it insisted on precision; it attacked artifice and moralizing. And during an important period Pound found this programme almost wholly salutary. He had revised his own poetic practice in its direction, and his developing theory drew heavily on Ford's critical injunctions.

But where Ford's Impressionism offered a new rigour for existing literary techniques, the aesthetic theories in the fine arts promised a fundamental rupture. This is certainly the enthusiasm that had struck Hulme in Berlin, and it animates Pound's February essay on "The New Sculpture." Literary realism has become anachronistic, "has had its run." Four months earlier, the artistic goal had been "true witness." Now Pound writes that "To the present order of things, we have nothing to say but *merde*; and this new wild sculpture says it."[70]

The movement in the fine arts had severed realistic correspondence and realistic responsibility. (This we have considered in Hulme.) It substituted a pursuit of abstraction for the pursuit of representation; it deserted "life." It inclined to primitivism, and assaulted the primacy of the human form. "Dehumanization," wrote Lewis in *Blast*, "is the chief diagnostic of the Modern World." Or, as he would later put it, "Man was not the hero of our universe."[71] The formal relation of colours and forms was the movement's consuming preoccupation.

And what did literature learn from this? That it was no longer obliged to justify its technical experiments on the grounds of greater realism, that it might now insist on the autonomy of form. In 1912 Kandinsky published *Über das Geistige in der Kunst*, and in 1914 the work was translated into English as *On the Spiritual in Art*. Pound used it much the way Hulme used Worringer. Kandinsky formulated a definition of modern art on a strict abstractionist basis. "The emancipation from dependence on nature," he announced, "is only just beginning."[72] Among the immediate London circle, Pound identified this impulse with Lewis, Wadsworth, Epstein and, especially, Gaudier-Brzeska, who was only twenty-two at the time and would live just one year more. In *Blast*, appearing in July, Gaudier-Brzeska published a sculptural manifesto in which he wrote that

> Sculptural feeling is the appreciation of masses in relation.
> Sculptural ability is the defining of these masses by planes.[73]

Pound took these slogans as definitive and cited them frequently; they characterized for him a pure devotion to form. From this point of view the realist and representational emphasis of Impressionism was unnecessary, obsolete and diversionary. Vorticism, wrote Pound, is interested in the "creative faculty as opposed to the mimetic." What need was there for a work of art to resemble something? "You do not demand of a mountain or a tree that it should be like something; you do not demand that 'natural beauty' be limited to mean only a few freaks of nature, cliffs looking like faces, etc."[74] Although Pound continued to praise Impressionist precision – for this he would always acknowledge a debt to Ford – he came increasingly to attack the more general programmatic goals. Impressionism, he complained, "has set a fashion of passivity"; Impressionism and Futurism (I have cited this) "DENY the vortex. They are the CORPSES of VORTICES."[75] This last, most vehement, remark came in *Blast* in July.

The sequence of events would, I suspect, bear summary. *Des Imagistes* was accepted for publication in the summer of 1913. In October Pound began publishing his essay "The Serious Artist" in the *Egoist*, and this was also the month of Lewis' break with Roger Fry. Hulme's attack on Ludovici appeared in late December. The Quest Society lectures were delivered on January 22, 1914, and Pound's "The New Sculpture" appeared on February 16. The Rebel Art Centre was established in April; the contention with Marinetti occurred in June. *Blast* appeared in July with considerable eclat, and Pound's essay on Vorticism was published in the *Fortnightly Review* in September. The more closely one looks at this notable year in the history of the avant-garde, the more striking become the changes in attitude. It becomes clear, for instance, that Imagism must be conceived in two phases. The first, up to the compilation of the anthology and before Pound's swerving to the plastic arts, was characterized by the predominant influence of Ford. The second phase, the one under present consideration, dates roughly from the beginning of 1914 and involved the *rewriting* of Imagism in line with new aesthetic commitments.

In the spring Pound delivered an informal lecture at the Rebel Art Centre on the relation of Imagism to experiments in the fine arts. The talk was later elaborated into the *Fortnightly Review* essay, which is perhaps his central statement on the subject (Pound said that it contained the "general theory of the new art . . .")[76] and which argues that Vorticism refers not only to a style of painting but to a parallel movement in several arts. What has been called Imagism might just as well be called "Vorticist Poetry," since it is simply the manifestation in literature of an underlying aesthetic commitment common to the painting of Lewis and the sculpture of Gaudier-Brzeska. We mistake the point of the essay, if we see Pound as merely explaining Vorticism to a reluctant public. He is equally intent to legitimize the place of literature within the general movement in the arts. Years later, Lewis would claim "that *vorticism* was purely a painters' affair (as imagism was a purely literary movement, having no relation whatever to *vorticism*, nor anything in common with it)."[77] In 1914, of course, he was far more sympathetic to collaboration. Still, one can understand the pressure on Pound to establish a shared artistic programme. "The image," he writes, "is the poet's pigment" and "with that in mind you can go ahead and apply Kandinsky, you can transpose his chapter on the language of form and colour and apply it to the writing of verse."[78] But can you?

In the second issue of *Blast* appeared the following poem by Pound, under the title "Dogmatic Statement on the Game and Play of Chess."

> Red knights, brown bishops, bright queens
> Striking the board, falling in strong "L's" of colour,
> Reaching and striking in angles,
>   Holding lines of one colour:
> This board is alive with light
> These pieces are living in form,
>   Their moves break and reform the pattern:
> Luminous green from the rooks,
>   Clashing with "x's" of queens,
>   Looped with the knight-leaps.
> "Y" pawns, cleaving, embanking,
> Whirl, centripetal, mate, King down in the vortex:
> Clash, leaping of bands, straight strips of hard colour,
> Blocked lights working in, escapes, renewing of contest.[79]

"The pictures proposed in the verse," wrote Pound to Harriet Monroe, "are pure vorticism."[80] It is not difficult to see what he means. Indeed, this is one of the few poems of Pound's Vorticist phase whose relation to the fine arts is clear. When Imagism was reformulated in 1914, the new emphasis fell on energy and movement; in place of the static implications of an "intellectual and emotional complex," the image now appears as a confluence of powers, "a radiant node or cluster . . . a VORTEX, from which, and through which, and into which, ideas are constantly rushing."[81] Such a description was inspired in large measure by the painting and sculpture which Pound admired – in particular the work of Lewis, who set out to correct the "passivity" of Picasso's cubism. The frenzy of Pound's chess pieces recalls Lewis' fractured forms – propelled across the canvas as though from an explosion somewhere in the gallery. One of the goals of Vorticist painting was to create simultaneous impressions of pattern and activity. The chess board gives Pound an image of structure on which he can project continuous movement.

If this study were tracing a different line of development, Ernest Fenollosa would play a large role. But here he makes only a brief appearance in virtue of one particular idea pertinent to Pound's revision of Imagism. In *The Chinese Written Character as a Medium for Poetry*, Fenollosa attacked the primacy of the noun. "It might be thought," he writes, "that a picture is naturally the picture of a *thing*, and that therefore the root ideas of Chinese are what grammar calls nouns." In fact, "examination shows that a large number of the primitive Chinese characters, even the so-called radicals, are shorthand pictures of actions or processes." For Fenollosa this insight becomes the basis for a metaphysic – and for Pound "a whole basis of aesthetic." A true noun, both hold, "does not exist in nature." No more does a pure verb. Instead, nature consists of "things in motion, motion in things," and the power of the Chinese written character is that it stays "close to nature" by depicting objects in process.[82] Pound, we remember, had originally presented Imagism as "direct treatment of the *thing*." But with the example of Lewis and the theory of Fenollosa, he moved from thing to process, noun to verb. Clearly enough, "Dogmatic Statement" is a poem dominated by verbs and verb forms. By taking chess as his subject, Pound, as it were, equips himself with ready-made nouns – knights, bishops, queens – which, because they exist in virtue of the game's conventions, need not occupy his attention further. The board and pieces are *given*; the interest of the poem lies in the predicates which they invite.

Such a form of presentation amounts to an assault on the game of chess which, after all, is a game in which abstract position is essential and in which the physical movement between positions scarcely matters. But here is no patient unfolding of strategy, only a rapid dance of counters swarming all at once, released from a guiding mind. Accidental features – the colour of the pieces, the light that strikes them, the shapes they make – become primary. The poem, in short, is a dogmatic statement on the play of chess, whose governing conceit is to make sensuous the abstract relations of the game.

When the poem first appeared in *Blast*, it had a subtitle: "Theme for a Series of Pictures," and one can easily imagine a painting along these lines. And yet this raises a provoking question. Pound had defined the Vorticist attitude as a recognition that "we go to a particular art for something which we cannot get in any other art."[83] Each art has what he calls a "primary pigment" – that is, an essential component which it does not share with any other. For form and colour we go to painting; for form in three dimensions to sculpture; for pure sound, to music; and for the image we go to poetry. Pound would later relax this astringent demand for the primary pigment, expanding his definition to permit the well-known taxonomy of three poetic kinds: melopoeia, phanopoeia, logopoeia. But in 1914, an astringent year, he wanted the image alone to serve as the differentia of poetry, and this is where the problem arises. For, despite talk of "energies" and "nodes," the image retains primarily visual suggestions. Imagist poems typically depend on striking visual metaphors, and certainly the force of "Dogmatic Statement on the Game and Play of Chess" derives not primarily from metre or metaphor but from its evocation of complex forms derived from the visual arts.

In May of 1914 Ford summarized the state of the avant-garde, which he referred to as Futurism, using the term to indicate artistic experiment in general. On the one hand, wrote Ford, "whilst all the literary, all the verbal manifestations of Futurism are representational, and representational, and again representational, all the plastic-aesthetic products of the new movements are becoming more and more geometric, mystic, non-material, or what you will."[84] By "verbal manifestations" Ford clearly means his own literary Impressionism, and he is probably also thinking of the Imagists, whom he had placed in the "category of realists." In the opposing "geometric" strain no doubt belongs the work of Picasso and Kandinsky, as well as the painting of Lewis, Bomberg and Wadsworth, and the sculpture of Gaudier-Brzeska and Epstein.

Pound, in his essay "Vorticism," had drawn a similar distinction, but he had proposed a different arrangement of avant-garde sects. He places Impressionism in one camp and in the other Vorticism, "which is, roughly speaking, expressionism, neo-cubism, and imagism gathered together . . ." In other words, in the division between an increasingly representational literature and the increasingly formal plastic arts, Pound places himself on the side of the fine arts. Kandinsky had suggested that painting learn from the dance: "conventional beauty must go, and the literary element, 'storytelling' or 'anecdote' must be abandoned." In the Vorticism essay Pound puts that point this way: "Whistler and Kandinsky and some cubists were set to getting extraneous matter out of their art; they were ousting literary values."[85] He endorses that enterprise, and it is a striking thing for a poet to do.

Pound, of course, is using "literary values" to refer to unnecessary verbiage, but the choice of phrase itself is revealing. For it is clear that in attempting to develop a revolutionary aesthetic, he looked to the example of revolutionary painting and sculpture. When Pound explains how Imagism differs from "lyricism," he suggests that in Imagist poetry "painting or sculpture seems as if it were 'just coming over into speech.'"[86] One can see here the fragility of his "primary pigment." Pound wants a poetry which will provide something that we cannot get in any other art, but when he comes to formulate his poetic, he relies on concepts borrowed from the fine arts. That he would give a poem the subtitle "Theme for a Series of Pictures" itself reveals a great deal. Kermode has astutely remarked that behind much of the modernist poetic lies the "wish that poetry could be written with something other than words."[87] In the present instance, one is tempted to say that here is a poem which would rather be a painting. As it is, the poem has a quality of blueprint about it, almost as though Pound harboured the secret hope that Lewis would paint that series of paintings, for which he has given the theme.

What Pound embraces in the work of Lewis and Gaudier-Brzeska is the commitment to form as such, "form, not the *form of anything*."[88] This new sculptural form, writes Pound, "What is it? It is what we have said. It is an arrangement of masses in relation. It is not an empty copy of empty Roman allegories that are themselves copies of copies. It is not a mimicry of external life."[89] But it is far from clear how literature can adopt an analogous programme. And when Pound attempts to suggest formal values in his own poem, he depends not on features of language but on the painterly qualities of line and colour. Notably, in that remark to Monroe, Pound describes as "pure Vorticism," not the verse rhythm or verse structure but "pictures proposed."

In this he strains against his linguistic medium. Although it is obvious what kind of image Pound means to evoke, he can scarcely achieve the precise definition that a painting would allow. These pieces, we are told, are "living in form" – what form? Their moves, we learn, "break and reform the pattern" – which pattern? Pound relies, as he must, on such abstract characterizations since no verbal description, however precise, can hope to attain the *density* of a properly visual form. Although Pound's poem has its own power, it seems plain that modernist poetry could not continue to develop by emulating the methods of painting and sculpture.

One way to give order to the critical frenzy of these few years, and to this chapter which has described that frenzy, is to see the rapid changes as a result of a confusion over the roots of literary meaning. Through all the critical turnings, an implied question hangs in the air: What does the literary word signify? A number of relationships competed: word and essence, word and world, word and the poet who utters it. As a rough way of organizing these terms, one might imagine them in a chain of signification.

$$poet \rightarrow word \rightarrow world \rightarrow essence$$

Yeats had insisted on carrying literature all the way through this chain, from the poet's intuition to the spirit's essence. The poet spoke the word to evoke an object that might symbolize an essence. Pound and Ford had, in effect, refused this last step, halting at the natural object, content to disregard the invisible essence. They made their attack on symbolism from the point of view of realism, and through the Imagist and Impressionist propaganda of 1912 and 1913 runs an aggressively mimetic assumption. Words name things. Or, in Fenollosa's revision, words name actions.

But the mimetic justification, it is now plain, proved no more stable than the symbolist, and the natural world came to appear just as superfluous as the higher essence. The realist position endured attack from two directions. On the one side, the Fordian side, the real collapsed into the perceived, and the artist began to usurp the place of the world. Pound's dictum that the natural object is the adequate symbol was implicitly reformulated: the impression became the adequate object. The chain of meanings thus began to close upon itself. The world was no longer distinct from the poet who renders it. When Pound praises Ford because he has "expressed himself and mirrored the world," it is unclear whether he thinks Ford has done one thing or two.

The second threat to mimesis came from the word itself, the word freed from the need to signify at all. The introduction of abstract forms into modern painting seemed to open a similar opportunity for poetry. No more than the line and colour of a painter would the image, the poet's pigment, be obliged to represent the world. The practical difficulties of an "abstract" literature have already appeared, but nothing stood in the way of revolutionary critical utterance. Thus May Sinclair insisted that "in no case is the Image a symbol of reality (the object); it is reality (the object) itself." [90] In short, from the perspective of either the autonomous poet ("reality is in the artist") or the autonomous word ("reality . . . itself"), the obligation to depict the world loses its hold. These two extreme formulations, so prevalent during the Vorticist spring and summer of 1914, mark a culmination of the major lines we have followed: the increasingly radical egoism and the similarly extreme formalism. On one side the representative figures have been Pater, Bergson, Stirner, Upward and Ford, who, despite divergences in detail, shared a fundamental outlook: each offered a sceptical critique of traditional beliefs and institutions, and a renewal through retreat to the self – the existing order criticized from the standpoint of the ego. On the other side stood Worringer, Husserl, Lasserre, Maurras, G. E. Moore, Gaudier-Brzeska and Lewis, all denying the ultimacy of the human subject and insisting on the autonomy of art, logic, politics and ethics, whose laws were independent of human will and whose values were intrinsic – the existing order criticized from the standpoint of objective truth and objective value.

That is the theoretical distinction, whose historical enactment I have attempted to trace. The early apologies for modernism (in early Hulme, in Ford) had been frankly egoistic; radical individualism was to be the basis for literary advance. Art would be set free of its moral and political entanglements, and its value would depend only on its adequacy to the demands of personality. But from 1912 onward – for the complex of reasons we have considered – this emphasis was overlaid with a renewed attention to the internal structure of art, and in the nine months before the war, the outlines of an extreme formalist aesthetic were drawn. The value of a work lay in its technical properties; realism, vitality, humanity were irrelevant considerations. "Why," asked Hulme in an essay on David Bomberg (July 1914), "if you are only interested in form, should you be asked . . . to add to it the alien elements which would make it into a solid realistic representation?"[91] And Bomberg himself showed how far this tendency to abstraction might be taken: "My object is the *construction of Pure Form*. I reject everything in painting that is not Pure Form."[92]

"My object," "Pure Form" – the warm-blooded ego demands cold abstraction. Bomberg's remark, like his painting, expresses the vehemence of both individualism and formalism. Indeed, a striking aspect of the pre-war period was the intensification of these often competing values. In Pound's *Blast* essay he traces the ancestry of Vorticism through a series of three quotations.

> All Arts approach the conditions of music.
>
> (Pater)

> An image is that which presents an intellectual and emotional complex in an instant of time.
>
> (Pound)

> You are interested in a certain painting because it is an arrangement of lines and colours.
>
> (Whistler)[93]

The Pater and the Whistler remarks are both statements of the internal and abstract character of art: as such they fall naturally together. But Pound's own definition stands uneasily between these two. The notion of "an intellectual and an emotional complex" points back from the world and toward the psychology of the creating artist. One can, after all, think of Whistler's "lines and colours" as independent of personality, but it is difficult to think of intellect and emotions in that way. Indeed, the psychological implication was made explicit in the early definition of the image, when Pound announced that he used the term "complex" in the "technical sense employed by the newer psychologists, such as Hart . . ."[94] The configuration of the three quotations, then, might be seen as Pound's attempt to bring Imagism in line with the new abstract art, as an implicit insistence that his literary experiments were part of the same aesthetic movement. But his own remark reminds us of the personal and psychological basis on which the formalist experiments depend. "We observe," Hugh Kenner has written, "that *Imagisme* was named for a component of the poem, not a state of the poet, and that its three principles establish technical, not psychic, criteria."[95] Certainly, Pound was technically-minded from the start, and he would increasingly emphasize the technical aspects of his poetic campaign. But Kenner may be too quick to exclude "psychic criteria." As "that which presents an intellectual and emotional complex," the image cannot be firmly dissociated from "the state of the poet," and Pound's writings on the subject continually return to the relation of poetry to psychology and individual consciousness. In 1912, the year he founded Imagism, he wrote that the poet was "the advance guard of the psychologist on the watch for new emotions"; what "the analytical geometer does for space and form, the poet does for the states of consciousness." In 1913, he claimed that the artist was responsible for supplying the "data of psychology." "The author must use his *image*," he said in 1914, "because he sees it or feels it . . .," and in "As For Imagisme" in January 1915 he wrote that "emotion is an organiser of forms" and that "emotional force gives the image."[96]

All of these remarks attest to a psychological emphasis, but the last instance is perhaps the most telling. By 1915 Pound had enthusiastically embraced the primacy of form independent of all representation: "form, not the *form of anything*." But for all his celebration of formal values, he does not eliminate the constitutive role of the "creative emotion." He calls the image a "Vortex or cluster of fused ideas . . . endowed with energy," and says that "The Vorticist is expressing his complex consciousness." [97] For Pound, then, the art-work is a formal structure whose components nevertheless are essentially psychological constituents: energy, emotion, idea.

Here, then, is a persistent ambiguity in early modernism: the desire for the autonomy of form and the claim that the root source and justification for art is individual expression. The power of these two ideas led to a fitful oscillation between artist and art-work as the decisive value. Thus Edward Wadsworth, defending Kandinsky in *Blast*, argues that "the artist can employ any forms (natural, abstracted or abstract) to express himself, if his feelings demand it." [98] The aim is to make a point about form, the legitimacy of abstraction, but the defence is mounted in psychological terms, the artist's need for self-expression. "Objectivity and again objectivity and expression . . .," enjoined Pound, thus giving terse expression to these divided aims in the critical programme. [99] Insofar as the movement celebrates "pure form," then it appears to overturn anthropocentric values, to stake itself upon objective principles wholly distinct from human will, and to mark a break with a romantic aesthetic. But insofar as its basis remains the freedom of the artist and the absolute priority of personal vision, then it appears as only an extreme romantic individualism. Up to the outbreak of the war, and somewhat beyond, these two principles remained entangled. Pure form was a goal; individual will was its underpinning. If human values disappeared from the art, they simply reappeared in the aggressive and self-dramatizing artist.

The argument throughout this chapter has had both a conceptual and an historical aim: conceptually, to make some further discriminations among the many critical positions; historically, to show how the aspiration to literary revolution remained bound by some traditional premises. As a final point in this connection, we might reflect for a moment on the very notion of an artistic movement in the modern era. These early English moderns – in particular that American–English modern Ezra Pound – were quick to understand the value of association. In an age of publicity the solitary artist was at a disadvantage, and Pound, Lewis and their confederates learned from Marinetti the benefit of a collective war-cry, ringing loudly. "Vortex" was not only a notion of form but also an ideal for the flourishing creative centre; *Blast* was the "Review of the Great London Vortex." All through the writing of this period runs the talk of schools, gangs, movements, camps, parties, in line with the principle that "all civilisation has proceded from cities and cénacles."[100] But this inclination to form schools, to start journals, to write manifestos, to *name* oneself and one's compeers, had to compete with another powerful ideal, namely the supremacy of individual genius. Romantic notions of the solitary creator continued to form a powerful undercurrent, and an ever more insistent and aggressive egoism threatened the unity of the movement. In 1917 Pound wrote that "the last few years have seen the gradual shaping of a party of intelligence, a party not bound by any central doctrine or theory."[101] He wants, in other words, the unity of a party without its constraints, a shaping intelligence without central doctrine. Such an arrangement can only be fragile, and when Pound announces that Vorticism is "a movement of individuals, for individuals, for the protection of individuality," one must wonder how long these individuals will move together.

III. Consolidation

CHAPTER 8

The war among the moderns

The avant-garde in retreat

Imagism began with two poets and a poet-impresario. Pound willed it into being, wrote it into doctrine and publicized it into prominence. As he would put it later: "I ordered 'the public' (i.e. a few hundred people and a few reviewers) to take note of certain poems."[1] Still, Imagism began as a fragile success, its big splash confined to little magazines. Then, in early 1914, Pound closed ranks with Lewis and Gaudier-Brzeska, and the poetic movement became part of a general aesthetic programme. A number of artists had been struck with mutual enthusiasm, and they recognized the advantages of alliance. In Pound's more stirring formulation: "We worked separately, we found an underlying agreement, we decided to stand together."[2] While their numbers were never large, their notoriety became great. By the spring and early summer of 1914, the London avant-garde had advanced into the general cultural consciousness. The popular press, never very attentive to the nuances of doctrine, was eager to follow controversy, and when controversy flagged, to provoke it. The *New Weekly* recruited Chesterton to attack Futurism, and then recruited Lewis to attack Chesterton. In the six months before the war, recalled Lewis, the avant-garde moved from obscurity to renown: "Exhibitions were reviewed in column after column. And no illustrated paper worth its salt but carried a photograph of some picture of mine or of my 'school,' as I have said, or one of myself, smiling insinuatingly from its pages."[3] Ford confirmed the point: "in 1914, Les Jeunes had succeeded in interesting a usually unmoved but very large section of the public – and had forced that public to take an interest not in the stuff but the methods of an Art."[4] The public,

137

says Ford, treated the avant-garde "with great seriousness and unparalleled avidity."[5]

The members of the avant-garde, for their part, treated the public (and often one another) with contempt. During the first six months of 1914, the rhetorical din reached its greatest intensity. It was the period of Hulme's verbal assault on Ludovici and Fry, Pound's bitter denunciations of the reading public, the disrupting of Marinetti's lecture and, most notably, *Blast* itself. "War and art," wrote Lewis, "in those days mingled, the features of the latter as stern as – if not sterner than – the former."[6] The provocation was deliberate and relentless, a desire to outrage that without question succeeded. After the publication of *Blast*, G. R. Prothero of the *Quarterly Review* sent a note to Pound. "Many thanks for your letter of the other day. I am afraid that I must say frankly that I do not think I can open the columns of the Q. R. – at any rate at present – to anyone associated publicly with such a publication as *Blast*. It stamps a man too disadvantageously."[7] Pound's response, of course, was not to hide the slight but to cite it in print.

Plainly, these two characteristics are bound together: it was insofar as the avant-garde achieved the status of a recognized *movement* that it confidently adopted its antagonistic stance. But we cannot explain the vehemence of the rhetoric as simply the exuberance of success. The venom is too poisonous. The polemical violence of the avant-garde is only understandable when linked to a vision of the larger social whole, a vision of that whole as moribund, decadent and stifling to creative endeavour.

In *The Servile State* of 1912, Hilaire Belloc had placed the problem in its starkest aspect, prophesying the elimination of freedom under the pressures of social organization. Liberal welfare and liberal reform – originally intended to promote greater freedom – were, according to Belloc, leading to the opposite result. Material needs, "food, housing and clothing, promised subsistence for old age," would be met, but the framework of existing inequality would remain. An "unstable equilibrium" would lead to a "stable equilibrium," demanding more compulsion and "servility," even as basic wants were satisfied. The socialist aim, argued Belloc, had been assimilated and redefined by the dominant capitalist order:

the Socialist whose motive is human good and not mere organisation is being shepherded in spite of himself *away* from his Collectivist ideal and *towards* a society in which the possessors shall remain possessed, the dispossessed shall remain dispossessed . . . but in which the special evils of insecurity and insufficiency . . . have been eliminated by the destruction of freedom.[8]

Belloc, in short, envisions the triumph of bureaucratic constraint and "mere organization": material well-being at the expense of freedom, safety at the expense of spontaneity. And the pre-war avant-garde defined itself against just such a vision. Ford thus satirized the "mawkish flap-doodle of culture, Fabianism, peace, and good will"; Pound fulminated against the modern "race . . . of rabbits"; and Lewis wrote that "we all foresee in a century or so everybody being put to bed at 7 o'clock in the evening by a State Nurse."[9]

The dominant perception was not of anarchy but of complacency, not of too little control but of too much. The rhetorical violence of the early modernist polemic – the taunts, the insinuations, the deliberate scandalizing – should be seen as a response to these constraints. One month before the war, Lewis wrote an essay in the *Outlook* with the splashy title "Kill John Bull With Art." John Bull, he pointed out, "has seen a lot of art lately. He is getting restive." And Lewis delights in the conflict.

The existence of this ferocious national animal is an excellent thing for the art of this country. It renders the artists and other people who create new things more agile and energetic than they otherwise would be . . . We should be proud of the particular protagonist of our misfortunes. Every exceptionally inane remark in the Press should send a thrill of pride through us. "No Press could be so obtuse and ridiculous as that!" we should say. But it is hardly ferocious enough as yet . . . It has not yet realised, either, what a lot of art is being flourished under its nose.[10]

In his later reflections on the period, Lewis would explain that the "organized disturbance" of the arts had been necessary "seeing how 'bourgeois' all Publics were".[11] "'Kill John Bull with Art!' I shouted. And John and Mrs. Bull leapt for joy, in a cynical convulsion. For they felt as safe as houses. So did I."[12]

All of this the war changed. Its first cultural consequence was its most obvious: the abrupt shift in popular attention. "The war," wrote Lewis, "was like a great new fashion": "Everything was become historical – the past had returned. Romance had oozed up and steeped everything in its glamours. Also this was a People's World once more, racy, rich and turbulent."[13] The complacency which had typified the bourgeois public was suddenly converted into the manic energy of wartime tension. It ought to surprise no one that the need to discriminate between Vorticism and Futurism became less pressing.

The effect on the artists themselves was in large part delayed. Ford kept at work on *The Good Soldier*, completing it in 1915. Lewis kept at home, nursing an illness and attempting to complete *Tarr*, his first novel, so that, in case of his wartime demise, "the world might have a chance of judging what an artist it had lost."[14] Pound maintained his incessant propagandizing. Nevertheless, it soon became plain that the war had transformed the position of the avant-garde. The arts withdrew into the recesses of popular consciousness; the polemic rang hollow. "To the war," Ford would write later, "went all that was *tapageur*, careless, and uncalculating of Les Jeunes: to the war went the Futurists, the Cubists, the Imagists, the Vorticists – even the poor old Impressionists. The Eminent Middle-Aged remained in undisturbed possession of the fauteuils of Parnassus . . ." And Lewis would write that "All Europe was at war and a bigger *Blast* than mine had rather taken the wind out of my sails." "The War had washed out the bright puce of the cover of the organ of 'the Great London Vortex.' Too much blood had been shed for red, even of the most shocking aniline intensity, to startle anybody."[15]

Whereas pre-war English society had seemed to drift towards state-controlled welfare, the outbreak of the war made violence and barbarism the more urgent concern. The shift from the Servile State to the Militant State was abrupt and thoroughgoing, and necessitated, among other things, a rethinking of the relation of art to society. Before the war, the modernists had assumed the role of violence-inciting artistic *provocateurs* whose aim was to startle the culture out of lethargy. But after August 1914, lethargy was no longer the dreaded ill. The problem for the moderns became what posture to adopt in the face of general social disarray. This would have an important effect on the development of artistic doctrine, and to this I will shortly turn. But at the moment I want to discuss a change in modernist *tone*.

In January 1915 Pound published yet another essay on

Vorticism, in which he observed; "The political world is confronted with a great war, a species of insanity. The art world is confronted with a species of quiet and sober sanity called Vorticism."[16] The remark is a revealing sign of the shift in polemical style. "Quiet" and "sober" are perhaps the last epithets one would have associated with Vorticism, and Pound's tack reflects an interesting change of strategy. The aim is no longer a rousing assault on a stagnant culture; there are no more calls for the artist to recognize that "the war between him and the world is a war without truce."[17] The avant-garde becomes a source of "sanity."

This should not be misunderstood. Pound was not temperamentally equipped to abandon his propagandizing fervour; we are not to suppose that he became polite or discreet. The point rather is that the social changes required a change in the polemical strategy, which is manifest, for instance, in the second, and last, number of *Blast*, published in June of 1915. It is scarcely half as long as the initial number, and while there has been no obvious chastening of the Vorticist inspiration, there is an evident fatigue and a certain blurring of the critical focus.

Whereas the first number had proclaimed utter detachment from social and political concerns – "We want to leave Nature and Man alone" – the second finds itself obliged to acknowledge the general crisis. *Blast* 2 thus calls itself a "War-Number," and its opening editorial tries to close the gap between war and art, making the military struggle into a conflict between opposed aesthetics. Germany represents "Traditional Poetry and the Romantic Spirit"; Vorticism, committed to the "Reality of the Present," stands against the "Poetry of a former condition of life." Moreover, "the Kaiser, long before he entered into war with Great Britain, had declared merciless war on Cubism and Expressionism." "Under these circumstances, apart from national partisanship, it appears to us humanly desirable that Germany should win no war against France or England."[18] No gesture of solidarity could be more tepid, and it points to the difficulties and ambiguities of the avant-garde position. A year earlier Lewis had called England "a marked country in Europe: the great, unimaginative, cold, unphilo-sophic, unmusical bourgeoise."[19] But now he comes grudgingly to England's defence. In the context of general, and international, violence, it became implausible to insist on the *particular* imbecilities of British culture.

In fact, far from sustaining their assault on the British bourgeoisie, the Vorticists found themselves obliged to defend their art. *The Times* had run a short notice on "Junkerism In Art" in which the following appeared: "Should the Junker happily take to painting, instead of disturbing the peace of Europe, he would paint pictures very similar to those of Mr. Wadsworth, Mr. Roberts and Mr. Wyndham Lewis."[20] Lewis takes some pains to defend the group against the charge: he rejects the idea that the paintings are "ferocious and unfriendly" and while conceding that the Vorticists remain committed to pictorial "rigidity," he denies that this connects them to the Junker temperament.[21] But the shift in the cultural balance of power is noteworthy. The Vorticists suddenly found themselves with decreased prestige, position and leverage, regarded either as distractions or as enemies.

Pound's memoir for Gaudier-Brzeska, published in 1916, is instructive in this regard. Gaudier-Brzeska was killed in battle on June 5, 1915. He was not yet twenty-four, and his death disturbed Pound deeply ("One is rather obsessed with it").[22] There is no need to doubt the sincerity of his regret. We should all regret. But what begins as a memoir passes rapidly into an exposition and review of Vorticism. Pound hurriedly reviews the early life, dutifully reprints the available correspondence and then settles on the subject which most interests him: Gaudier, Pound and the vicissitudes of an aesthetic movement. The text concludes with a set of Pound's own recent essays on Vorticism.

Pound is sensitive to the potential awkwardness of such theorizing in the midst of reminiscences; his justification, however, is straightforward: insofar as critical discussion is "likely to lead to a clearer understanding or a swifter comprehension of Brzeska's work, in just so far will the general topic of vorticism be dragged into the present work."[23] By the conclusion of the memoir, it seems rather as if Gaudier-Brzeska is being dragged into the work. In the last pages he virtually disappears from the text. It becomes plain that the pamphlet exists as much to legitimize Vorticism as it does to memorialize

Gaudier-Brzeska, a point made particularly obvious when Pound, shortly afterwards, writes to John Quinn of his plan for a companion volume on Wyndham Lewis.[24] Lewis was alive and in combat, and certainly in no imminent need of a memorial volume (he would live another forty years). Pound, of course, was not thinking of an elegy but of a critical study concerned with Lewis' work and its relation to Vorticism.

The noteworthy point is not Pound's personal indifference, but the new set of pressures on the artistic movement. As much as anything to that time, the death of Gaudier-Brzeska had made plain its precariousness. (After the loss was duly noted in *Blast*, James Douglas of the *Star* had castigated Lewis for making up names: "Mr. Lewis kills the great Gaudier-Brzeska. The joke is not too seemly . . ."[25] Understandably, this was a source of bitterness to the moderns.) Perhaps the most notable aspect of Pound's memoir, then, is the consistent attempt to secure some greater stability for avant-garde art. In identifying Gaudier-Brzeska so thoroughly with Vorticism, Pound is aiming at a permanence for both.

This accounts for the change in tone. There is no longer the aggressive provocation; Pound speaks with scorn of "Journalistic squabbles." "I am not over-anxious to enter upon long quibbles either about his work or the group-name he chose to work under. The fact remains that he chose to call himself a 'vorticist,' as Wyndham Lewis, and myself, and Edward Wadsworth and several others have chosen, for good reasons enough."[26] Not many months earlier, Pound had been more than eager to encourage "squabbles" and "quibbles" in pursuit of polemical advantage. But now he expresses contempt for partisan debate: "The fact remains that he chose to call himself a 'vorticist'"; Pound's new inclination is to chronicle such "facts," which give the movement an historical legitimation. The structure of Pound's memoir – the reproduction of Gaudier-Brzeska's sculptures, the bibliography of his work, the inclusion of Pound's early essays – is best seen as an effort toward documentation, an attempt to amass *evidence*, to give proof of the movement's weight and presence. The aesthetic assault had faltered; in its place was an attempt to make a fragile position more secure. Even as Gaudier-Brzeska's contribution was receding into the Vorticist past, Pound was offering new names for consideration, among them Joyce and Eliot.

Ford Madox Ford provides a somewhat comic instance of this shift in orientation. His pre-war attitude had been a "social agnosticism" which regarded the modern world as too complex for political decision, and Ford had defended James against the charge of narrowness by insisting that nobody knew enough to judge.[27] But with the outbreak of hostilities, Ford's scepticism was painlessly transmogrified into conviction. He rushed an attack on Germany into publication: *When Blood Is Their Argument*. The book was a loose compendium of sociological data, philosophic critique and personal anecdote, all designed to dramatize the threats of the Teuton. It concluded with a ringing statement of the choice which the war posed.

We have in fact to decide whether our children and our children's children shall be monomaniacs or graceful and all-round beings; we have to plump for professionalism or amateurism in politics, the arts, the universities, and every department of life. We have to decide whether the future of the race shall be that of organised, materialist egoism, or that of what I would call the all-round sportsmanship of altruistic culture.[28]

Ford was the one who had insisted that "all art must be the expression of an ego," and who had scorned the "official altruism" of the Victorian age. His is a gross instance of reversal, but it indicates the kind of demands descending upon artists and the arts in this period. The threats to the cultural order were no longer routine, safety and complacency, but the possibility of thorough social disintegration. And this provoked a change in modernist bearing. In the face of actual violence, it was no longer rhetorically effective to present modern art as a call to arms, as a savage assault on traditional values. In Ford's case there was even relief at being freed from the burdens of opposition. "I have never felt such an entire peace of mind," he wrote to his mother, "as I have felt since I wore the King's uniform," and he mentioned his delight at being sent to places, "where I shall be precluded from uttering injunctions to find le mot juste."[29]

Pound was never so enthusiastic as this, but as the war progressed, he increasingly identified with the English position. In 1913 he had expressed contempt for the state of English culture (and had for this reason drawn great hostility), but in 1917 he writes that "England and France are civilisation . . . Neither nation has been coercible into a Kultur; into a damnable holy Roman Empire, holy Roman Church orthodoxy, obedience, Deutschland über Alles, infallibility, mouse-trap." "If," says Pound, "I care for anything in politics I care for a coalition of England, France and America." As opposed to his earlier attraction to artistic violence, he now writes that "Civilisation means the enrichment of life and the abolition of violence . . ." He attacks "dehumanization," defends "personal liberty" and the "humanist belief that a man acquires knowledge in order that he may be a more complete man . . ."[30] In short, though never conventional, Pound inclines toward a less bilious demeanour.

Certain more immediate effects of the war demand mention. Most fundamental was the dispersion of the movement, which did not happen immediately, but happened steadily. Gaudier-Brzeska was the first to leave, departing to enlist almost as soon as the war began. Ford left to serve in the summer of 1915, Lewis that same year. Aldington tried to enlist just after the outbreak of hostilities, but was turned away; he was successful when he tried again in 1916. Hulme joined the army in late 1914, but then, when he was overlooked by the War Office, he briefly resumed his London life, writing now, however, more about the war than art. He went back into service in 1916 and was killed in September 1917.

Not surprisingly, artistic possibilities contracted even for those who remained out of combat. "Literary papers," wrote Richard Aldington, "quietly disappeared, literary articles were not wanted, poems had to be patriotic."[31] *Blast*, which had been conceived as a quarterly, managed one more issue, the "War-Number" of 1915. The *Egoist* became a monthly, and then a bi-monthly. As for the painters and sculptors, commissions were virtually non-existent.[32] But this point must be made carefully, because, while it is true that the scale of activity was vastly reduced, and that attention to modern art waned, the art did not disappear altogether. Its character, however, changed. For one thing, while many of the English writers and artists became engaged in the war, the two American émigrés, Pound and Eliot, remained civilians. For another, it happened that the most articulate supporters (and practitioners) of experiment in the fine arts (Hulme, Lewis and Gaudier-Brzeska) became involved in the war – and only one of them survived. This circumstance meant, among other things, that the aesthetic dominance of painting and sculpture now diminished. Not only were the literary figures able to keep working, they assumed the task of defining the modernist position. Moreover, that definition was pursued again in literary terms and not in terms of the plastic arts. The shift is by no means inessential. We have seen the extent to which Kandinsky, Worringer, Marinetti, Lewis, Gaudier-Brzeska and Epstein had determined the lines of literary development. The immediate result was that Pound became the leading exponent of the new art – a role he had previously shared with Hulme and Lewis. The longer-range effect was that Pound and Eliot moved into a literary alliance.

Pound and Eliot, a counter-current

Eliot met Pound in September 1914, that is, shortly after the war began, and the political and social confusion has naturally obscured the extent to which the artistic movement was then in disarray. The war itself, of course, was foremost among the disrupting circumstances. As we have seen, it markedly diminished the prominence of the new movement and caused the dispersion of the avant-garde group; those who survived and remained in London were placed on the cultural defensive. But the artistic difficulties were not merely a matter of external circumstance. Internally, the movement had reached a point of crisis, and Eliot's appearance was serendipitous.

Amy Lowell had travelled to London in the summer of 1914. Unhappy with her very modest place in the first Imagist anthology (only one of Lowell's poems had been included, against ten of Aldington's), she had contrived a new plan for organizing publication, suggesting that a volume appear annually, along the lines of *Georgian Poetry*, and that the contributing poets be allotted equal space. Pound, who correctly saw the suggestion as a threat to his editorial control, resisted the idea. Refusing to participate himself, he tried to persuade Lowell to avoid the Imagist rubric, use of which, he insisted, "would deprive me of my machinery for gathering stray good poems and presenting them to the public in more or less permanent form . . ." Furthermore, he told her, the "present machinery was largely or wholly my making . . ."[33] But having won the support of H. D. and Aldington, Lowell was adamant. After an angry exchange of letters, the rivals became irreconcilable and when Harriet Monroe asked about the quarrel in September, Lowell responded, "It is not a quarrel now, it is a schism."[34] Over Pound's protests, an anthology was published on Lowell's terms the following year, with the title, *Some Imagist Poets*, representing a minor concession to Pound's demands. Aldington, H. D., Lawrence and Flint were participants in the new group, which Pound referred to as a "democratic beer-garden."[35]

The terms of the dispute are intriguing, revealing as they do some of the complex cultural politics within an avant-garde movement. Notice that in the confrontation with Lowell, Pound does not resist the split within Imagism but the threatened appropriation of the *name*. He advises her that it would be "wiser to split over an aesthetic principle. In which case the new group would find its name automatically, almost."[36] He suggests that the new anthology be called "Vers Libre," so as to be distinguished from "what I mean by 'Imagisme.'"[37] But Lowell refuses to abandon Imagism ("Having been given the name of Imagiste I shall certainly not repudiate it."), and Pound's fear is that the Imagist programme will thus be weakened "by making it mean *any* writing of vers libre." He writes to Harriet Monroe that "the very discrimination, the whole core of significance I've taken twelve years of discipline to get at, she expects me to accord to people who have taken fifteen minutes' survey of my results."[38]

Pound's anxiety is telling. His fear is not that good verse will no longer be written, but that without a specifying identity, it will be lost in the onrush of vulgarity. The success of the movement will thus become precarious, since it will invite imitators who share the superficial trappings of Imagism (free verse) without its essential characteristics ("hard light, clear edges").[39] Lowell quickly became impatient with Pound's proprietary attitude, observing wryly at one point that he could not copyright the name. But here is a small historical irony. A year later, after the publication of *Some Imagist Poets*, Imagism became vastly fashionable in the United States, and Lowell was confronted with the circumstance that had tormented Pound, the loss of literary identity in the wash of imitators. Fearing that she might lose control of the movement, she herself considered copyrighting the name "Imagist," forming a "business association" which would be able to exclude the casual imitator.[40]

At issue here, especially in Pound's case, is the fear that widespread diffusion will undermine the essentially elite nature of the modern renaissance. In a letter to Harriet Monroe he had written that "My problem is to keep alive a certain group of advancing poets, to set the arts in their rightful place as the acknowledged guide and lamp of civilization.'[41] The sentiment is standard Poundian doctrine, most famously expressed in his remark that artists are the "antennae" of the race.[42] But this attitude, it is worth noting, stands in uneasy relation to his relentless propagandizing. On the one hand his inclination is to publicize and to legitimize new aesthetic doctrine; on the other, the aim is to avoid the democratization of art, since once democratized it loses the force of a cultural vanguard. In order to "keep alive" the movement Pound exploits the particular character of mass culture – its susceptibility to publicity, celebrity and fashion – but at the same time he defines himself against the logic of mass appeal, the dissemination of high cultural values. This ambiguity has led to a familiar pattern in the history of modernism, the unbroken succession of new methods which are aggressively advertised, but whose acceptance leads only to their obsolescence.[43]

With the Imagist split and the Vorticist dispersion, Pound was briefly threatened with isolation and Eliot arrived on the literary scene as a *deus ex machina*. That he was a potential ally, Pound recognized from the start, and was eager to swear blood-brotherhood. (When Eliot returned to London after having spent time at Oxford, Pound wrote relievedly to Harriet Monroe, "Eliot back here, thank God.")[44] The energies that had been lavished on Aldington, H. D. and Vorticism found a new object, with Pound arranging the publication of "Pruf-rock" in *Poetry* and "Portrait of a Lady" in the *Catholic Anthology*. He introduced Eliot to Lewis; in the second, and last, edition of *Blast* (1915), "Preludes" and "Rhapsody on a Windy Night" appeared. Pound likewise undertook the defence of Eliot's work, refusing even to pass along Harriet Monroe's criticisms ("Neither will I send you Eliot's address in order that he may be insulted").[45]

Still, for all of Pound's enthusiasm, Eliot's entrance into the literary arena was gradual. He had come to England in order to complete work on his doctoral dissertation in philosophy and went to Oxford for that reason. In 1915 he married Vivien Haigh-Wood and in 1916 the two moved to London. Eliot submitted the dissertation but abandoned his philosophic career; he took a position at the High Wycombe Grammar School and began contributing essays to the *International Journal of Ethics* and the *New Statesman*. This period seems to have been particularly difficult for Eliot; his poetic production was meagre and his critical essays slight. Only in 1917 did his situation improve. He found a position in the foreign department of Lloyd's Bank, and through Pound's intervention he became literary editor of the *Egoist* when Aldington left for the war. Also through Pound, he began contributing to Margaret Anderson's *Little Review*. With these new outlets his critical work proliferated, and in the literary wars that so eerily reflected the real war he became an active ally of Pound.

The chapter "Symbol, impression, image, vortex" registered the shifting ground of a revolutionary aesthetic which some-times justified its experiments on the basis of the artist's freedom and sometimes on the basis of purity of form. These two principles had been aggressively conjoined in Vorticism, which celebrated an artistic individualism as extreme as any to be found in a romantic credo, while prescribing a technical regimen which held merely human values in contempt. One consequence of the split within Imagism was that these conflated principles became rudely separated. Lowell's *Some Imagist Poets* was published in April 1915. Its editorial preface, written by Aldington and amended by the others, refers to the *Des Imagistes* of the previous year, acknowledging it as the beginning of Imagism. "Differences of taste and judgment, however, have arisen among the contributors to that book . . ."[46] The preface proceeds to outline a poetic position based largely on this remark of Remy de Gourmont:

Individualism in literature, liberty of art, abandonment of existing forms . . . The sole excuse which a man can have for writing is to write down himself, to unveil for others the sort of world which mirrors itself in his individual glass . . . He should create his own aesthetics and we should admit as many aesthetics as there are original minds . . .[47]

All art, continues the preface, "is an attempt to express the feelings of the artist," and poetry is "the vision in a man's soul which he translates as best he can with the means at his disposal."[48]

To create new rhythms – as the expression of new moods – and not to copy old rhythms, which merely echo old moods. We do not insist upon "free verse" as the only method of writing poetry. We fight for it as a principle of liberty. We believe that the individuality of a poet may often be better expressed in free-verse than in conventional forms.[49]

Liberty, novelty, individuality – these are not new demands but Lowell's group expresses them so unabashedly and so clearly as to turn them into easy targets.

Eliot had arrived in London after a period of intense critical debate, in which he had not participated and towards which he remained somewhat detached. Imagism, Vorticism and *Blast* had become incontrovertible, if not always welcome, cultural facts. Pound would later remark that Eliot "displayed great tact, or enjoyed good fortune, in arriving in London at a particular date with a formed style of his own."[50] But more was at issue than a formed style; it was equally a matter of literary and intellectual attitudes not bound to existing opinion. This enabled Eliot to overturn acknowledged modernist premises. Never having been an Imagist or a Vorticist, he was perhaps more inclined to radical resection.

He began with a consideration of free verse, "Reflections on Vers Libre," in the *New Statesman*, March 1917:

It is assumed that *vers libre* exists. It is assumed that *vers libre* is a school; that it consists of certain theories; that its group or groups of theorists will either revolutionize or demoralize poetry if their attack upon the iambic pentameter meets with any success. *Vers libre* does not exist, and it is time that this preposterous fiction followed the *élan vital* and the eighty thousand Russians into oblivion.[51]

This is coy, but there is a careful strategy behind the pose. The intention – it is everywhere in Eliot's work of the period – is to alter the terms of the literary debate. As the most obvious feature of the new poetry, *vers libre* was where the issue had been met; critical discussion had centred on the merits of complete freedom as to literary form. But for Eliot, and also for Pound, this had become a great awkwardness. It blurred distinctions. Eliot's tack is to deny the importance, or at least the salience, of the *vers libre* question: "*Vers libre* has not even the excuse of a polemic; it is a battle-cry of freedom, and there is no freedom in art."[52]

Eliot is placing himself at a great distance from the early modernist position. Ford, Hulme, Lewis and Aldington had consistently defended their formal experiments on the grounds of freedom for the individual artist. Freedom was a justification for the deliberate confrontation with established forms, for the abandonment of realistic subject-matter, for the defiance of social involvement. And in the Lowell faction of Imagists, freedom continued as a clarion call. Eliot, of course, is not suggesting metrical rigidity. He wants rather to see metrical innovation as progress toward a new discipline, not a new freedom. He concludes his essay with the ironic and famous words: "the division between Conservative Verse and *vers libre* does not exist, for there is only good verse, bad verse, and chaos."[53]

John Gould Fletcher wrote an aggrieved letter in response to Eliot's essay, castigating what he took to be its conservatism and defending the cause of *vers libre*: "The English *vers librists* aim at destroying the numerous and not uninfluential collection of pedants that still talk about the 'rules of versification,' or tell you that verbal music is impossible without a rhyme-structure."[54] Fletcher reaffirms the principle of unfettered artistic freedom and claims that *vers libre* is written precisely "to evade the bounds of regularity." Free verse is a refusal of "metrical servitude."[55]

Eliot was unmoved. He wrote a short critical appreciation

of Pound, *Ezra Pound: His Metric and Poetry*, published anonymously the following year because, as Pound put it, "it would be extremely unwise for him, at this stage of his career, with the hope of sometime getting paid by elder reviews, and published by the godly, and in general of not utterly bitching his chances in various quarters, for him to have signed it."[56] The volume was intended to introduce Pound's poetry to a larger public, and what is striking is the basis Eliot offers for appreciation. He stresses Pound's distance from a literary or academic establishment, pointing out that he arrived in London as "a complete stranger, without either literary patronage or financial means," and that he deserted his thesis (as Eliot was then doing) "and the Ph.D. and the professorial chair, and elected to remain in Europe."[57] Eliot, that is, wants to emphasize the unconventional, even renegade, aspect of Pound's position. But he is also eager to distinguish innovation from freedom. Again he attacks *vers libre*, denying its suitability for describing Pound's work. "Any verse," he writes, "is called 'free' by people whose ears are not accustomed to it," but in fact Pound's verse is rigorous and severe, laying "so heavy a burden upon every word in a line that it becomes impossible to write like Shelley, leaving blanks for the adjectives, or like Swinburne, whose adjectives are practically blank."[58] This is far from the justification which Ford had offered for *vers libre*, as allowing "a freer play for self-expression," or the "principle of liberty" which Lowell and her allies had embraced.[59] For Eliot the metrical experiments reflect a disciplined pursuit of form, and as he had in "Reflections on Vers Libre" he denies the general coherence of the concept "free verse": "There are not, as a matter of fact, two kinds of verse, the strict and the free; there is only a mastery which comes of being so well trained that form is an instinct and can be adapted to the particular purpose in hand."[60]

Reflecting on this period Pound would later write that

at a particular date in a particular room, two authors, neither engaged in picking the other's pocket, decided that the dilutation of *vers libre*, Amygism, Lee Masterism, general floppiness had gone too far and that some counter-current must be set going. Parallel situation centuries ago in China. Remedy prescribed "Émaux et Camées" (or the Bay State Hymn Book). Rhyme and regular strophes.

Results: Poems in Mr. Eliot's *second* volume, not contained in his first . . .
also 'H. S. Mauberly.'

Pound calls the activity of these few years "a movement to
which no name has ever been given."[61] Eliot's most recent
biographer regards it as an aberration.[62] That it has a special
character will soon be apparent.

In part, the remarkable energy for criticism in the early
modern movement reflects the zeal to explain and to publicize
literary innovation. As Eliot put it, "novelty meets with
neglect; neglect provokes attack; and attack demands a
theory."[63] Pound saw some work of H. D., coined the name
"*Imagiste*" and proceeded to formulate a doctrine to justify
what she had written by instinct. But it would be a mistake to see
this large body of critical material as simply *ex post facto*
rationalization. And in the present instance, in the "movement
to which no name has ever been given," what is striking is the
way the literature itself seems *ex post facto*. Pound and Eliot
adopted a task for themselves, to counter the "dilutation" of
modern verse, and then set out to write poems accordingly.
Eliot would later comment that Imagism was primarily a critical
movement, but as much can be said of the post-Imagist
experiments. They often appear less as manifestations of a
creative urge than as self-conscious efforts to satisfy a critical
programme. What is more, the demand is incited from without.
The advance of Amy Lowell *must* set going a "counter-
current." But why? Why should any work of Lowell and her
colleagues determine the direction of Pound and Eliot?

Since the controversy surrounding the avant-garde often
assumed a theological character, it may be useful to borrow a
distinction from Christian disputation. *Apologetics* might then
refer to the defence of literary doctrine against hostile opponents (especially heathen worshippers of Tennyson), while
polemics would indicate the rooting out of errors within the
movement. Early modernist criticism, in the period stretching
from roughly 1908 to 1913, was largely apologetic in character.
Its urgent aim was to defend the right of innovation against the
hasty dismissal of both the literary establishment and the
general public. There existed at least an appearance of unity
among the embattled few who challenged artistic orthodoxy.

But not surprisingly, as the movement grew, it became factionalized and entered a polemical phase in which violent disputes erupted over arcane points of doctrine that only initiates could understand. No longer was there a need to safeguard the right to experiment; that was a battle obviously won. "Up to very recently," wrote Eliot in 1917, "it was impossible to get free verse printed in any periodical except those in which Pound had influence . . . now it is possible to print free verse (second, third, or tenth-rate) in almost any American magazine."[64] Eliot is echoing Pound's fear that the dissemination of a literary method will work toward its vulgarization. His aim, it was Pound's as well, became an assertion of rigorous standards and the establishment of a literary identity which would distinguish the genuine from the spurious modern. From such a standpoint, admirers were almost as dangerous as detractors, since the enthusiastic epigone threatened to turn experiment into dogma. This fear is what led Eliot and Pound to challenge former allies such as Lowell, while they took steps to keep their own work inimitable. The Lowellites had fought for *vers libre* as a "principle of liberty"; Pound and Eliot set out to show that "there is no freedom in art."

In 1918 Pound wrote an essay called "The Hard and the Soft in French Poetry." He apologizes for "using these metaphorical terms 'hard' and 'soft,'"[65] but he need not have. One way to capture nuances in the literary sensibility is to notice the variety of metaphors for modernity. A broad distinction seems to obtain. On the one hand, there is the frequent image of life and art as essentially amorphous – misty, hazy, fluid. Thus Hulme calls for a poetry which will suggest a "vague mood," and Ford wants an "infinite flicker of small vitalities." Conrad describes the meaning of Marlow's tales as emerging in the way that "a glow brings out a haze, in the likeness of one of those misty haloes that sometimes are made visible by the spectral illumination of moonshine" – an image that recalls Woolf's description of life as a "luminous halo."[66] All of these metaphors imply an art that rejects precise statement and moral certainty in favour of the suggestiveness and imprecision usually associated with symbolism or Impressionism. Pound, on the other hand, opposed all "mushy technique" and "emotional slither," preferring a poetry "as much like granite as it could possibly be." Hulme later came around to this view in his celebration of classical literature as "dry and hard." In related images, Eliot praises Jean de Bosschère for "an intense frigidity . . . altogether admirable" and commends Sacheverell Sitwell for his "distinguished aridity."[67] Within this strain of metaphor the values are clarity and distinctness, and there is a positive dislike for the soft, the damp and the misty.

But it is one thing to choose a metaphor; it is another to apply it to the writing of verse. Imagism had begun by attacking rhetoric, adjectives and the superfluous word, and by insisting upon "efficient writing" and "straight talk." As compared to the gauziness of the nineties, it no doubt seemed as adamantine as poetry could get. But by the time of *Some Imagist Poets* all kinds of things passed as *des images*, including the following lines from Aldington's "Round/Pond":

> Water ruffled and speckled by the galloping wind
> Which puffs and spurts it into tiny pashing breakers
> Dashed with lemon/yellow afternoon sunlight.
> The shining of the sun upon the water
> Is like a scattering of gold/crocus/petals
> In a long wavering irregular flight.[68]

Imagism, it is clear, had begun to stand for any short poem with a striking (or strained) image. Pound did not respond by changing his metaphor; hardness remains "a quality which is in poetry nearly always a virtue,"[69] but its defining features began to alter. During the "counter-current" the emphasis on a single concentrated image gave way to rhythmical precision. "Rhyme and regular strophes" became the criteria for the hard. It was as though when the image could no longer impose an adequate rigour, Pound and Eliot turned to the severity of a demanding metre, as if to purify the movement through the fineness of their ears. Théophile Gautier emerged as a presiding influence, and Eliot would later describe the advantages of "metrical servitude": "We studied Gautier's poems and then we thought, 'Have I anything to say in which this form will be useful?' And we experimented. The form gave the impetus to the content."[70] In fact, the form almost supersedes the content. Gautier wrote of Inès de las Sierras and Eliot writes of Sweeney, but these differences seem insignificant beside the strong similarities in metre and syntax.

> Impassible et passionnée,
> Fermant ses yeux morts de langueur,
> Et comme Inès l'assassinée
> Dansant, un poignard dans le coeur!
>
> (Gautier, "Inès de las Sierras")

> Apeneck Sweeney spreads his knees
> Letting his arms hang down to laugh,
> The zebra stripes along his jaw
> Swelling to maculate giraffe.
>
> (Eliot, "Sweeney Among the Nightingales")

> Carmen est maigre, – un trait de bistre
> Cerne son oeil de gitana.
>
> (Gautier, "Carmen")

> Grishkin is nice: her Russian eye
> Is underlined for emphasis
>
> (Eliot, "Whispers of Immortality")

The language of poetry, Pound had written not long before, "must be fine language, departing in no way from speech save by a heightened intensity (i.e. simplicity). There must be no book words, no periphrases, no inversions   nothing that you couldn't, in some circumstances, in the stress of some emotion, actually say."[71] These strictures had undoubtedly helped to reform poetic style, but so now did their antitheses. Eliot came to argue that conversational style was no antonym to rhetoric; a conversational style had a rhetoric of its own. In place of "the language of common speech," so sedulously cultivated in *Some Imagist Poets*, Eliot offered a deliberate and exaggerated artifice, characterized precisely by book words, periphrases and inversions, and by things that one would never actually say (e.g. "Polyphiloprogenitive").

One of the persistent subjects of modernist dispute, the relative positions of poetry and prose, thus flared again. Hulme, it will be recalled, had seen prose as a barrier to genuine literary expression, because it continually reduced fresh images into worn clichés. Only the "intuitive language" of poetry could startle speech into evocation, and the task of modern literature was to rehabilitate a language ravaged by prose. Pound, on the other hand, followed Ford, arguing that "poets should acquire the graces of prose" – namely, the virtues of efficiency and precision. In "The Serious Artist" he cited Stendhal's blithe dismissal of poetry: "La poésie, avec ses comparaisons obligées, sa mythologie que ne croit pas le poète, sa dignité de style à la Louis XIV, et tout l'attirail de ses ornements appelés poétiques, est bien au-dessous de la prose dès qu'il s'agit de donner une idée claire et précise des mouvements du coeur; or, dans ce genre, on n'émeut que par la clarté."[72] Pound welcomed this challenge and agreed that if poetry could not attain the clarity of prose, then it should cease to be written. The emergence of Gautier, however, occasioned still another reversal. Gautier in his time had defended the distinctive character of verse, attacking those "utilitarians, progressive and practical, or simply clever men, who think with Stendhal that verse is a childish form that was good enough for the primitive ages, but who insist that poetry should be written in prose, as beseems an age of common-sense."[73] In the same spirit half a century later Eliot dealt a heavy blow to the prose tradition in his essay "The Borderline of Prose," in which he insisted upon sharp differences between verse and prose rhythms and disparaged the prose poem as a dangerous mixing of modes. "The distinction between poetry and prose," wrote Eliot, "must be a technical distinction; and future refinement of both poetry and prose can only draw the distinction more clearly . . . Both verse and prose still conceal unexplored possibilities, but whatever one writes must be definitely and by inner necessity either one or the other."[74] With the poems in the manner of Gautier, Eliot wrenched poetry free from its deference to prose.

But the commitment to rhyme and strophes was more than a formal decision. It reflected a new turning toward literary history. Damon has suggested that Pound, in tying himself to Lewis and Vorticism, cut himself off from his early historical enthusiasms; certainly, Lewis' "Gospel of the Present" jeopardizes a passionate interest in the troubadours. And even before his association with Lewis, Pound was asserting baldly that "No good poetry is ever written in a manner twenty years old," a remark that recalls Hulme's call for the destruction of "all verse more than twenty years old."[75] But just as Hulme rediscovered Racine, Byzantium and Egypt, so Pound returned to his "pawing over the ancients." He made a hasty retreat from his defence of *vers libre*, writing that it "has become a pest . . . as rabbits are a pest in Australia," and suggesting that literary progress now lies "in an attempt to approximate classical quantitative metres."[76] Eliot himself had not joined the attack on tradition. He had not chanted with the Vorticists that "Life is the Past and the Future. The Present is Art." He thus entered the debate at an opportune moment to assert the need for the regenerating example of past forms. Free verse in his view was only a local fashion which had no special claim on the modern poet and not only were Gautier's quatrains still pertinent but "we only need the coming of a Satirist – no man of genius is rarer – to prove that the heroic couplet has lost none of its edge since Dryden and Pope laid it down."[77] The pastiche of Pope in the drafts to *The Waste Land* suggest that Eliot entertained brief thoughts of himself as that satirist of genius.

He was not. But the very proposal of satire was enough to signal another point of difference from his Imagist contemporaries who valued exact statement and displayed little interest in the indirections of irony or satire. The Lowellites claimed "for their work only that it is sincere."[78] Pound, too, in his early programme for Imagism had depended on values of literary sincerity. Technique, he writes, is "the test of a man's sincerity" and in good writing "the writer says just what he means."[79] Indeed, it is noteworthy that during his Imagist phase, Pound's reliance on a speaking mask diminished, as though the commitment to "straight talk" and "direct treatment" were incompatible with a persona. Eliot had passed through no Imagist phase; he had never praised direct treatment; and he was eager to attack the cult of poetic sincerity.

Late in 1917, Eliot took up this issue in a review of *The New Poetry: An Anthology*, edited by Harriet Monroe and Alice Corbin Henderson. Of the poetry itself he had comparatively little to say, choosing instead to discuss the volume's introduction, which offered its own characterization of literary modernity. Monroe and Henderson had claimed that what animated the modern experiment was "an ideal of absolute simplicity and sincerity," in line with Yeats' demand for a "'style like speech as simple as the simplest prose, like a cry from the heart.'"[80] This demand, according to the editors, allowed modern poets to avoid the pitfall of rhetorical verse. Eliot meets that claim directly. He insists that even this volume contains rhetoric, and that a "style like speech" and a "cry from the heart" are not the appropriate ways to modernize verse: "I am inclined to believe that Tennyson's verse is a 'cry from the heart' – only it is the heart of Tennyson, Latitudinarian, Whig, Laureate. The style of William Morris is a 'style like speech,' only it is the speech of Morris, and therefore rather poor stuff. The 'Idylls of the King' sound often like Tennyson talking to Queen Victoria in heaven; and the 'Earthly Paradise' like an idealized Morris talking to an idealized Burne-Jones."[81]

Notice that Eliot is not concerned to dispute the *value* of the new poetry; he is rather intent to provide a different explanation of that value. Those contemporary poets "who have avoided rhetoric," he argues, "have done so chiefly by the exercise, in greater or less degree, of intelligence, of which an important function is the discernment of exactly what, and how much, we feel in any given situation."[82] In other words, Eliot is denying self-expression as the criterion of success, and is insisting on the need for a controlling intelligence behind poetic creation. He is attacking the view, inherited from the romantics, entertained by the pre-war moderns and still held by the Lowellites, that art is primarily a matter of mirroring the soul. On the contrary, argues Eliot, it involves selection, suppression, control and order.

These early critical essays are best understood as efforts to revise and reorder the prevailing modernist ideas, to free them of contradiction, to provide for them an adequate theoretical base and to distinguish them from rival attitudes. Eliot systematically undermined a series of formerly dominant concepts: sincerity, simplicity, freedom, expression, emotion. In his essay on Rostand, he even went so far as to defend the place of rhetoric, which had been the most assailed target of the literary reformers. Thus his critical task took shape: an assault on unconstrained personal expression and an insistence on order, intelligence and form. But to assert a need is not to satisfy it. How can verse be intelligent? What will provide its order? And how must its form change?

Gautier seemed to offer an answer to these questions. He once explained that his title *Émaux et Camées* reflected his intention "to treat slight subjects within a restricted space": "Every poem was to be a medallion fit to be set in the cover of a casket, or a seal to be worn on the finger . . ." Needing a verse form appropriate to his aim and finding Alexandrines "too mighty for such modest ambitions," Gautier settled upon octosyllabic lines in quatrains, which he "polished and chiselled with all possible care," renewing an old form "by the rhythm, the richness of the rimes and the accuracy to which any workman may attain when he patiently and leisurely works out some small task . . ."[83] Eliot set about his own quatrains with a similar ambition, and the poems he composed are notable for the precision of their rhythms and the fastidiousness of their rhymes. But as Eliot himself recognized, more was at issue than technical hygiene: "To create a form is not merely to invent a shape, a rhyme or rhythm. It is also the realization of the whole appropriate content of this rhyme or rhythm. The sonnet of Shakespeare is not merely such and such a pattern, but a precise way of thinking and feeling."[84]

> Morning stirs the feet and hands
> (Nausicaa and Polypheme).
> Gesture of orang-outang
> Rises from the sheets in steam.
>
> ("Sweeney Erect")

The short lines and tense rhythms do not permit the extended introspection of a speaking voice or the slow accumulation of emotional effect. The poems in quatrains are the most impersonal work of Eliot's career. The speaker either remains aloof (as in "The Hippopotamus") or plays a diminished and elusive role (as in "A Cooking Egg"). In earlier poems Eliot had relied on the responses of a character as a principle of structure. Now, with no individual consciousness at the poetic centre, he begins to experiment with other forms of order. Specifically, he begins to use the past to orient complex responses. In 1918 he registered his admiration for Joyce's method of allusion, noting that Joyce "uses allusions suddenly and with great speed, part of the effect being the extent of the vista opened to the imagination by the lightest touch."[85] Eliot himself works out a similar method. His early work had also involved allusion, but there Eliot depended on more familiar antecedents, such as Hamlet or Lazarus, placing them within extended conceits. In the later poems he develops the technique he will use in *The Waste Land*. He passes much more rapidly among his allusions, and like Gautier frequently uses them as shorthand descriptions.

> Un vrai château d'Anne Radcliffe,
> Aux plafonds que le temps ploya,
> Aux vitraux rayés par la griffe
> Des chauves-souris de Goya
>
> (Gautier, "Inès de Las Sierras")

> I shall not want Pipit in Heaven:
>   Madame Blavatsky will instruct me
> In the Seven Sacred Trances;
>   Piccarda de Donati will conduct me.
>
> (Eliot, "A Cooking Egg")

The strong accents, the unlikely rhymes, the rapid movement of thought, the casual appropriation of a cultural past, these are devices well suited to the methods of irony, and if the quatrain form represents a "precise way of thinking and feeling" for Eliot, it is the way of irony – not the incidental ironies of "Prufrock," but irony as the structural principle of the whole. ("Delicate irony," wrote Pound, "the citadel of the intelligent.")[86] These poems are built out of certain violent contrasts – Grishkin and the jaguar, Pipit and Lucretia Borgia, the hippopotamus and the True Church – and their development consists in the unfolding of stark antitheses. "What cruel irony," wrote Gautier, "in a palace next to a hovel," and the sensibility that delights in such juxtapositions is the sensibility that controls this phase of Eliot's career. In "Sweeney Among the Nightingales" Eliot turns irony to its most supple purposes, but even here the poem has to struggle to rise above the bathetic contrast between Sweeney and Agamemnon. Although Eliot displays great virtuosity in the quatrains, virtuosity is almost all that he displays. The aridity and frigidity that he praised he found. No more than the prose of Ford or the painting of Lewis would the octosyllabics of Gautier provide a solution to the problem of poetic form.

Still, the poems have their place in the ongoing development of a modernist style. After the direct statements of Imagism, irony must have seemed an expansive mode. And in one respect the most immediate problem confronting Pound and Eliot was how to expand their forms. With its mania for concentration, Imagism had threatened to reduce poetry to confines so narrow that they become constraints. Harold Monro had been among the first to recognize the limitations of such a compressed style. In a special issue of the *Egoist* devoted to Imagism, Monro took up the case of H. D. "She presents *one* image," wrote Monro,

That is all. It can be said in the one minute before lunch. There is no mould to be filled, no risk of padding, no fear of words being exploited to complete a rhyme . . . It is petty poetry; it is minutely small: it seems intended to be. Such images should appear by the dozen in poetry. Such reticence denotes either poverty of imagination or needlessly excessive restraint.[87]

Poems such as "A Cooking Egg" or "The Hippopotamus" would scarcely delay lunch longer, but their ironies, much like the ironies of Pound's "Mauberly," open beyond the confines of the single perception. The simplest ironic gesture – a statement offered then withdrawn – signals the beginning of development past the image. The movements of these poems, arch though they may be, are nonetheless movements; they are no longer restricted to that once-prized "instant of time." Pound had tried to adapt Imagism to larger purposes, holding that nothing stood in the way of a long Imagist poem. But it became steadily apparent that the long poem would have to have another basis than the integrity of a single image, no matter how generously that is conceived, and the counter-current implied an attack not only on the icons of free verse, direct treatment and sincerity, but more importantly on the kind of unity associated with an intellectual and emotional complex. Perhaps the most important legacy of that brief counter-current was the unravelling of the one-image poem, its direct statements tangled in a web of irony.

Eliot, of course, had begun his career, not with *des images*, but with the dramatic monologue, with "The Love Song of J. Alfred Prufrock," and "Portrait of a Lady." It would take us too far afield to approach these poems, which have in any case been well treated by others. But one specific point is worth mentioning – the weakness of the voices that hold these monologues together. Prufrock is from the start a "you and I," and certainly, by the time of "Gerontion," the reflecting consciousness has become so attenuated that it can scarcely count as a self. In part, this reflects simply the fragility of personal identity but, seen from another point of view, it signals a new opening to experience. The weaking of a central consciousness becomes a way of enlarging the poetic domain. Gerontion dissolves into history and, in losing a character, we gain a culture. The single consciousness is thus subjected to the same pressures that assail the single image. It, too, had threatened to impose narrow limits and a false homogeneity on the literary universe, and increasingly Eliot came to demand a method that will take "variety and complexity" into account. In the essay on Blake, he writes that "you cannot create a very large poem without introducing a more impersonal point of view, or splitting it up into various personalities."[88] He thus implicitly marks the limits of the monologue form and prepares himself for the act of will that makes possible *The Waste Land*.

The main line of Eliot's early development stretches from "Prufrock" through "Gerontion" to *The Waste Land*. These are the substantial works of the first phase of his career. But in paying serious attention to the poems of the counter-current, I have meant to suggest that they are not divagations from his proper calling but a second line of development. The poems in quatrains, after all, represent a reaction, not only to Imagism, but to Eliot's own previous methods. To the confessional aspect of the monologues they oppose the studied reticence of impersonal ironies and, in freeing Eliot from his former stylistic habits, these poems helped him to develop some of his most characteristic techniques: the abrupt juxtapositions, the reliance on temporal oppositions, the rapid shifts in point of view, the impersonal voice and the more tightly controlled rhythms. Eliot once laid down a "necessary condition of all art: the counter-thrust of strict limitations of form and the expression of life."[89] Whether that is in fact a necessary condition of art is difficult to say, but it undoubtedly gives us a useful way to understand his own early poetic development. He wants to enlarge the expressive range of his verse; this leads to the progressive refinements within the monologue. At the same time he seeks the "counter-thrust" of form, and this carries him to the experiments in quatrains. More expression, more limitation, more life, more form   out of such conflicting demands was *The Waste Land* made.

CHAPTER 9

The Waste Land

Speakers and ghosts

In early 1922 Eliot returned to London after several months away and resumed the "London Letter" which he had contributed to the *Dial* during the previous year. These brief essays had been relaxed, even jaunty commentaries in which Eliot had noted current London fashions, while indulging his taste for the crisp dismissal: "I cannot see in the Georgian Anthology any such influence as Wordsworth, Keats, and Shelley had upon Arnold, Tennyson, and Browning. The dulness of the Georgian Anthology is original, unique; we shall find its cause in something much more profound than the influence of a few predecessors. The subtle spirit inspiring the ouija-board of Mr. J. C. Squire's patient prestidigitators is not the shattered Keats but the solid and eternal Podsnap himself." [1] But the letter, published after his return, perhaps the first piece of criticism he wrote after a five-month hiatus, stands apart from the rest. Indeed, it is like nothing else in Eliot's criticism. It drops the clever tone of the previous letters and almost entirely disregards its ostensible aim, to report on the contemporary literary scene. Eliot dutifully begins to discuss two new anthologies of verse, one American, one English. But he gives them only the most perfunctory attention. In the space of one sentence, he dismisses Vachel Lindsay, Edgar Lee Masters, Amy Lowell and Robert Frost, and then like the typist in *The Waste Land* gives an exhausted sigh, "There, that is done." He is even more cursory with the English anthology, which he condemns without even identifying its contributors. "This should have been a London letter," he apologizes; instead it is a fiercely bitter assault on London, unrelieved by any note of hope. After a separation, writes Eliot, "one is disposed to generalize about impressions; so I have been led to contemplate, for many moments, the nature of the particular torpor or deadness which strikes a denizen of London on his return."[2]

There is certainly, in the atmosphere of literary London, something which may provisionally be called a moral cowardice. It is not simply cowardice, but a caution, a sort of worldly prudence which believes implicitly that English literature is so good as it is that adventure and experiment involve only unjustified risk; lack of ambition, laziness, and refusal to recognize foreign competition; a tolerance which is no better than torpid indifference; not cowardice merely, but still a composition of inertias which is usually to be found in general cowardice . . . in London these poisons are either more pernicious, or their effects more manifest, than elsewhere. Other cities decay, and extend a rich odour of putrefaction; London merely shrivels, like a little bookkeeper grown old.[3]

On medical advice Eliot had taken leave from his bank and had left London in October of 1921. He had travelled first to Margate and then to the now famous rest-cure at Lausanne. But the rest-cure, it would appear, had brought him little rest. The "London Letter" seems the work of an enervated personality and comes as close to a *cri de coeur* as Eliot ever allowed himself in his critical writings. For a moment he risks losing that cherished separation between "the man who suffers and the mind which creates." We know enough of his personal situation to suspect that Eliot had begun to worry that he, like London, was shrivelling and that he, too, resembled a "little bookkeeper grown old." But we do not need the hypothesis of private unhappiness to make sense of this dreary letter. More to the point, and more in line with our prevailing concerns, is the strain that Eliot sees between poet and audience – in particular, the strain between a poet who cares to experiment and a culture which asks to be flattered and soothed.

The instinct for safety it may be – as in the bird the ostrich, not always a safe instinct – or a complexity of causes, which seems to make the English poet take refuge in just those sentiments, images, and thoughts which render a man least distinguishable from the mob, the respectable mob, the decent middle-class mob. An appearance of daring, even a real daring in non-literary respects (for political courage is still respected) may do no harm, and may even please; for it makes the reader feel that he is daring too. But a truly independent way of looking at things, a point of view which cannot be sorted under any known religious or political title; in fact, the having the only thing which gives a work pretending to literary art its justification; the having something which the public have not got: this is always detested. Sometimes it is not recognized, sometimes it can be ignored; and then a man may have a deserved immediate popularity; but when it is recognized and cannot be ignored, it is certainly feared and disliked.[4]

When he composed this letter, Eliot knew what his readers did not, that he had recently completed a poem called *The Waste Land*, which had cost him the greatest pains and which he was now prepared to release to that "decent middle-class mob." No doubt this accounts for the tone of dread. His earlier verse had attracted no wide following, and *The Waste Land*, whatever else it might be, was not safe. The sullenness of the "London Letter" reflects Eliot's anticipation of the howl which would greet his poem. He was right about the howl. But what he could not have anticipated was the subsequent canonization. This radical experiment which indeed could not be "sorted under any known religious or political title" gave Eliot just what he doubted could be attained: a victory over reigning taste and at the same time an accommodation with the established literary order.

The "London Letter" thus captures a telling moment in English modernism. It reveals Eliot on the point of his poetic success, with the keenest fear of failure. After the publication of *The Waste Land* he moved steadily and rapidly toward a position of literary dominance. If he never won popular affection, he at least inspired popular awe. But the letter to the *Dial* reminds us of the estrangement that preceded acceptance. As such it establishes the terms of our own argument. For, as the headings indicate, in the last section of the study we will consider a shift from provocation to consolidation. In order to do so, we will have to change the scale of argument and adjust its focus. Our closing movement will offer a foreshortened view of the later developments, just as we began with a foreshortened view of the early years. Eliot, who has become prominent recently, will continue to be so, since he came to exemplify English modernism, since he presided over the changes in its definition and presentation, and since he wrote its most celebrated work. In a significant sense, he inherited the mantle of the London avant-garde, and it is our task to see what he made of the legacy.

The Waste Land will serve as the illustrative, if not representative text. Pound called the poem "the justification of the 'movement,' of our modern experiment, since 1900."[5] I am inclined to concur. But the poem did more than justify the movement; it revised, even as it consolidated, the work of two decades. In part, then, the poem deserves attention simply as a specimen-instance, revealing what modernist theory might be a theory *of*, what the doctrine might seek to explain, what the modernist apology might seek to justify. In greater part, though, *The Waste Land* has a claim on our interest because it stands as itself a doctrinal act, the poem as a critical gesture. In overturning old norms so thoroughly, the work cannot fail to raise the critical question: what norms are now appropriate? In replacing old forms, it cannot help but imply new conceptions of poetic form. It is not a matter of the radical creation *inviting* theory; the genuinely radical work is already implicated in theory. The process of literary change is at once sensuous and conceptual – as Eliot himself realizes. He writes that he looks forward to a day "when the dogma, or *ideology*, of the critics is so modified by contact with creative writing, and when the creative writers are so permeated by the new dogma, that a state of equilibrium is reached."[6] In one sense, the present study has followed the history of that search after equilibrium, and, as equilibrium is a two-term relation, a consideration of literary forms themselves is not only convenient but necessary. *The Waste Land* will permit us to place modernist doctrine where we want it, hard between cultural institutions and literary forms.

> April is the cruellest month, breeding
> Lilacs out of the dead land, mixing
> Memory and desire, stirring
> Dull roots with spring rain.[7]

Who speaks these lines? – presumably whoever speaks these next lines:

> Winter kept us warm, covering
> Earth in forgetful snow, feeding
> A little life with dried tubers

since the subject-matter (the life of the seasons) persists, as does the distinctive syntactic pattern (the series of present participles) and the almost obsessive noun–adjective pairings ("dead land," "spring rain," "little life," "dried tubers"). The second sentence, of course, introduces a new element, a narrating personal consciousness. But surely this need not signal a new speaker; it suggests rather that there is and *has been* a speaker, the unspecified "us," who will receive greater specification in the next several lines.

> Summer surprised us, coming over the Starnbergersee
> With a shower of rain; we stopped in the colonnade,
> And went on in the sunlight, into the Hofgarten,
> And drank coffee, and talked for an hour.

Certainly we want to identify the "us" that winter kept warm with the "us" that summer surprised, and with the "we" who stop, go on, drink coffee and talk. That is how we expect pronouns to behave: same referents unless new antecedents. But if the pronouns suggest a stable identity for the speaker, much else has already become unstable. Landscape has given way to cityscape. General speculation (April as the "cruellest month") resolves into a particular memory: the day in the Hofgarten. And the stylistic pattern shifts. The series of participles disappears, replaced by a series of verbs in conjunction: "And went . . . And drank . . . And talked." The adjective–noun pattern is broken.

What can we conclude so far? – that a strain exists between the presumed identity of the poem's speaker and the instability of the speaker's world. If this is the speech of one person, it has the range of many personalities and many voices – a point that will gain clarity if we consider the remaining lines of the sequence:

> Bin gar keine Russin, stamm' aus Litauen, echt deutsch.
> And when we were children, staying at the arch-duke's,
> My cousin's, he took me out on a sled,
> And I was frightened. He said, Marie,
> Marie, hold on tight. And down we went.
> In the mountains, there you feel free.
> I read, much of the night, and go south in the winter.

The line of German aggravates the strain, challenging the fragile continuity that has been established. Here is a new voice with a new subject-matter, speaking in another language, resisting assimilation. Is the line spoken, overheard, remembered? Among the poem's readers no consensus has emerged. Nor is consensus to be expected. In the absence of contextual clues, and Eliot suppresses such clues, the line exists as a stark, unassimilable poetic datum.[8]

And yet, after that line a certain continuity is restored. The first-person plural returns; the pattern of conjunction reappears: "And when . . . And I . . . And down." Even that startling line of German, let us notice, had been anticipated in the "Hofgarten" and "Starnbergersee" of the previous lines. Discontinuity, in other words, is no more firmly established than continuity. The opening lines of the poem offer an elaborate system of similarities and oppositions, which might be represented in the following manner:

April is the cruellest month, *breeding*
Lilacs out of the dead land, *mixing*
Memory and desire, *stirring*
Dull roots with spring rain.
Winter kept *us* warm, *covering*
Earth in forgetful snow, *feeding*
A little life with dried tubers.
Summer surprised *us*, coming over the *Starnbergersee*
With a shower of rain; *we* stopped in the colonnade,
And went on in the sunlight, into the *Hofgarten*,
And drank coffee, and talked for an hour.
Bin gar keine Russin, stamm' aus Litauen, echt deutsch.
And when *we* were children, staying at the arch-duke's,
My cousin's, he took *me* out on a sled,
And I was frightened. He said, Marie,
Marie, hold on tight. *And* down we went.
In the mountains, there you feel free.
I read, much of the night, and go south in the winter.

The diagram should indicate the difficulty. Lines 1–6 are linked by the use of present participles, lines 5–18 by personal pronouns, lines 8–12 by the use of German, lines 10–16 by the reiteration of the conjunction "and." The consequence is that in any given line we may find a stylistic feature which will bind it to a subsequent or previous line, in this way suggesting a continuous speaker, or at least making such a speaker plausible. But we have no single common feature connecting all the lines: one principle of continuity gives way to the next. And these overlapping principles of similarity undermine the attempt to draw boundaries around distinct speaking subjects. The poetic voice is changing; that we all hear. Certainly we hear it when we compare one of the opening lines to those at the end of the passage. But the changes are incremental, frustrating the attempt to make strict demarcations. How many speak in these opening lines? "One," "two" and "three" have been answers, but my point is that any attempt to resolve that issue provokes a collision of interpretive conventions. On the one hand, the sequence of first-person pronouns – an "us" that becomes a "we," a "me" an "I," and then "Marie" – would encourage us to read these lines as marking the steady emergence of an individual human subject. But if the march of pronouns would imply that Marie has been the speaker throughout, that suggestion is threatened in the several ways we have considered: the shift from general reflection to personal reminiscence, from landscape to cityscape, from participial connectives to conjunctions, the disappearance of the noun–adjective pattern, the use of German. Attitudes, moreover, have undergone a delicate, though steady, evolution. Can the person who was "kept . . . warm . . . in forgetful snow . . ." be that Marie who prefers to "go south in winter?" Can the voice which solemnly intones the opening and explosive paradox: April is cruel, utter such conversational banalities as: "In the mountains, there you feel free"?

Perhaps – but if we insist on Marie as the consistent speaker, if we ask her to lay hold of this complexity, we can expect only an unsteady grasp. The heterogeneity of attitude, the variety of tone, do not resolve into the attitudes and tones of an individual personality.[9] In short, the boundaries of the self begin to waver: if we can no longer trust our pronouns, what can we trust? Furthermore, though we find it difficult to posit one speaker, it is scarcely easier to posit many, since we can say with no certainty where one concludes and another begins. Though the poem's opening lines do not hang together, neither do they fall cleanly apart. Here, as elsewhere, the poem plays between bridges and chasms, repetitions and aggressive novelties, echoes and new voices.

In the opening movement of *The Waste Land*, the individual subject possesses none of the formal dominance it once enjoyed in Conrad and James. No single consciousness presides; no single voice dominates. A character appears, looming suddenly into prominence, breaks into speech, and then recedes, having bestowed momentary conscious perception on the fragmentary scene. Marie will provide neither coherence nor continuity for the poem: having been named, she will disappear; her part is brief. Our part is larger, for the question we now face is the problem of boundaries in *The Waste Land*.

Has there been sufficient emphasis (I think not) upon the peculiar angle of vision that governs the first line of *The Waste Land*? Spring comes not to men and women, nor to trees and birds, but to lilacs, which do not flower as one might expect, but which are bred out of the earth. The view, that is, settled toward the ground. To be more precise, it looks at spring from beneath the ground, a fact that becomes clear in the next few lines, which specify that there are "roots" that are stirred and "tubers" that nourish. The eye here sees from the point of view of someone (or some thing) that is buried. In what other circumstances would snow act as a cover? How else could tubers feed a "little life"? Grover Smith has traced this latter image to James Thomson's "To Our Ladies of Death," in which there appears the line, "Our Mother feedeth thus our little life," and, more pertinent still, the line that follows: "That we in turn may feed her with our death." Thomson goes on to imagine his body after death, mingling with the soil: "One part of me shall feed a little worm . . . One thrill sweet grass, one pulse in bitter weed."[10] Given these considerations, may I be permitted my speculation, that the opening of *The Waste Land* looks at spring from the point of view of a corpse? Only here is a corpse that has not died, that retains its little life. We recall that the title of this opening section is "The Burial of the Dead" and already we have a fierce irony. These buried are not yet dead. Moreover, as the poem continues, the visual standpoint moves above ground, as much as to imply a rising from the grave.

Resurrection, of course, is one of the major themes of *Adonis, Attis, Osiris*, on which Eliot relied so heavily. Frazer attempted to show how "the peoples of Egypt and Western Asia represented the yearly decay and revival of life, especially of vegetable life" as the personification of a god "who annually died and rose again from the dead."[11] It should not then be surprising to find a vegetal consciousness as the image for the "dead and risen" spirit. To approach the first lines in these terms is to provide a context for the burial of the dead as an initially controlling motif and in particular for that otherwise anomalous remark from later in the first section:

> "Stetson!
> "You who were with me in the ships at Mylae!
> "That corpse you planted last year in your garden,
> "Has it begun to sprout?

The opening of the poem can be seen precisely as the sprouting of a corpse.

The poem's critics have been uneasy with the notion of a buried corpse planted in order to grow, and it has frequently been neutralized through the resources of paraphrase. Matthiessen takes the corpse as a memory.[12] But to psychologize so quickly is to remove the power from an image which suggests that the barriers between life and death are not firm and that what has already died can yet revive. No talk of buried memories can replace the image of the god risen from the dead.

The topos of the reviving god is, however, not the only significant pattern associated with the rising of the dead and not the only one on which Eliot depends. In *The Golden Bough*, Frazer describes a number of myths that chronicle the return of the dead as wandering ghosts that haunt the living. Eliot himself was much preoccupied with this more chilling aspect of a return from the grave, and the drafts of *The Waste Land* contain several sustained evocations of a death that is unable to put an end to life. In an early version of "What the Thunder Said," the protagonist comes upon a man who "lay flat upon his back, and cried/'It seems that I have been a long time dead:/Do not report me to the established world.'"[13] In "Elegy," a poem included with *The Waste Land* manuscripts, the speaker bids his dead lover to "stay within thy charnel vault!" but nevertheless sees "sepulchral gates flung wide," revealing the "features of the injured bride" – a situation, notes the speaker, "as in a tale by Poe."[14] "One cannot be sure," wrote Eliot, "that one's own writing has not been influenced by Poe."[15] The evasion is enticing. Poe is a forgotten figure behind *The Waste Land*, and to remember Poe is to recover the gothic element that is too often explained away, the waste land as a chamber of horrors. One of the poem's cancelled lines is a response to the question "What is the wind doing?" The protagonist replies "Carrying/Away the little light dead people" – a chilling line that would have reminded us of what we should not in any case forget: namely that *The Waste Land* is a kind of ghost story with protagonists both haunted and haunting. Indeed, there is a distinctly disembodied aspect to consciousness in the poem, which watches without being watched and seems not so much to inhabit the world as to float upon it.

Eliot regarded the original epigraph from Conrad –

Did he live his life again in every detail of desire, temptation, and surrender during that supreme moment of complete knowledge? He cried in a whisper at some image, at some vision, – he cried out twice, a cry that was no more than a breath –

"The horror! the horror!"[16]

– as "somewhat elucidative," and commentators have usually assumed that this remark refers to Kurtz's celebrated cry. But the reader, who scarcely needs Kurtz to elucidate the poem's horror, might find the opening of Conrad's sentence more germane than its close. For, in important respects, *The Waste Land* is the record of one who must, like Kurtz, live life again "in every detail of desire, temptation, and surrender." The unifying notion here is the theme of the *retrospect*, which pervades the poem and which receives its consummate expression in Tiresias, who is obliged to return to old scenes and to witness old failures – in short, to endure the agony of retrospection helpless to change what it vividly sees.

Dante is another figure needed in this configuration, specifically Dante as author of the verse that becomes line 63 of *The Waste Land*: "I had not thought death had undone so many." In Canto III of the *Inferno* death has "undone" the Neutrals, not only in the sense of ruined or destroyed but also in the sense of cancelled or reversed – as a deed or a knot may be undone. The Neutrals, who have been "undone" by death are also said "to have no hope of death."[17] In this respect, Dante's Neutrals belong to the pattern that includes the Cumaean Sibyl and the ghosts of Poe, all of whom suffer a repulse by death and an obligation to live without hope of rest.

The image of a corpse that sprouts thus captures a startling ambiguity in the poem's opening movement, standing as it does at the point where two powerful topoi converge: the reviving god and the wandering dead. A triumphant return to life is made to coincide with an inability to die. The situation of Adonis and the situation of Dante's Neutrals, the fate of gods and the fate of ghosts, merge.

Such considerations have bearing on how we organize the poem's motifs, but also, and this is the immediate issue, on how we understand its form, because to take seriously the loss of clear boundaries between life and death and to acknowledge the disembodied character of consciousness is to approach the extent of the poem's formal provocation. If a corpse can sprout, then no boundaries are secure, and just here the thematic issue joins with the earlier structural concern: the ambiguity of pronouns and the dissolution of boundaries around the self. We may take as our starting point, both textually and historically, the recognition that the poem oversteps boundaries, moving among voices, between bodies, over space and through time. And how, we may ask, does it move?

Conrad Aiken, for one, thought that it moved as a kaleidoscope does, "as a series of sharp, discrete, slightly related perceptions and feelings, dramatically and lyrically presented, and violently juxtaposed (for effect of dissonance), so as to give us an impression of an intensely modern, intensely literary consciousness which perceives itself to be not a unit but a chance correlation or conglomerate of mutually discolorative fragments."[18] F. R. Leavis provided an early and influential defence, reading the poem as the record of an "inclusive consciousness" – specifically, the consciousness of Tiresias.[19] The various literary manifestations become then the manifestations of a single mind. If there are sudden movements, abrupt shifts of attention, discontinuities, these are the movements of an individual mind. Such unity is cheaply purchased. Like many another patent nostrum, it harms little but helps less. Notice that we do not solve the problem of disorder by making it the problem of a disordered self. To draw a circle of consciousness around fragmentation is not to transform fragmentation into coherence, and if we avail ourselves of Leavis' "inclusive consciousness," we must yet ask what that consciousness includes. Then we are confronted with the same heterogeneity, the same fragmentation (now, admittedly a psychic fragmentation) which has always struck and discomfited the poem's readers. Surely we want to acknowledge that heterogeneity. Such considerations may seem to throw us back to the Aiken *Waste Land*, the poem as a kaleidoscopic confusion. But the problem I pose for myself is how to negotiate between the two assessments: the poem as a submerged unity and the poem as a chaos of fragments. If I am correct, a resolution of this problem will not only assist the interpretation of the text, it will help us with our genealogical concerns. With such ambitions must go patience. The problem will remain while we equip ourselves to confront it.

The theory of points of view

Accustomed as we are to strain after the connections between philosophy and literature – chasing down stray references to Nietzsche, suggesting that Kant must have been "in the air," spinning precarious threads of inference – we are not sure what to make of a fully explicit, detailed and technical piece of philosophy, conceived and written at the beginning of a literary career. Since its publication in 1964, and even before its publication, Eliot's dissertation on F. H. Bradley has done little but stir controversy. There has been overenthusiasm, one commentator claiming that Bradley's mind "lies behind the structuring principles of Eliot's poetry, as well as behind every major theoretical concept appearing in his literary criticism," and there has been indifference, but there has been nothing like a measured assessment.[20] Nor can I hope to correct matters, though I will clarify where I can. I am restricting myself to an issue that bears closely on the history I have been tracing: Eliot's critique of Bradley's notion of the Absolute.

F. H. Bradley, brother of the Shakespearean scholar A. C. Bradley, was perhaps the most distinguished of the British Idealists who briefly gained philosophic sway at the end of the nineteenth century, and his *Appearance and Reality*, published in 1893, is probably the movement's most distinguished work. Bradley calls it a "sceptical study of first principles," and it represents a sustained attack on the conceptual apparatus of the empiricist worldview. It rejects the primacy of self, of science and of experience. As such, it is part of the dismantling of Victorian ideology.

Reduced to its most austere essentials, the metaphysic of F. H. Bradley follows this outline. The groundwork of all reality lies in "immediate experience," a state of experience prior to any division into self and other, or self and world, a state in which no consciousness is distinguishable from its object: "In the beginning there is nothing beyond what is presented, what is and is felt, or rather is felt simply. There is no memory or imagination or hope or fear or thought or will, and no perception of difference or likeness. There are, in short, no relations and no feelings, only feeling."[21] From one point of view the central task of philosophy this century has been an effort to eradicate the hypostatization of subject and object, and Bradley's doctrine of immediate experience is an early and important contribution to that task. Compare the above quotation with the following remark of William James: "The instant field of the present is always experience in its 'pure' state, plain unqualified actuality, a simple *that*, as yet undifferentiated into thing and thought, and only virtually classifiable as objective fact or someone's opinion about fact."[22]

For Bradley, as for James, the world of common-sense reality – the realm of subject and object, concept and category – is only a construction out of this initial amorphous whole. For James this poses no great difficulties; reason is derivative but effective. But Bradley, much like Bergson, sees ordinary rational thought not only as derivative but as a contradictory and unstable derivation. The concepts which we employ to apprehend the world are "a makeshift, a device, a mere practical compromise, most necessary, but in the end most indefensible."[23] All the fundamental notions on which rationality depends – time, space, causality, motion, change – disclose mere appearance while concealing reality. We divide the world into distinct things and objects, but this plurality is artificial and finally unsatisfying "Reality is one. It must be single, because plurality, taken as real, contradicts itself."[24]

This consummate oneness Bradley calls the Absolute. It is not a God nor any identifiable entity; it is not something we can ever fully know. It is simply the final synthesis of all diversity, the supra-rational state past the reach of common sense which integrates and transcends contradiction. Ordinary thought contents itself with a certain set of concepts and categories, but if we submit them to a test of their theoretical validity, they prove in each case to terminate in self-contradiction. Immediate experience at the beginning and the Absolute at the end are the two cases where contradictions are overcome – immediate experience because it exists *prior* to any divisions into terms and relations, and the Absolute because it *transcends* such division. This, then, is Bradley's philosophic topology: non-relational immediate experience at the foundation, then the ordinary pluralistic world of common sense, replete with contradiction, and finally the Absolute as the integration of plurality into unity and harmony. "There is nothing," writes Bradley "which, to speak properly, is individual or perfect, except only the Absolute."[25]

Such an attitude puts Bradley in roughly the same ideological terrain in which we have previously positioned Worringer, Husserl, Maurras and the later T. E. Hulme. Like these others, Bradley scorns the idea that the self can be the foundation or the centre of reality, and scorns, too, a dependence on scientific rationality. "Our principles may be true," he writes in a favourite passage of Eliot's, "but they are not reality. They no more *make* that Whole which commands our devotion, than some shredded dissection of human tatters *is* that warm and breathing beauty of flesh which our hearts found delightful."[26] Bradley's continual aspiration, in short, is towards a reality which transcends the self and transcends rationality.

This sets him, for instance, in severe antagonism to Arnold's religious programme. Arnold, after all, had accepted the rational standards of science and had depended on the self as the basis for religious sensibility. Wanting to avoid any step beyond these limits, he had ended by conceiving God as a matter of personal experience. In his *Ethical Studies*, Bradley bitterly satirized this position:

"Is there a God?" asks the reader. "Oh, yes," replies Mr. Arnold, "and I can verify him in experience." "And what is he then?" cries the reader. "Be virtuous, and as a rule you will be happy," is the answer. "Well, and God?" "That is God," says Mr. Arnold; "there is no deception, and what more do you want?" I suppose we do want a good deal more. Most of us, certainly the public which Mr. Arnold addresses, want something they can worship; and they will not find that in an hypostatised copy-book heading, which is not much more adorable than "Honesty is the best policy," or "Handsome is that handsome does," or various other edifying maxims, which have not yet come to an apotheosis.[27]

The notion that we can construct all that we require of religion, morality, politics and philosophy on the basis of individual psychology – this notion that was so compelling to Arnold, Mill and Huxley – was anathema to Bradley. He was a lifelong opponent of empiricist individualism; his Absolute towered majestically above it; and certainly this accounts for much of Eliot's initial attraction to his philosophy.[28] Eliot began his formal study of philosophy in 1910, travelling to Paris to study at the Sorbonne, where he listened to Bergson's lectures. The following year he returned to Harvard and entered the philosophy department; he remained there for the next three years. In 1913 he began preliminary work on his dissertation, purchasing his copy of *Appearance and Reality* in June of that year. In 1914 he travelled to Europe on a Sheldon fellowship, beginning in Germany and then moving to Oxford. He would continue work in philosophy until 1916. At Harvard Eliot had attended a seminar which Bertrand Russell had given while visiting the school. The two became friends and, when Eliot took up residence in England, Russell tried to see him through some serious personal difficulties. More important here is their intellectual relation. For if Eliot came to Bradley to escape empiricism, he came away from Bradley thinking that some form of empiricism was inescapable.

Since the turn of the century Russell and G. E. Moore had been pursuing a vigorous attack on idealism, an attack which would ultimately have the effect of restoring empiricist hegemony in British philosophy. Bradley's Absolute was a particular object of vituperation, and on this issue, though not on many others, William James was one with Russell and Moore. James called the Absolute a "metaphysical monster"; Russell and Moore were scarcely more sympathetic.[29] To the generation of analytic and pragmatic philosophers, the supposed justification for the Absolute was embarrassingly insufficient. By Bradley's own admission, we can never know the Absolute itself, only its intellectual necessity. Ultimately, the decisive argument is that only the Absolute satisfies the requirement of non-contradiction. To pragmatists and empiricists, this was the worst sort of sophistry. As the bibliography of his dissertation attests, Eliot was well-read in the anti-idealist literature of the day. Indeed, we might see his brief philosophic career as an attempt to accommodate the empiricist critique within the idealist perspective, maintaining certain key Bradleyan propositions while quietly abandoning what had become untenable.

In the dissertation Eliot is plainly uneasy about Bradley's Absolute. In the first chapter he indicates that "the ultimate nature of the Absolute does not come within the scope of the present paper," and then dispenses with the concept in the rest of his argument.[30] But in an article published in the *Monist* shortly after he finished work on the dissertation, Eliot's tone slides unmistakably into suspicion. For Eliot – as for James, Russell and Moore – the Absolute has become a quaint metaphysical canopy, all too securely encompassing the diversity below.

Here one further concept from Bradley's metaphysic needs introduction: the notion of the "finite centre." Though this is only a peripheral element in Bradley's system, it will become crucial for Eliot, who describes a finite centre as a "unity of consciousness," a "universe in itself," the whole world as it exists for an individual consciousness.[31] But a finite centre, as Eliot will emphasize, is finite. It is a "monad," isolated and impervious, a single momentary unity of consciousness, the perceptual (and conceptual) totality of a single point of view – thus a "universe in itself." Though it is a temporary point of view, while it lasts, it constitutes the whole of reality. Eliot will point out that it is not to be confused with a "self" or "soul"; it exists prior to any such determination, it is the stuff of which selves are made. In short, the finite centre is something like the fundamental constituent of knowledge and experience, and if we look for a helpful parallel, we might see it in the "image" in Pound's early definition, "an intellectual and emotional complex in an instant of time."[32]

If Bradley attended so little to the finite centre, that was because it mattered so little in the grand scheme of his philosophy. Finite centres, like time, space, causality, things and selves were provisional and limited and ultimately overcome in the ineluctable progress toward metaphysical unity.[33] But Eliot hesitated before that progress. He accepted Bradley's undermining of the self; he accepted the idea that momentary glimpses of the world were more fundamental than individual personalities. But, a reluctant hostage to the new empiricism, Eliot could not accept the leap past such glimpses, past experience, past finite centres, and he writes in the *Monist* article that: "The Absolute responds only to an imaginary demand of thought, and satisfies only an imaginary demand of feeling. Pretending to be something which makes finite centres cohere, it turns out to be merely the assertion that they do."[34]

This remark should be read for the radical restatement of doctrine that it is. The whole tendency of *Appearance and Reality* had been toward an insistence on the necessity of the Absolute. Now Eliot blithely observes that such necessity is only imaginary. Eliot had faithfully adopted the notions of immediate experience and the finite centre. So far as these two concepts lead us, however, experience is simply a *plurality of perceptual moments*, out of which the more complex realms of subject and object, reality and unreality can later be construed. Bradley, of course, is unalterably opposed to remaining at this stage of the argument. The sum and substance of monism is the disallowal of such a plurality, and Bradley proceeds to insist on the integration of this diversity into the Absolute.

This Eliot resists. The title of the October essay is "Leibniz'

Monads and Bradley's Finite Centres"; and even to begin to compare Leibniz and Bradley is to take a long step away from monism. Leibniz' monadology is one of the most severely pluralist systems in the history of philosophy.[35] The monads which constitute his universe are absolutely individuated entities, utterly distinct from one another, "windowless and doorless," impenetrable, and in these respects, argues Eliot, the monads resemble Bradley's finite centres. But like Bradley, Leibniz was dissatisfied with the incoherence which he assumed such a pluralism would imply. He therefore completed his metaphysic by positing a 'pre-established harmony' among the monads; Eliot rejects this as he had rejected Bradley's leap to the Absolute: "just as Leibniz' pluralism is ultimately based upon faith, so Bradley's universe, actual only in finite centres, is only by an act of faith unified. Upon inspection, it falls away into the isolated finite experiences out of which it is put together . . . Bradley's Absolute dissolves at a touch into its constituents."[36]

So, too, at this moment, does Eliot's own metaphysical position dissolve – from monism into monadism, unity into plurality. His opposition between "faith" and "inspection" provides still another version of the contest between traditional belief and scientific verifiability, and in light of Eliot's subsequent conversion, it is worth alluding to his early empirical-tending position. For the Eliot of 1915–16 "actual" knowledge depends on the immediate and finite experience, and he refuses to take the last and crucial step in Bradley's argument – refuses, in short, to entrench the finite comfortably within the infinite.

In an essay of 1915, Richard Aldington, by way of elaborating the Imagist attitude, had defined it against the "'cosmic' crowd" and the "'abstract art' gang." Imagism, insisted Aldington (following Pound), had nothing to do with such flights of rhetorical excess; it was down-to-earth and immediate, depending on "direct treatment" of its poetic subject.[37] I mention this because Aldington's particular hostility to the "cosmic crowd" stands usefully alongside Eliot's antipathy toward Bradley's Absolute. In both cases the drive toward transcendence is rejected as sentimental and archaic. But we have seen that the literary consequences of the Imagist critique involved certain problems. In his 1915 assault on Imagism, Harold Monro had complained that the Imagists were so terrified at Cosmicism that they ran away into a kind of exaggerated Microcosmicism, and found their greatest emotional excitement in everything that seemed intensely small . . . The forms they still felt they might use, the vocabulary that remained at their disposal, were so extremely limited; so much good material had to be thrown into the large waste-paper basket of Cliché, that they remained now almost unprovided with a language or a style.[38]

And if on one side the charge was triviality, on the other it was egoism, the Imagists having retreated so far toward immediacy that they fell, according to Padraic Colum, into personal idiosyncrasy. In an essay called "Egoism in Poetry," Colum wrote that "it seems right that the thing that inspired the poem should not be dwarfed by the poet's vision of himself."[39]

Given such criticisms the poetic problem then became how to negotiate between cosmic poetry and egoism, between rhetorical overstatement and the limits of the single image. Such is the problem which Eliot addresses in the 1917 literary countercurrent, and it was the intricacies of this issue which led us to philosophy and will keep us with philosophy for a moment longer. For Eliot's philosophy risks the same charge of egoism which came to plague the Imagists. If the Absolute is relinquished, then the risk is the loss of extra-individual standards and a collapse into solipsism. That is the movement we have witnessed from Pater to Ford and the Stirnerians, the retreat to the self as the only sure measure of evaluation. Eliot acknowledges the difficulty of the issue. The "conclusions already reached," he concedes in the dissertation, "demand an examination of Solipsism."[40] For if a finite centre is self-contained and isolated, if within it everything is equally real, how is reality to be separated from illusion? A good statement of the difficulty is found in the quotation from Bradley that Eliot includes as a note to *The Waste Land* (Eliot also quotes the passage in his *Monist* article):

My external sensations are no less private to myself than are my thoughts or my feelings. In either case my experience falls within my own circle, a circle closed on the outside; and, with all its elements alike, every sphere is opaque to the others which surround it . . . In brief, regarded as an existence which appears in a soul, the whole world for each is peculiar and private to that soul.[41]

Now, for Bradley, this situation does not pose serious problems; finite centres, like everything itself, resolve themselves within the Absolute. Eliot, for his part, tries to solve the matter from a more empirical standpoint, and to that end he develops what he calls "the theory of points of view."

The argument runs like this. While it is true that, within the confines of any given finite centre, reality and unreality, subjectivity and objectivity, cannot be distinguished, a comparison among a *number* of finite centres makes such distinctions possible. The self, writes Eliot, "passes from one point of view to another . . ."; no single point of view is sufficient for knowledge; only in multiple perspectives does the world become real: "So that the reality of the object does not lie in the object itself, but in the extent of the relations which the object possesses without significant falsification of itself." [42] Eliot cites, as an example, the case of a child who mistakes a shadow for an attacking bear. At the moment of misconception and terror, argues Eliot, that shadow *is* a bear. Only when the shadow/bear is submitted to further relations – when it doesn't growl, when it disappears in the light – does its unreality become manifest: "the difference between real bear and illusory bear is a difference of fullness of relations, and is *not* the sort of difference which subsists between two classes of objects . . ." [43] Or as Eliot would put it elsewhere: "Whatever is gathered together in consciousness equally is, and is real or unreal only in relation." [44] If we situate such an attitude in the history we have been following, it becomes evident that Eliot is proposing a new theory of meaning. Meaning is no longer identified with presence to an individual consciousness (as in the various instances of Pater, Conrad and Ford). Nor is meaning considered autonomous and self-sufficient (as in Husserl or Hulme). It is the product of multiple perspectives, "of various presentations to various viewpoints." [45]

I have shown, I have tried to show, that Eliot's attack on the rational ego proceeded from two directions. He insisted on something simpler and more fundamental: the immediate experience (the particular points of view) out of which the self only subsequently emerged. The ego was as much a construction as the world or other people; as Eliot put it, "We have not only to interpret other souls to ourself but to interpret ourself to ourself." [46] But Eliot also insisted on something more complex than the self, the developing *system* of points of view which extends beyond the ego and within which alone it is possible to speak of reality, truth, meaning, value, self. The human subject, then, was neither primary nor ultimate; experience did not begin in the ego, nor did judgment end there.

Eliot's philosophy, though mannered and difficult, though conceived in Bradleyan terms and executed technically, nevertheless enacts the intellectual struggle we have been considering and faces the same compelling questions: How might we construct an intellectual position which acknowledges the scientific critique of transcendence (of the Absolute)? And how, once transcendence is relinquished, might we avoid a precipitous fall into solipsism? That is to say, how acknowledge the force of a sceptical science and the need for authority and order?

To this point in modernist development, there has been little in the way of resolution. In general, we can say that the modernist apology has embraced one of the two tendencies: either an extreme egoism (in the Stirnerians, in early Hulme, in Ford) or an equally radical absolutism (in Hulme, Worringer). Lewis and Pound veered alternately in both directions, but at any one point, in any one manifesto, the explicit embrace of one tendency precluded the other. This led to much of the instability and incoherence of the pre-war literary position.

The position which Eliot developed was a well-considered attempt to avoid the difficulties of such an opposition, rejecting, as it did, the primacy of both the individual and the Absolute. The "theory of points of view" maintained an experiential basis – it involved no leap into transcendence – while avoiding dependence on the individual and individual consciousness, since a point of view was more fundamental than an individual. It furnished a principle of authority, the system of points of view, without violating empiricist constraints of verifiability. The theory, in short, can be recognized as a legitimate third term, neither egoist nor objectivist. This is not to see it as an Hegelianized synthesis, although that would be tempting and not wholly wrong. But Eliot's theory did not make obsolete the competing attitudes. Moreover, Eliot himself would ultimately find this an inadequate solution; his conversion to Anglo-Catholicism represented, among many other things, an overturning of his early philosophic premises. Still, I am describing a precise historical moment, within which Eliot's formula was the most successful formula and accordingly achieved cultural dominance – as will become clear, when we put the matter in literary terms.

The painful task of unifying

The history traced in this study has been a history of oppositions, disproportions and asymmetries, a history of distinctions drawn then dramatized, a doctrinal struggle waged often between mutually excluding extremes. Apostles of freedom contended with guardians of order, realists with abstractionists, sceptics with dogmatists, subjectivists with anti-humanists. The instability of the movement, its persistent doctrinal revisions, must be linked to the incompatibility of these rival imperatives. If Eliot has come to prominence in these pages, if he came to prominence in the twenties, it was in large part because he revised this habit of the modernist mind. His critical efforts ought to be seen as attempts to restore equilibrium, to effect a satisfactory poise among competing aesthetic demands, to achieve, in Eliot's phrase, "a moment of stasis,"

His notion of tradition aimed at just such a critical poise, avoiding egoism on the one side and severe dehumanization on the other, not denying the individual ego but severely restricting its claims. The self was to be positioned among other selves; consciousness was to be corrected by a tradition of consciousnesses. The vision was not one of individuals versus authority, but of an authority composed of individuals. The totality of individuals – individual poets, individual poems – *was* the requisite authority. In short, what the "theory of points of view" effected on the philosophic plane, "tradition" effected on the plane of literary judgment. Both provided standards within the world but beyond the self. Compare the following two quotations – the first from Eliot's dissertation, the second from "Tradition and the Individual Talent":

I have tried to show that there can be no truth or error without a presentation and discrimination of two points of view; that the external world is a construction by the selection and combination of various presentations to various viewpoints.

No poet, no artist of any art, has his complete meaning alone. His significance, his appreciation is the appreciation of his relation to the dead poets and artists. You cannot value him alone; you must set him, for contrast and comparison, among the dead.[47]

There is no question of *deriving* the critical concept from the philosophic. That would be misleading and would in any case explain little. The point rather is the continuity of Eliot's intellectual perspective, the structural homology between his epistemological position and his attitude toward aesthetic evaluation. In both cases, he rejects the possibility of intrinsic judgment. Truth, like poets, cannot be assessed alone. And yet just this had been a tendency among the early moderns, art as *sui generis* and *sui temporis*. The Futurists had dismissed tradition, and the Stirnerians dismissed other people. Insofar as modernist art participated in this tendency, it inclined towards the self-sufficiency of the individual aesthetic gesture ("Reality is in the artist"); it valued liberty, sincerity, "speech from the heart."[48] Such was the current against which Pound and Eliot positioned their 1917 counter-current; in the context of their self-conscious reaction, tradition became a secularized authority, a way of escaping literary solipsism without relying on an Absolute. Like the "points of view" in the dissertation, tradition depended on inspection not faith.

Tradition is not, insists Eliot, an "indiscriminate bolus," an accumulated mass of literary endeavour.[49] It is rather a meaning-giving system. The value of any particular artist, of any particular work, cannot be determined in isolation – just as no object, no person, no fact, can be perceived in isolation. There must exist, already exist, a scheme into which the new phenomena can fit. Two more quotations – again from the dissertation and "Tradition and the Individual Talent" – should make the point clear.

Facts are not merely found in the world and laid together like bricks, but every fact has in a sense its place prepared for it *before it arrives*, and without the implication of a system in which it belongs the fact is not a fact at all.

The existing order is complete *before the new work arrives*; for order to persist after the supervention of novelty, the *whole* existing order must be, if ever so slightly, altered; and so the relations, proportions, values of each work of art toward the whole are readjusted.[50]

No meaning without relations; no truth, no reality, no value without order, without system. Eliot's tradition, then, is not the product of a mere sentimentalizing nostalgia for the past. As he himself will remark a few years later, the problem of tradition is "a problem of order" and he speaks of the need to conceive of literature as "systems in relation to which, and only in relation to which, individual works of literary art, and the works of individual artists, have their significance."[51]

The issue of tradition has not been exhausted; we will return to it; but it would be pointless to wait any longer to consider *The Waste Land* in the light of these conceptual distinctions. Another coincidence of phrasing will ease our way back to the poem. In the note to line 218 Eliot writes:

Tiresias, although a mere spectator and not indeed a "character," is yet the most important personage in the poem, uniting all the rest. Just as the one-eyed merchant, seller of currants, *melts into* the Phoenician Sailor, and the latter is *not wholly distinct* from Ferdinand Prince of Naples, so all the women are one woman, and the two sexes meet in Tiresias.

The phrases that I have emphasized establish the issue which we are in a position to address: what does it mean to call characters "not wholly distinct"? How can they "melt into" one another? How can the many become one? And how is this to be reconciled with the poem's polyphony?

In his dissertation, as in his second *Monist* article, Eliot had taken pains to stress the analogy between the philosophies of Bradley and Leibniz. Both, he pointed out, had posited fundamental self-contained units as the basis of reality, isolated finite experiences which were the ground of all knowledge, in Leibniz' words, "the true atoms of nature and, in a word, the elements of things."[52] For Bradley, these were "finite centres," for Leibniz the "monads;" in each case a set of rigorously bounded fragments was the foundation of reality.

Eliot himself — we considered this in the last chapter — attached great significance to these concepts. He, too, held that the basis of knowledge was immediate and finite experience. But the error of both Leibniz and Bradley, according to Eliot, lay in their supposing that these basic atoms of experience remained irrevocably separate: in Leibniz' well-known phrase, "windowless and doorless." Such a belief, argued Eliot, implied that order in the universe could not derive from the monads themselves: order must come from elsewhere, and thus Leibniz "lets himself in for the most unnecessary of his mysteries – the pre-established harmony."[53] The pre-established harmony, the fore-ordained order of the monads, an order established by divinity in order to ensure a "perfect mutual agreement" among the monads – this does for Leibniz what the Absolute does for Bradley: it provides an encompassing, integrating pattern for the individual isolated experiences.

Eliot, as we have already seen, rejects the need for any such integrating Absolute as a way of guaranteeing order. His theory of points of view means to obviate that need. Points of view, though distinct, can be combined. Order can emerge from beneath; it need not descend from above. And thus in the *Monist* he says of Leibniz' theory of the dominant monad: "I contend that if one recognizes two points of view which are quite irreconcilable and yet *melt into* each other, this theory is quite superfluous." And in the dissertation he writes that "the pre-established harmony is unnecessary if we recognize that the monads are *not wholly distinct.*"[54]

My italics are tendentious, dramatizing the repetitions in phrase. But the repetition is more than a chance echo; it identifies a problem which both the philosophy and the poetry address. How can one finite experience be related to any other? Put otherwise, how can difference be compatible with unity? Moreover, the poetic solution is continuous with the philosophic solution: individual experiences, individual personalities are not impenetrable. They are distinct, but not wholly so. Like the points of view described in the dissertation, the fragments in *The Waste Land* merge with one another, pass into one another.

Madame Sosostris, for instance, identifies the protagonist with the drowned sailor ("Here, said she/Is your card, the drowned Phoenician Sailor"). But the sailor, Phlebas, is also identified with Mr Eugenides: recall Eliot's phrase, "the one-eyed merchant, seller of currants, melts into the Phoenician Sailor." But, as Langbaum has shown, if the protagonist is identified with Phlebas and Phlebas with Eugenides, then it is difficult to escape the conclusion that the protagonist and the Smyrna merchant are, themselves, "not wholly distinct."[55] What, then, do we make of these lines?

> Under the brown fog of a winter noon
> Mr. Eugenides, the Smyrna merchant
> Unshaven, with a pocket full of currants
> C.i.f. London: documents at sight,
> Asked me in demotic French
> To luncheon at the Cannon Street Hotel
> Followed by a weekend at the Metropole.

The protagonist, as Langbaum points out, "stands on both sides of the proposition," and such a conclusion will unnerve us only if we hold fast to traditional concepts of self, personal identity, personal continuity and the barriers between selves. But in *The Waste Land* no consistent identity persists; the "shifting references" alter our notions of the self.[56] The characters are little more than aspects of selves or, in the jargon of Eliot's dissertation, "finite centres," "points of view." Here are the concluding lines of "The Fire Sermon":

> To Carthage then I came
>
> Burning burning burning burning
> O Lord Thou pluckest me out
> O Lord Thou pluckest
>
> burning

Lines from Augustine alternate with lines from the Buddha, and, as Eliot tells us in the footnote: "the collocation of these two representatives of eastern and western asceticism, as the culmination of this part of the poem, is not an accident." Of course it is not. It is the way the poem works: it collocates in order to culminate. It offers us fragments of consciousness, "various presentations to various viewpoints," which overlap, interlock, "melting into" one another to form emergent wholes. The poem is not, as it is common to say, built upon the *juxtaposition* of fragments: it is built out of their *interpenetration*. Fragments of the Buddha and Augustine combine to make a new literary reality which is neither the Buddha nor Augustine but which includes them both.

But at my back from time to time I hear
The sound of horns and motors, which shall bring
Sweeney to Mrs. Porter in the spring.

The echo from Marvell passes into an echo from Day: the poetic effect depends on amalgamating these distinct sources, on recognizing them as not wholly distinct. For we know, argues Eliot, "that we are able to pass from one point of view to another, that we are compelled to do so, and that the different aspects more or less hang together." The movement of *The Waste Land* is just such a movement among points of view: Marvell and Day, the Buddha and St Augustine, Ovid and Virgil.

We find ourselves in a position to confront a problem, which, though distant, is not forgotten: the problem of the poem's unity, or what comes to the same thing, the problem of Tiresias. We may begin to see how Tiresias can serve the function of "uniting all the rest," without that obliging us to conclude that all speech and all consciousness are the speech and consciousness of Tiresias. For, if we rush too quickly to Tiresias as a presiding consciousness, along the lines established by Conrad or James, then we lose what the text clearly asks us to retain: the plurality of voices that sound in no easy harmony. What Eliot says of the Absolute can be said of Tiresias, who, also, "dissolves at a touch into . . . constituents." But this does not leave us with a heap of broken fragments; we have seen how the fragments are constructed into new wholes. If Tiresias dissolves into constituents, let us remember the moments when those constituents resolve into Tiresias. Tiresias is, in this sense, an intermittent phenomenon in the poem, a *subsequent* phenomenon, emerging out of other characters, other aspects. The two sexes may, as Eliot suggests, meet in Tiresias, but they do not begin there.

"The life of a soul," writes Eliot in the dissertation, "does not consist in the contemplation of one consistent world but in the painful task of unifying (to a greater and less extent) jarring and incompatible ones, and passing, when possible, from two or more discordant viewpoints to a higher which shall somehow include and transmute them." Tiresias functions in the poem in just this way: not as a consistent harmonizing consciousness but as the struggled-for emergence of a more encompassing point of view. The world, Eliot argues, is only sporadically accessible to the knowing mind; it is a "felt whole in which there are moments of knowledge."[57] And so, indeed, is *The Waste Land* such a felt whole with moments of knowledge. Tiresias provides not permanent wisdom but instants of lucidity during which the poem's angle of vision is temporarily raised, the expanse of knowledge temporarily widened.

The poem concludes with a rapid series of allusive literary fragments: seven of the last eight lines are quotations. But in the midst of these quotations is a line to which we must attach great importance: "These fragments I have shored against my ruins." In the space of that line the poem becomes conscious of itself. What had been a series of fragments of consciousness has become a consciousness of fragmentation: that may not be salvation, but it is a difference, for as Eliot writes, "To realize that a point of view is a point of view is already to have transcended it." And to recognize fragments *as* fragments, to name them as fragments, is already to have transcended them – not to an harmonious or final unity but to a somewhat higher, somewhat more inclusive, somewhat more conscious point of view. Considered in this way, the poem does not achieve a resolved coherence, but neither does it remain in a chaos of fragmentation. Rather it displays a series of more or less stable patterns, regions of coherence, temporary principles of order – the poem not as a stable unity but engaged in what Eliot calls the "painful task of unifying."

Within this perspective any unity will be provisional; we may always expect new poetic elements, demanding new assimilation. Thus the voice of Tiresias, having provided a moment of authoritative consciousness at the centre of the poem, falls silent, letting events speak for themselves. And the voice in the last several lines, having become conscious of fragmentation, suddenly gives way to more fragments. The polyphony of *The Waste Land* allows for intermittent harmonies, but these harmonies are not sustained; the consistencies are not permanent. Eliot's method must be carefully distinguished from the methods of his modernist predecessors. If we attempt to make *The Waste Land* conform to Imagism or Impressionism, we miss its strategy and miss its accomplishment. Eliot wrenched his poetry from the self-sufficiency of the single image and the single narrating consciousness. The principle of order in *The Waste Land* depends on a plurality of consciousnesses, an ever-increasing series of points of view, which struggle towards an emergent unity and then continue to struggle past that unity.

Myth, tradition, classicism

When he first met Eliot, Pound commented admiringly that here was a young poet who had "modernized himself." [58] But perhaps even more impressive is that slightly older poet who historicized himself. Eliot had begun his critical career immersed in the local disputes of the modernist polemic and, in comparing the uncollected essays of these early years with those of his maturity, one is immediately struck by the partisan tone of the earlier work and its caustic wrangling over minor points. But one is also struck by its narrow historical range. Eliot's characteristic subjects included *vers libre*, the prose poem, the virtues of Pound and the vices of Amy Lowell. He wrote a series of articles for the *Egoist* called "Reflections on Contemporary Poetry," another called "Studies in Contemporary Criticism," and all of his work might have fit comfortably under these rubrics. Baudelaire and Flaubert marked a rough beginning to the modern period and a rough limit to Eliot's critical concerns. He wrote appreciations of James and deprecations of the Georgians, while scarcely considering the darker ages before the symbolists.

In the academic year 1918–19 he gave a course of lectures on Elizabethan drama, which seems to have been the occasion for a stirring of his historical sense. He would not have been the first to find that the promise to give a lecture is a great prod to learning. In any event, the year 1919 saw Eliot's first important works of criticism: the studies of Jonson and Marlowe, the *Hamlet* essay, and "Tradition and the Individual Talent." Over the next two years Eliot expressed some of his most influential historical opinions, writing essays on Blake, Dante and Massinger in 1920 and on Dryden and the metaphysical poets in the following year. In short, he gave himself a literary past. Pound had offered the movement an antiquarian's zeal, but Eliot provided the rudiments of a continuous literary history. Given his notion of tradition, he could scarcely aspire to less. If the "historical sense" compels a poet to write with a feeling for "the whole of the literature of Europe," then the task of criticism is never done.[59] It must always extend its range in pursuit of the whole. It must always widen the historical compass. Such commitments led Eliot into the more obscure corners of Elizabethan drama and led him as well to anthropology.

"Within the time of a brief generation," wrote Eliot, "it has become evident that some smattering of anthropology is as essential to culture as Rollin's Universal History."[60] Eliot had read Lévy-Bruhl for his dissertation; he knew the work of Gilbert Murray and Jane Harrison; and week-end exegetes continue to find good sport in tracing *The Waste Land*'s many references to *The Golden Bough* and Jessie Weston's *From Ritual To Romance*. My own interest is not with these works as literary sources but with something prior: the relation between Eliot's poetic and the anthropological temper.

One of Eliot's chief targets in his criticism is that much-abused figure, the "ordinary man," who stands for all that the artist must not. "It is important," writes Eliot in the essay on Blake, "that the artist should be highly educated in his own art; but his education is one that is hindered rather than helped by the ordinary processes of society which constitute education for the ordinary man. For these processes consist largely in the acquisition of impersonal ideas which obscure what we really are and feel, what we really want, and what really excites our interest." We learn in the essay on the metaphysical poets that the ordinary man is not only insensible to ideas, feelings, desires and interests, but also that "the ordinary man's experience is chaotic, irregular, fragmentary." In the introduction to Pascal, he reveals himself incapable of both doubt and faith, for "when the ordinary man calls himself a sceptic or an unbeliever, that is ordinarily a simple pose, cloaking a disinclination to think anything out to a conclusion." And in Eliot's review of Lewis' *Tarr*, the novel is praised at his expense:

The artist, I believe, is more *primitive*, as well as more civilized, than his contemporaries, his experience is deeper than civilization, and he only uses the phenomena of civilization in expressing it. Primitive instincts and the acquired habits of ages are confounded in the ordinary man. In the work of Mr. Lewis we recognize the thought of the modern and the energy of the cave-man.[61]

This last formulation throws more light on Eliot's attraction to anthropology. In trying to establish a standpoint for artistic innovations, Eliot places it at a steadily more distant remove from "ordinary" experience. In an immediate and striking way anthropology represented the furthest reach of tradition, the greatest distance from the ordinary man and, in this respect, an incitement to art. Eliot's pursuit of the historical sense culminated naturally in the anthropological search for origins:

The maxim, Return to the Sources, is a good one. More intelligibly put, it is that the poet should know everything that has been accomplished in poetry (accomplished, not merely produced) since its beginnings – in order to know what he is doing himself. He should be aware of all the metamorphoses of poetry that illustrate the stratifications of history that cover savagery.[62]

But Eliot, unlike some of his contemporaries, cautiously avoids a celebration of atavism. The artist, though the first to see the merits of studying the primitive, must be the last to see it "in a romantic light, or to yield to the weak credulity of crediting the savage with any gifts of mystical insight or artistic feeling that he does not possess himself."[63] Eliot, that is, wants not to emulate the primitive but to assimilate it. In his review of *Le Sacre du Printemps* he praises Stravinsky's music but criticizes the ballet for remaining merely a "primitive ceremony": "one missed the sense of the present." And "even The Golden Bough can be read in two ways: as a collection of entertaining myths, or as a revelation of that vanished mind of which our mind is a continuation."[64]

Eliot insists on that continuation, looking to the vanished mind not as an alternative but as a precursor, knowledge of which might keep the modern mind from a crippling isolation. He takes Blake as an example of what happens to the poet when he is left too much alone. Blake "was naked and saw man naked, and from the centre of his own crystal": "What his genius required, and what it sadly lacked, was a framework of accepted and traditional ideas which would have prevented him from indulging in a philosophy of his own, and concentrated his attention upon the problems of the poet." As always, Dante is Eliot's example of a poet who had the great benefit of a coherent culture, and "the concentration resulting from a framework of mythology and theology and philosophy is one of the reasons why Dante is a classic, and Blake only a poet of genius."[65] A framework is what Eliot himself seeks. His immediate predecessors had aspired to density and compression, to increasingly concentrated units of meaning: the image, the impression, the epiphany. But Eliot looks for meaning in "systems," "wholes" and "frameworks," not in bristling instants. In his sketch of English literary history, what he regrets most is the loss of the larger coherences. The task he sets for modernity is not to generate a host of new particulars; there are particulars enough; but to find a way to organize the exhausting diversity: "If we are to digest the heavy food of historical and scientific knowledge that we have eaten we must be prepared for much greater exertions. We need a digestion which can assimilate both Homer and Flaubert."[66] Here, then, is another form – historical now, rather than epistemological – of that problem which so preoccupied Eliot. How may we widen our view and how at the same time may we give order to what we perceive? In that Edenic period before Milton ate the apple of magniloquence and "a dissociation of sensibility set in," poets had "possessed a mechanism of sensibility which could devour any kind of experience."[67] This is what modernity must seek to restore. The bearing of anthropology should be evident. It is that modern discipline which offers the broadest view and which through its "comparative method" hopes to bring pattern into the heterogeneity of human culture. It thus provides a framework for the modern mind; it is a prosthesis for the dissociated sensibility.

These considerations carry us to "the mythic method." Others, too, have been carried to the mythic method. It is one of the phrases most frequently quarried from Eliot's criticism and carted to his poetry. But my concern is not to apply the concept but to address a puzzle that it creates. The mythic method, Eliot tells us with some relish, is a "way of controlling, of ordering, of giving shape and significance to the immense panorama of futility," a way of "making the modern world possible for art." Less exuberantly, but perhaps more significantly, he writes that the mythic method involves "manipulating a continuous parallel between contemporaneity and antiquity."[68] Indeed, *The Waste Land*, quite obviously, is constructed out of such parallels: tradition repeatedly projected onto modernity, antiquity as a source of context. At one point in "Ulysses, Order, and Myth," Eliot suggests that the new method is the happy result of modern scientific disciplines. "Psychology . . . ethnology and *The Golden Bough* have concurred to make possible what was impossible only a few years ago." When Eliot specifies what has become possible, the problem appears. "Instead of narrative method," he writes, "we may now use the mythical method."[69] But why "Instead of?" Myth is not ordinarily opposed to narrative; a familiar definition of myth characterizes it as a "purely fictitious narrative." In what sense then does myth represent an alternative to narrative? And, further, if *The Waste Land* employs the mythic method, if the mythic method is opposed to narrative method, then what becomes of the poem's narrative?

A way of beginning to answer is by offering refinements on an earlier point. We who think and write about the poem are in the habit of referring to its "protagonist," as though we confronted a being on the order of Orestes or Macbeth or El Cid. "Protagonist" may be inevitable, but with so tenuous a construction we cannot expect old effects of consistency or integrity. Eliot, however, is able to exploit circumstances which might constrain others. The dissolution of the boundaries of the self creates possibilities for new and powerful effects. The problem of disintegrating consciousness opens onto the problem of disintegrating culture, or, as Eliot will put it in 1928:

I believe that at the present time the problem of the unification of the world and the problem of the unification of the individual, are in the end one and the same problem; and that the solution of one is the solution of the other . . . The problem of nationalism and the problem of dissociated personalities may turn out to be the same.[70]

Until now, I have described the constituent units of the poem as fragments of consciousness, but we ought to recognize, as

Eliot's remark encourages us to do, that such fragments are *at the same time* fragments of culture. In a strong sense for Eliot, we are what our culture has been. Consider this remark from "Tradition and the Individual Talent": "Some one said: 'The dead writers are remote from us because we *know* so much more than they did.' Precisely, and they are that which we know."[71] The suggestion is clear; knowledge is identified with knowledge of the past – specifically, knowledge of past cultural achievement. And to investigate consciousness in *The Waste Land* is to investigate a cultural legacy which itself, too, becomes a mass of finite perceptions, individual points of view, aspects, distinct but not wholly so.

> The river's tent is broken: the last fingers of leaf
> Clutch and sink into the wet bank. The wind
> Crosses the brown land, unheard. The nymphs are departed.
> Sweet Thames, run softly, till I end my song.

These are the lines that begin "The Fire Sermon"; the last of them, as Eliot obligingly glosses, is from Spenser's "Prothalamion," a direct quotation. But notice that Eliot is not merely citing the verse as ornament, nor just as an illuminating counterpoint; he uses it to *constitute* the human consciousness, that unnamed "I" who now witnesses the river scene. Insofar as a protagonist is established here, that protagonist is an extraction from Spenser. Five lines later Eliot supplements the "Prothalamion" with versions of Psalm 137 and Marvell's "To His Coy Mistress"

> By the waters of Leman I sat down and wept . . .
> Sweet Thames, run softly till I end my song,
> Sweet Thames, run softly, for I speak not loud or long.
> But at my back in a cold blast I hear
> The rattle of the bones, and chuckle spread from ear to ear.

What is the status of this "I"? It has been given no name, no determinate personal history, no autonomous bearing. It exists embedded within a series of quotations; it derives from other texts. It is virtually epiphenomenal, a mere effect of literary history. Eliot, we might say, is borrowing subjectivity from his predecessors. In this sense his "I" is a creation of literary context, a construction out of Spenser, the Bible and Marvell.

The pronoun here does not refer so much as it links compatible
texts. The "I" becomes a measure of what these literary
ments have in common. "Amalgamating disparate ex-
ce," "forming new wholes" – these are the pressing tasks
that Eliot urges in "The Metaphysical Poets" and that in *The
Waste Land* fall to this "I," whose movement within the poem is
not so much toward an object as through a tradition. In place of
a bounded personality, the poem creates a consciousness that
emanates from the cultural past, and whose very fragility makes
it permeable to history. Now we can ask our earlier question
again, this time with the hope of answering it. Why does Eliot
oppose myth to narrative?

A solution lies, I think, in the notion of "continuous
parallel." "In the first part of Part v," says one of the poem's
notes, "three themes are employed: the journey to Emmaus, the
approach to the Chapel Perilous (see Miss Weston's book) and
the present decay of Eastern Europe." The journey to Emmaus
occupies a crucial place in the Biblical narrative, when the
promise of resurrection is met and the last doubts of the
disciples fade. In the poem Eliot alludes to the opening of the
episode, as the risen Christ appears to two of the disciples on the
road to Emmaus, and they fail to recognize him:

> Who is the third who walks always beside you?
> When I count, there are only you and I together
> But when I look ahead up the white road
> There is always another walking beside you
> Gliding wrapt in a brown mantle, hooded
> I do not know whether a man or a woman
> – But who is that on the other side of you?

The subsequent moment is, of course, the decisive one, when
"their eyes were opened and they recognized him." But Eliot
deserts the Biblical story without allowing it to come to
conclusion. He shifts instead to an evocation of the Russian
revolution:

> What is that sound high in the air
> Murmur of maternal lamentation
> Who are those hooded hordes swarming
> Over endless plains

The "hooded" Christ thus suffers the embarrassment of

generalization, linked here to the "hooded hordes" rising in the East. Attention then turns to the so-called Chapel Perilous scene, and if we "see Miss Weston" as Eliot advises, we discover that the scene stands in striking parallel to the passage to Emmaus. The questing knight, seeking shelter from a storm, enters a deserted chapel, where he pauses before going on to the Grail Castle itself. But no more than with the previous narrative threads does Eliot allow this thread to play itself out. He leaves the Quester in the Chapel; the Castle never emerges in the poem, nor, needless to say, does the Grail. *The Waste Land*, let us recognize, is a grail poem in which no grail appears. Eliot, to put the matter briefly, attends here to *incipient* phenomena ("journey," "approach," "decay") the stages that precede realization. He employs, he tells us, "three themes" in this section of the poem, but none of the three achieves dramatic resolution; they remain, indeed, poised in "continuous parallel." The result is a particular dramatic inconclusiveness. Parallels multiply, but they do not meet. The movement from Emmaus to the Russian revolution to the Chapel Perilous represents not so much a dramatic progress as the progress of analogy, of comparison, of context, and it ought to be clearer now why Eliot opposes myth to narrative. Where narrative has traditionally depended on convergence, convergence of incident, convergence of character, Eliot's mythic method extends *parallels*. At the end of "A Game of Chess," as the story in the pub approaches its climax, it is interrupted again, and this time left unfinished, unresolved, placed in the frame established by Ophelia's parting speech. Consistently, the poem withdraws from dramatic conflict to cultural context.

In his influential essay "Spatial Form in Modern Literature," Joseph Frank argued that modernists characteristically sought to replace temporal with spatial form. As a representative instance, he took Pound's notion of the image, "an intellectual and emotional complex apprehended in an instant of time." The aim of Pound and Eliot, argued Frank, was "to undermine the inherent consecutiveness of language, frustrating the reader's normal expectation of a sequence and forcing him to perceive the elements of the poem as juxtaposed in space rather than unrolling in time." Frank is certainly right to notice – and he was among the first to insist upon the fact – that modern literature represents a challenge to consecutive temporal development. He argues that, in *The Waste Land*, the "meaning-relationship is completed only by the simultaneous perception in space of word-groups that have no comprehensible relation to each other when read consecutively in time . . ."[72] Modern poetry, in this view, aspires to static simultaneity rather than to linear sequence. But, in casting out sequence, Frank casts out development of any sort, insisting instead on a "simultaneous perception." We might better claim, I think, that there is development in *The Waste Land*, only that it is not traditional narrative development, but what we might better call *contextual development*. The poem moves forward only as it moves sideways, toward new analogies, new parallels, new possibilities for comparison. The completion of the quest becomes of less central dramatic emphasis than the recognition of other quest-motifs in other cultural settings. The poem develops not by resolving conflicts but by enlarging contexts, by establishing relations between contexts, by situating motifs within an increasingly elaborate set of cultural parallels – by widening.

The activity of tradition is what makes Eliot's view most compelling, tradition not as an inert mass but as an ongoing process, something that "cannot be inherited" but that must be obtained through "great labour." The composition of *The Waste Land* involved a labour not unlike this obtaining of tradition. Indeed, to read through the succession of drafts is to witness the slow building of a tradition within the poem: Pope, no; Webster, yes; John, no; Tiresias, yes. No doubt Eliot was thinking of this task when he wrote in "The Function of Criticism" that probably "the larger part of the labour of an author in composing his work is critical labour; the labour of sifting, combining, constructing, expunging, correcting, testing: this frightful toil is as much critical as creative." But this critical act is not simply a telling feature of the poem's genesis. It is a striking aspect of its form. *The Waste Land* generates a wealth of cultural allusions, but it places them in no permanent order; the poem works and reworks its sense of the past. It gives us the Dante of the *Inferno*, mitigated by the Dante of the *Purgatorio*. It presents the Shakespeare of *Antony and Cleopatra*, qualified by the Shakespeare of *The Tempest*. In place of a consistent historical pattern, it adjusts the pattern as it proceeds. The poem itself, that is, engages in the toil of sifting, combining, constructing, expunging, correcting, testing, and much of our excitement comes from a curiosity as to what this nascent historical structure can finally contain. The poem is itself an inventive act of literary history.

In a sense, drama reappears in a new form. No longer a drama of event – will the Quester find the Grail? will the Fisher King recover? will the land bloom? – the poem becomes a drama among contexts: the relation between *The Tempest* and vegetation rituals, between the Buddha and Augustine, between Shakespeare and the "Shakespeherian rag," between the Fisher King and the London fishmen. In "Tradition and the Individual Talent" Eliot speaks of a need for a poet to fit in, to conform. And what is true of the poet is true of the fragments in this poem. Of each fragment the poem asks: Can this, too, be assimilated into pattern? Part of the drama of the poem is the attempt to bring diverse cultural contexts into satisfactory relationship, the effort to obtain a tradition.

Among diverse other things, then, *The Waste Land* is a product of the anthropological temper which understands by comparing, which sets systems of belief in relation to one another, and which disallows the special claims of any single system. Richards has said that Eliot "effected a complete severance between his poetry and all beliefs," but we might just as well see him as implicated in all belief.[73] The two come to much the same thing. "Wide reading," Eliot later wrote, is valuable not "as a kind of hoarding, an accumulation of knowledge"; it is valuable "because in the process of being affected by one powerful personality after another, we cease to be dominated by any one, or by any small number."[74] In *The Waste Land* Eliot acknowledges the greatest range of attitudes and faiths, with the consequence that none comes to final dominance.

In one of his notes, Eliot points out that the Buddha's Fire Sermon "corresponds in importance" to the Sermon on the Mount. The method of *The Waste Land*, like the method of anthropology, depends precisely on such correspondences, and in another note Eliot explains his use of "The Hanged Man" from the Tarot deck: "The Hanged Man, a member of the traditional pack, fits my purpose in two ways: because he is associated in my mind with the Hanged God of Frazer, and because I associate him with the hooded figure in the passage of the disciples to Emmaus in Part v." The anthropological temper conjoins and relativizes: the Hanged God *and* Christ. Christianity loses autonomy and becomes part of a still larger pattern which encompasses primitive vegetation rituals, medieval romance and the revolution in Russia. The continuous parallels are not then simply bland ornaments. Each new parallel represents an implied challenge to any enclosed body of beliefs and each forcibly obliges us to enlarge our notion of the cultural tradition.

In this connection, it is worth noticing a distinctive pattern in a number of Eliot's revisions of *The Waste Land*. He removed the original epigraph from *Heart of Darkness* in favour of the existing one from the *Satyricon*. For the heading of the second section, he replaced the Jamesian "In the Cage" with "A Game of Chess" derived from Middleton. He changed the poem's title from Dickens' "He Do the Police in Different Voices" to the present title with its allusion to pre-Christian nature cults. No doubt different reasons pertain to each of these emendations, but they share one feature which bears on our present concern. In each instance, a more recent reference has given way to a reference more remote: Conrad to Petronius, James to Middleton, Dickens to a vegetation ritual. Pound had complained that the quotation from Conrad was not "weighty enough." Eliot, after some hesitation, agreed. But it is not clear why Petronius should be any weightier. He is certainly more *distant*, and in all these cases what seems to be at issue is an instinct toward a wider historical compass. Kenner has usefully invoked Dryden as an abandoned model for the poem; we know too that a pastiche of Pope was discarded.[75] It becomes clear that as the poem took shape it stood at an increasing remove from its original sources in neo-classic and nineteenth-century English literature. The only recent allusions are those to the Continental tradition, and one might surmise that Wagner, Baudelaire, Verlaine and de Nerval provided the cultural distance that Pope, Dryden, Conrad, Dickens and James did not.

In a "Lettre d'Angleterre" which Eliot published in *La*

Nouvelle Revue Française after he had completed *The Waste Land* but before it had appeared, he wrote again of the isolation of the modern English poet: "Nous nous sentons aujourd'hui très abandonnés. Kipling . . . Wells, Bennett, Chesterton, Shaw, sont séparés de nous par un gouffre; dans leurs oeuvres nous ne pouvons plus puiser de subsistance. En dépit de notre admiration, ni James, ni Conrad ne sont très proches de nous."[76] This is not, Eliot goes on, because English literature is essentially anti-traditional; on the contrary, the present age is peculiar in feeling so little attachment to the one preceding it. It is clear, then, that Eliot felt the need to overcome the abandonment of the modern poet, by inventing a usable tradition. And it is equally clear that as the writing of *The Waste Land* proceeded, Eliot traced that tradition at a great distance from the more immediate English literary past – in recent Continental sources and, more importantly, in Dante, Spenser and Shakespeare and in the primitive rituals described by Frazer and Weston. Notably, when Eliot defines the mythic method, he sees it as presenting parallels, not simply between past and present but between *antiquity* and contemporaneity, as though only remote references could provide a sufficient counterweight to modernity.

In the preface to *The Golden Bough*, James Frazer described how his work grew. "In attempting to settle one question," he wrote, "I had raised many more: wider and wider prospects opened out before me."[77] Much the same might be said of Eliot, whose historical sense underwent a steady widening, which manifests itself not only in his criticism but in the process of creation, and still more provocatively in *The Waste Land* as it finally stands. History in the poem is not some consistent or continuous inheritance but something that the poem constructs and whose unity can no more be assumed than the unity of personality. *The Waste Land* expands its historical view and just when it seems to have established a coherent temporal standpoint it expands again. At the opening of "The Fire Sermon," the lines from the "Prothalamion" seem to point to an ideal of Elizabethan romance now regrettably lost, while by the end of that section the romantic "nonsense" of Elizabeth and Leicester suggests a re-evaluation of that ideal, which has been itself superseded by the more distant and more severe images of Augustine and the Buddha. Tiresias seems to embody the wisdom of the past until the poem invokes the still more ancient wisdom of the Thunder. The widening perspectives cannot be regarded as concentric circles which enclose and confirm one another: Eliot threw not one but a handful of stones into the pond. History in *The Waste Land* exists as the complex product of overlapping traditions, and "antiquity," that source of parallels, carries its own ambiguity. To the facile opinion that *The Waste Land* opposes the present to the past, one must immediately rejoin, which past?

In considering the work of T. E. Hulme, we were able to tease out a veiled opposition: modernism as a classicism and modernism as an attempt to escape from the classical, modernism as a renewal of the Western tradition and as a rejection of that tradition. This opposition bears on *The Waste Land*, which itself depends on two kinds of cultural antecedents. On the one hand it invokes the monuments of Western culture: Dante, Shakespeare, Virgil, Ovid and Spenser. On the other hand, it looks beyond that canonical cultural legacy: toward the primitive rituals described by Frazer and Weston, and toward Eastern religion. What we learned from considering Hulme is that the two lineages, the Occidental and the Oriental, the neo-classical and the neo-primitive, exist in no easy compatibility; they struggle against one another.

In a submerged fashion they struggle within *The Waste Land*. In the final movements of the poem, the possibility of renewal, insofar as that possibility obtains, comes not from within Western culture but from without, from the Hindu. In the last lines of the poem, the images from Western literature are images of disintegration, while the fragments of Sanskrit provide tentative principles of moral structure: Datta, Dayadhvam, Damyata, Give, Sympathize, Control. And to bring the poem to completion, Eliot again depends on the East – "Shantih Shantih Shantih" – as much to imply that the European tradition could not provide adequate depth of expression. Eliot later revised his explanation of "Shantih," describing it as "equivalent" to the phrase "The peace which passeth understanding," but in the original note he was not so confident of European verbal range:

"Shantih. Repeated as here, a formal ending to an Upanishad. 'The Peace which passeth understanding' is a *feeble translation* of the content of this word." To read this as an embrace of Hinduism is to simplify, where simplicity is the least appropriate of attitudes. Still, the poem, we must concede, rejects the boundaries of the Western tradition; it resists Eurocentrism, insisting on a wider range of reference. It represents a challenge to the self-sufficiency of the European tradition.

In a sense Eliot was in flight from *The Waste Land* as soon as he completed it. A month after its publication he wrote that "As for *The Waste Land*, that is a thing of the past so far as I am concerned . . ."[78] He frequently disparaged the accomplishment, writing to Ford Madox Ford that only thirty lines were of any worth, and then later reducing the figure to twenty-nine. He gave away the drafts of the poem, and tended to underplay the significance of the work, calling the poem merely a piece of "rhythmical grumbling." Where Eliot had previously inclined to pursue experiments through a series of poems, the method of *The Waste Land* was not pursued again. He would never repeat its most distinctive devices: the severe discontinuities, the sustained mythic parallels, the reliance on Eastern belief and primitive ritual. We are not to assume that he thought the poem a failure, only that he recognized its peculiar demands: its difficulty, its provocation.

Much of that provocation, I have tried to show, may be linked to the anthropological habit of mind, if that is broadly conceived, so as to designate the *comparatist* temperament, which retains the widest angle of vision, which refuses to bestow privilege upon any culture or epoch, which regards no human manifestation as too lowly to bear study, which captures the "primitive" and the "civilized" in the same glance. But anthropology possesses a peculiar ambiguity that will lead us to an ambiguity in Eliot. The issue returns us to modernist doctrine: it will help clarify the divergence between Eliot's criticism and his poetry, and with luck it will allow us to conclude the study.

On the one hand the mere existence of anthropology has been a challenge to Europe. By the nature of the discipline it questions European isolation, insisting on a fundamental continuity in human culture, promising an escape from a complacent and optimistic rationalism. Frazer, Tylor and Lévy-Bruhl helped make plain what European culture had inclined to ignore or suppress: the irrationalism lurking beneath the canopy of respectability. Pound and Lawrence had greedily seized this implication, with Pound comparing the artist to a "bushman" and describing himself and his allies as "the heirs of the witch-doctor and the voodoo," and Lawrence writing this to Bertrand Russell:

I have been reading Frazer's *Golden Bough* and *Totemism and Exogamy*. Now I am convinced of what I believed when I was about twenty – that there is another seat of consciousness than the brain and the nerve system: there is a blood-consciousness . . . with the sexual connection holding the same relation as the eye, in seeing, holds to the mental consciousness. One lives, knows, and has one's being in the blood, without any reference to nerves and brain. This is one half of life, belonging to the darkness.[79]

"The art-instinct," wrote Lewis, "is permanently primitive," and he identified the Vorticists as "Primitive Mercenaries in the Modern World."[80] Eliot was never so rabid as Pound or Lewis nor so metaphysical as Lawrence, but he, too, as we have seen, used Frazer and Weston to suspend the dominance of a narrowly European tradition.

In another guise, however, anthropology offered a bulwark rather than a challenge: anthropology as a rational confrontation with the irrational, not an embrace of the primitive but an assimilation of the primitive facts into a now more inclusive rational scheme, not a challenge to the civilized mind but a triumph of that mind. Anthropology, in this aspect, far from challenging European attitudes, has remained Eurocentric. It is the European anthropologist, after all, who unravels the intricacies of the "savage mind" and who *knows* while the objects of his study only *act*. In the preface to *The Golden Bough*, Frazer proudly places himself in the tradition of Western scholarship.

The position of the anthropologist of to-day resembles in some sort the position of classical scholars at the revival of learning. To these men the rediscovery of ancient literature came like a revelation, disclosing to their wondering eyes a splendid vision of the antique world, such as the cloistered scholar of the Middle Ages never dreamed of under the gloomy shadow of the minster and within the sound of its solemn bells. To us moderns a still wider vista is vouchsafed, a greater panorama is unrolled by the study which aims at bringing home to us the faith and the practice, the hopes and the ideals, not of two highly gifted races only, but of all mankind, and thus at enabling us to follow the long march, the slow and toilsome ascent, of humanity from savagery to civilisation.[81]

Eliot was never so confident about human ascent. But his critical position reveals a similar commitment to European values and the European sensibility. In "Tradition and the Individual Talent," his tradition, when elaborated, proves to be the tradition of the "mind of Europe." He insists that poetry be regarded as a "living whole of all the poetry that has ever been written," but when that whole is specified, it turns out to be "the whole of the literature of Europe." And notice how, in praising *Ulysses*, he comes to identify "European" with "international":

. . . it is the first Irish work since that of Swift to possess absolute *European significance*. Mr. Joyce has used what is racial and national and transmuted it into something of *international value*; so that future Irish writers, measured by the standard he has given, must choose either to pursue the same ideal or to confess that they write solely for an Irish, not for a European public.[82]

In *The Sacred Wood* he makes the same identification. He praises Irving Babbitt's ability "to perceive Europe as a whole," then adds immediately, "he has the cosmopolitan mind."[83] The cosmos thus shrinks to the size of Europe. It is a significant transformation, more significant still when opposed to the method of *The Waste Land*, which points so repeatedly beyond Europe. In his criticism, in short, Eliot reasserts the centrality of the European tradition, making modernism, as it were, safe for that tradition.

In April 1924 Eliot published a brief note on T. E. Hulme, whom he described as a "forerunner" of the "classical."[84] Now *Speculations*, as we have seen, is by no means self-evidently classical. In fact, the volume contains a lexicon of modernist possibilities, principal among which are Bergson's subjectivism and Worringer's anti-humanism, with classicism receiving somewhat less emphasis and, moreover, enduring explicit attack. Indeed, as his career progressed, Hulme had placed himself at an increasingly distant remove from the dominant values in European culture. Following Worringer, he came to see Western art, from classical Greece to the present, as only one phase in a larger development – and by no means the most impressive phase. He used an Oriental tradition to contest the ascendancy of the West; he used primitivism to contest European civilization. Hulme, in short, offered the kind of challenge which Eliot implicitly put forward in *The Waste Land*: the sudden enlarging of a cultural perspective within which the particular claims of a Western and classical tradition would occupy only a limited, and often inglorious, place. Hulme would call classicism a "half-measure." But Eliot is intent to see Hulme as a forerunner of the classical, placing him alongside Maurras and Lasserre. He ignores the attacks on humanism, the defence of geometric art, the Bergsonism; needless to say, he ignores the attacks on classicism. He reads Hulme as classical, and this is how Hulme has since been read. Eliot's interpretation of Hulme amounts to a taming of Hulme, just as his criticism might be seen as a tempering of his own literary challenge – a fact which Pound, for one, would sorely resent. But before we view this as a weakness of will, we ought to recognize it as strategically apt: it was Eliot's presentation of the modernist position, after all, which won widespread cultural recognition and assured the legitimacy of the avant-garde.

Eliot was preoccupied with the opposition between "romantic" and "classical" at least as early as 1916, when he served as Oxford University extension lecturer on the subject of modern French literature. The synopsis for the course survives and makes plain Eliot's interest in the contemporary French reaction against romanticism, an issue he addresses in his second lecture. He refers to the work of Maurras and Lasserre; he used Hulme's translation of Sorel. Although Eliot's suspicion of romanticism is sufficiently plain from the synopsis – romanticism, he writes at one point, "stands for *excess* in any direction" – he is not prepared to make classicism his published critical position. He neglects it in his essays of 1917–20, and in the fall of 1920 he submits a letter to the *Times Literary Supplement* criticizing the romantic/classical terminology and suggesting that "it would perhaps be beneficial if we employed both these terms as little as possible, if we even forgot these terms altogether, and looked steadily for the intelligence and sensibility which each work of art contains."[85]

During a period when the urge to manifesto seemed as great as the urge to poetry, Eliot kept himself free from party affiliation. But late in 1923, he is prepared to make public avowal of classicism. He had published *The Waste Land* a year earlier and had begun to edit the *Criterion*; having attained an eminent position, he decided to give that position a name. The essay on *Ulysses* begins with Eliot defending the work against the criticism of Richard Aldington, criticism which he finds especially regrettable because of the common position which he and Aldington share. "Mr. Aldington and I are more or less agreed as to what we want in principle, and agreed to call it classicism." Eliot uses the term, he will tell us, "with hesitation." Still, he uses it.

After its Impressionist, Imagist and Vorticist avatars, modernism returns to classicism. Eliot maintains magisterial loftiness, avoiding the technical stipulations of earlier programmes and avoiding polemical violence. In his somewhat coy distinction, classicism is a "tendency" rather than a "programme."[86] Nevertheless, what Eliot means is plain enough. His classicism develops along the lines suggested by Lasserre, Maurras and Babbitt: the suspicion of progress, the hostility towards individualism and modern democracy, the insistence on hierarchy and order. In Eliot himself two preoccupations dominate: first, the ascendancy of reason over emotion – "a higher and clearer conception of Reason, and a more severe control of the Emotions by Reason" – and second, the need for an outer authority to restrain inner caprice. It is worth noting how these interests converge. Both imply a resistance to the view of poetry as direct, sincere speech, most effective insofar as it is most direct, most sincere. Authority and reason are *correctives* to immediate experience; both indeed provide ways to mediate experience. Reason acts from within, constraining the expression of emotion, and if these inner defences yield, there remains an "Outer Authority" to combat the "Inner Voice."

We have been committed to a close scrutiny of incremental changes in modernist doctrine, but now it is worth briefly taking the large view, if only to emphasize how much the dominant tone has altered in a decade. Consider how far we have come from the early definitions of Hulme and Ford in the period 1908–12. They had conceived modern art as the communication of a "vague mood," a "tentative and half-shy" expression, the "tenuous and momentary reflection" of the "dance of midges" that is contemporary life. Art in this view was obliged to exemplify the impressionistic disarray of society. Eliot, on the other hand, firmly positions modern art against modern society; the relation is meant to be antagonistic and therefore tonic; from modern social reality we can only learn how not to be. Art – even as it may employ superstition, taboo, myth, dream, irrationality – works these into pattern and supplies what the modern world lacks: coherence, form, control, order.

A fundamentally individualist perspective has become aggressively anti-individualist. The cult of inner experience has passed to outer control; personal expression has given way to critical discipline. In the place of freedom and spontaneity, art is now characterized in terms of order, restraint and authority. A revolutionary justification is exchanged for a traditionalist. Self-expression yields to self-suppression. The primacy of emotion yields to the primacy of reason.

Within the wide set of possibilities which modernism had generated, Eliot's classicism should be seen as a kind of *via media*, a way of leading modernism back towards a *rapprochement* with England, Europe and their traditions. Among the early moderns, these traditions were frequently ignored or subverted, but Eliot's critical labours of the early twenties amounted to a revival of an ignored lineage. He offered a reappraisal of the Elizabethans; he took the Metaphysicals with a renewed seriousness; he praised Dryden, calling him "one of the tests of a catholic appreciation of poetry."[87] "People with any guts in them," Hulme had challenged, "do not have catholic tastes."[88] But as Eliot's prominence increased his taste grew only more catholic. He would come to mistrust the clash of sensibilities which had thrilled the early moderns, as it had thrilled their opponents. He eliminated an adversary relation between epochs, styles and artists (though his own preferences show luminously through). His classicism will be a "state of equilibrium," a "moment of *stasis*." Individual accomplishments become part of a single "simultaneous order" and, in any case, art "never improves." Classicism is not just one party among others; it becomes "a goal toward which all good literature strives."[89] Classicism thus absorbs its rivals.

Epilogue. The editor and the loathed disturber

> The Vorticist movement is a movement of individuals, for individuals, for the protection of individuality.
>
> (Ezra Pound)[1]
>
> I am not an individual but an instrument.
>
> (T. S. Eliot)[2]

If we look for a mark of modernism's coming of age, the founding of the *Criterion* in 1922 may prove a better instance than *The Waste Land*, better even than *Ulysses*, because it exemplifies the institutionalization of the movement, the accession to cultural legitimacy. The journal provided Eliot, its editor, with a capacious forum; it had financial stability and intellectual weight; it constituted a respectable vessel for sometimes suspicious contents. *The Waste Land* appeared in the first issue of the journal, and its entry into the literary arena was no doubt eased by this context. If the poem threatened to outrage, the intellectual pedigree of the adjacent essays provided reassurance. These were reputable, restrained, even staid. To set the *Criterion* next to *Blast* is to underscore the extent of the change in eight years. The titles alone suggest the shift: measured evaluation replaces polemical salvo. Where *Blast* had printed its manifestos in screaming capitals, the *Criterion* kept its editorials in miniaturized type. With such changes went benefits: *Blast* survived for two issues, the *Criterion* for seventeen years.

In 1932, after the death of Harold Monro, Eliot asked Pound to write an obituary notice for the *Criterion*. Pound agreed, but the essay that emerged settled only fitfully on the subject of Monro and contained, among other things, Pound's brief description of his own 1917–18 "counter-current" with Eliot. Pound recalls the causes of the alliance and its literary consequences, and then abruptly halts the description with a curt two-word conclusion: "Divergence later."[3]

This is a hard slap at Eliot who, in soliciting the essay, had suggested that Pound discuss the

proposition . . . that Monro's work "did on the whole steadily improve up to the last (which is a poem in the *Criterion* of a few months ago), that it has a character which clearly distinguishes it both from the Georgian work on the one hand and our own on the other and finally that he received very little appreciation in his lifetime either for the poetry or for his social work."[4]

With characteristic indiscretion, Pound quotes Eliot's request in his essay, calling it "the words of authority." "I am not an authority," he continues, "I am but a loathed disturber; but my memory covers a period of Monro's life inaccessible to the Editor, and from it I have attempted to draw certain explanations of causes." Pound extracts from Eliot's note the phrase "our own," insisting that "Here we find a term really needing definition."[5] Plainly, Pound resents Eliot's easy implication of literary solidarity – and with reason. For from the end of the war, a distinctive aspect of the modernist movement was a new distance between Pound and Eliot, which resulted in the gradual ascendancy of Eliot and with him the ascendancy of his literary perspective. Though nothing like a formal break developed between the two, there was a perceptible shift in the balance of literary power.

They had met, as we have seen, in 1914. Pound was in the full flush of Vorticism, propagandizing vigorously and eager to assimilate Eliot to the movement. Protective and solicitous, he defended Eliot against criticism, secretly paid to publish a volume of his verse, and later, as is well known, suggested extensive emendations for *The Waste Land*. But such enthusiasm was never quite mutual. Even as Pound was telling Harriet Monroe that Eliot had produced "the best poem I have yet had or seen from an American," Eliot was writing to Conrad Aiken that Pound's work was "touchingly incompetent."[6] Later and in public he would say many kind things, but the reservations were detectable. Towards Vorticism, he remained distant and uninvolved. Still, we are not to assume cynicism or distaste on

Eliot's part. He saw a basis of literary agreement and recognized the virtues of alliance.

The essential history of that alliance has been traced: its departure from pre-war aesthetic principles, its new formal strategies, its antagonism to rival groups. But in 1919 signs of strain appeared. Eliot reviewed Pound's *Quia Pauper Amavi* for the *Athenaeum*, on the whole a distinctly lukewarm appraisal of the work, with Eliot commenting at one point that it was still possible "to argue that Mr. Pound's method is due to timidity rather than to a great integrity."[7] Obviously offended, Pound sent a letter to the editor, complaining that it was still uncertain whether Eliot *liked* the poetry. Pound went on to complain of Eliot's "*universitaire* tendency," suggesting that Eliot "seems to regard literature not as something in itself enjoyable, having tang, gusto, aroma; but rather as something which, possibly because of a non-conformist conscience, one *ought* to enjoy because it is literature (infamous doctrine)."[8] Eliot defended himself by saying that he had not considered his own enjoyment a "question of public interest."[9] The exchange is revealing. It points to Eliot's increasingly independent status as literary editor of the *Egoist*, and as a regular contributor to the *Athenaeum*. No longer obliged to depend on Pound's intervention or support, he had the occasion to develop his own critical attitude, and there rapidly appeared certain obvious differences in temperament and taste which would prove increasingly intractable.

This study must end with an irony, the modern movement consolidating its critical position, even as its leading figures discover irreconcilable differences among themselves. Individually, the English modernists would never want for an eager hearing, but they would never hear one another with the same sympathy. The muted conflict identified at the end of part II, the struggle between a desire for artistic alliance and a celebration of the individual artist, led finally to the dissolution of always fragile bonds. In 1928 Eliot offered a new assessment of Pound's contribution to modernism, tellingly entitled "Isolated Superiority," in which he asserted that Pound "has had, and has an immense influence, but no disciples."[10] In contrast, one recalls Pound's early statement that he was the only man in London "with guts enough to turn a proselyte into a disciple." But Eliot is intent to challenge the notion of Pound as the leader of a movement; indeed he challenges the very notion of a movement. He returns again to the *vers libre* question and notes that the "term *vers-libre*, never a happy one, is happily dying out. We can now see that there was no movement, no revolution, and there is no formula. The only revolution was that Ezra Pound was born with a fine ear for verse."[11]

Pound, for his part, had ceased to expect that "underlying agreement" which he had celebrated in the *Blast* days. In his own journal *Exile* he wrote still another consideration of the modern experiment, and this time his emphasis fell upon the contention among its principals: "I don't think I have ever agreed with Mr Lewis or Mr Joyce about anything, certainly not about any basic idea or 'relation to life' or anything of that sort. Neither do I find myself in agreement with Mr Eliot, on many occasions when Mr Aldington might think it prudent for me to be so."[12] Pound, so keen to find similarity in the early years, comes to affirm the advantages of difference: "It is of inestimable value that there be men who receive things in a modality different from one's own; who correlate things one wd. not oneself have correlated. The richness of any given period depends largely upon the number and strength of such men."[13] And Lewis introduces *his* journal, *The Enemy*, by declaring that "there is no 'movement' gathered here (thank heaven!), merely a person; a solitary outlaw and not a gang."[14]

These statements appeared within a year of one another and reveal the chastened ambitions of those who had once hoped for an ever-widening agreement in matters of artistic principle. A few years later Lewis went still further in expressing the disappointments of an avant-garde that had led but had not been followed: "We are not only 'the last men of an epoch' (as Mr. Edmund Wilson and others have said): we are more than that, or we are that in a different way to what is most often asserted. *We are the first men of a Future that has not materialized.* We belong to a 'great age' that has not 'come off.'"[15] That may appear an odd remark, given the individual accomplishments and the attention which those accomplishments have received. But Lewis is addressing another modernist ambition which it has also been our task to record: the aspiration to a comprehensive revaluation of taste, a movement of common sensibilities that would move an entire culture. Certainly, it is unclear what it would have meant for that future to have materialized. Lewis had no doubt hoped for too much and was not prepared to be grateful for what he got: namely a fertile period of exchange which created a new readiness to experiment, an alertness to the work of others, a contempt for easy solutions, and an eagerness to think the question of modernity to its roots. It may be the necessary illusion of the avant-garde that it can do more than this, that it can somehow *prevail*. Pound put the demand simply: "I want a new civilization."[16] But, though the literary achievement of English modernism is irreplaceable, the last thing one wants is a new civilization along the lines it proposed. And through the course of the century it has perhaps been the impertinent claim to be acknowledged legislators that has so frequently condemned the avant-garde to the margins of culture. Eliot was the one who recognized this and who was most prepared to make his peace with the old civilization. When Pound was calling himself the "exile" and Lewis was presenting himself as the "enemy," Eliot appeared as nothing more militant than the "criterion."

Donald Davie has suggested that Eliot owed his success on the London scene to his learning not to offend the English – something, says Davie, which Pound never learned.[17] Richard Aldington makes a similar point:

Ezra started out in a time of peace and prosperity with everything in his favour, and muffed his chances of becoming literary dictator – to which he undoubtedly aspired – by his own conceit, folly and bad manners. Eliot started in the enormous confusion of war and post-war England, handicapped in every way. Yet by merit, tact, prudence and pertinacity, he succeeded in doing what no American has ever done – imposing his personality, taste and even many of his opinions on post-war England.[18]

But Eliot's success was more than a matter of temperament, though it was no doubt partly that. It was equally a matter of an effectively contrived rhetoric. Pound, though by no means as rabid as in the *Blast* period, remained a partisan of "tang" and "gusto," of a passionate and contentious response to literature which acknowledged no extrinsic constraints. Eliot on the other hand was willing to concede imperatives which Pound ignored. After a period of polemics and apologetics, Eliot turned the movement toward an irenics that recognized the need for the avant-garde to reach accommodation with the general culture. What Pound called his "*universitaire* tendency" is better seen as Eliot's pursuit of a comprehensive, carefully established arrangement with the larger social whole – both personally and artistically. Of this pursuit Pound would later write,

I may in some measure be to blame for the extreme caution of his criticism. I pointed out to him in the beginning there was no use of two of us butting a stone wall; that he wd. never be as hefty a battering ram as I was, nor as explosive as Lewis, and that he'd better try a more oceanic and fluid method of sapping the foundations. He is now respected by the Times Lit. Sup. but his criticisms no longer arouse my interest.[19]

Eliot for his part was equally frustrated.

It is harder to help Pound than anyone else. Apart from the fact that he is very sensitive and proud and that I have to keep an attitude of discipleship to him (as indeed I ought) every time I print anything of his it nearly sinks the paper. And he offers more than I want, thinking that he is helping. I am willing to sink the ship for things like the cantos, which are great stuff whether anyone likes them or not, but it goes against the grain to do it for his articles. He always puts them in such a way that the errors stick out and the good points (there always are some) stick in, and he will imitate Hueffer, who writes vilely and who never omits to mention that he is an Officer (British) and a Gentleman.[20]

Plainly, this is not just a clash of personalities; it is a struggle over artistic deportment. Pound remained the Loathed Disturber while Eliot became the Editor of modernism.

Avant-garde movements always threaten to disappear, either shattering into a collection of individualities or ossifying into an old guard. And this is because within the avant-garde there inheres a permanent conflict: the need at once to subvert and to institutionalize. Without subversion a movement cannot justify itself; without some institutional stability it cannot survive. Pound felt the one risk clearly; Eliot felt the other. I have distinguished two broad phases within the period 1908 to 1922, provocation and consolidation. Pound was the chief agent of the former, and Eliot of the latter.

English modernism achieved its decisive formulation in the

early twenties – not only because of legitimizing masterworks such as *Ulysses* or *The Waste Land* but because there developed a rhetorically effective doctrine to explain and justify that body of work. For this rhetoric and doctrine Eliot was in large measure responsible. Not bound to earlier premises, he escaped grossly contradictory conclusions and reoriented the definition of modernism. The concluding phase of this study has attempted to show the movement towards balanced relations among constituent concepts: tradition, myth, point of view, individual, expression. In some sense, Eliot's most impressive achievement was the arrangement of these conceptual counters into a more stable literary doctrine. Partly, this was an intellectual achievement. But partly it was an achievement in cultural politics, a *rapprochement* between modernist literature and traditional authority. Where Vorticism, for instance, had depended on a severe anti-institutional assault, classicism involved an accommodation between artist and society, art and tradition. It is not therefore surprising that existing social and cultural powers would be more willing to give Eliot a sympathetic hearing. Pound was proud to be excluded, Eliot pleased to be included.

Thus the literary programme, as I have emphasized, merged with cultural irenics. Pound had been willing to dismiss the great preponderance of the reading public: "the mass, the half-educated simpering general, the semi-connoisseur, the sometimes collector ... the readers of the 'Spectator' and the 'English Review' ..."21 But Eliot avoided sweeping dismissal. The task he assumed was to oversee the integration of the modernist avant-garde into the general intellectual life. As editor of the *Criterion* he undertook to affirm the movement's seriousness, to establish its pedigree.

Pound had left London by the time the journal appeared, and at first he seems not to have understood the extent of Eliot's resolve. He wrote to a correspondent that " *The Criterion* has to be so heavily camouflaged as Westminster Abbey, that the living visitor is not very visible" – as though beneath the respectable exterior there remained a subversive sensibility.15 In fact, however, as Pound would come to recognize, subversion was not Eliot's aim. What Pound took as camouflage was not camouflage at all; it was Eliot himself. And this is a fit image with which to end: Eliot wilfully merging into his surroundings, no longer easily distinguishable from the established literary order, and modernism having thus won a place within that order.

Notes

Preface

1. T. S. Eliot, "The function of criticism," *Selected Essays* (New York: Harcourt, Brace, 1950), p. 15.
2. T. S. Eliot, "Dante," in *Selected Essays*, p. 225; Ezra Pound, *Gaudier-Brzeska* (New York: New Directions, 1970), p. 90; Ford Madox Ford, "Literary Portraits – XXXVI: Les jeunes and 'Des Imagistes'" (Second Notice), *Outlook*, XXXIII (May 16, 1914), p. 682; T. E. Hulme, "Modern art and its philosophy," in *Speculations*, ed. Herbert Read (New York: Harcourt, Brace, 1924), pp. 77, 78, 88; Hulme, "Humanism and the religious attitude," in *Speculations*, p. 55.
3. Wyndham Lewis, "A later arm than barbarity," *Outlook*, XXXIII (September 5, 1914), 299.
4. George Eliot, *Middlemarch* (Harmondsworth: Penguin, 1979), p. 225.
5. Ezra Pound, "Wyndham Lewis," *Egoist*, 1 (June 15, 1914), 234.

1. Consciousness

1. Joseph Conrad, Preface to *The Nigger of the "Narcissus"* (1897; rpt. New York: Doubleday, Page & Company, 1916), p. vii.
2. Ibid. pp. x, xi, x.
3. Ibid. p. viii.
4. Ibid. p. ix.
5. Ibid. pp. vii, xi, x, x.
6. Samuel Hynes, "Conrad and Ford: two Rye revolutionists," in *Edwardian Occasions* (New York: Oxford Univ. Press, 1972), p. 50.
7. Ian Watt, "Conrad's Preface to *The Nigger of the 'Narcissus,'*" *Novel*, 7 (1974), 103.
8. Conrad, "*Narcissus*," pp. 110, 28–29, 122.
9. See, for instance, Marvin Mudrick, "The artist's conscience and *The Nigger of the 'Narcissus,'*" *Nineteenth Century Fiction*, 11 (March 1957).
10. Conrad, "*Narcissus*," pp. 28–30.
11. Ibid. pp. 60–61.
12. Ford Madox Ford, "Joseph Conrad," *English Review*, X (December 1911), 76.

13. George Eliot, *Middlemarch*, p. 673.
14. Conrad, "*Narcissus*," pp. 213–14.
15. Conrad, "Henry James," in *Notes on Life and Letters* (Garden City, N.Y.: Doubleday, 1921), p. 13.
16. Matthew Arnold, *Literature and Dogma*, in *Dissent and Dogma*, vol. VI of *The Complete Prose Works of Matthew Arnold*, ed. R H Super (Ann Arbor: Univ. of Michigan Press, 1968), pp. 142–3.
17. Ibid. p. 149.
18. Ibid. p. 151.
19. Ibid. pp. 144, 149, 143.
20. Ibid. pp. 187, 176.
21. Lionel Trilling, *Matthew Arnold* (1939; rpt. New York: Columbia Univ. Press, 1965), p. 319.
22. Arnold, *Literature and Dogma*, pp. 149, 384.
23. Ibid. p. 190.
24. Ibid. p. 385.
25. George Eliot, as quoted in Basil Willey, *Nineteenth Century Studies* (New York: Harper & Row, 1966), p. 240.
26. Matthew Arnold, "The Study of Poetry," in *The Complete Prose Works of Matthew Arnold*, vol. IX (1973), p. 161.
27. Arnold, *Literature and Dogma*, p. 370.
28. John Stuart Mill, *Utilitarianism*, in *The Collected Works of John Stuart Mill*, ed. J. M. Robson (London: Routledge and Kegan Paul, 1969), p. 234.
29. Alfred Tennyson, as quoted in A. C. Bradley, *A Commentary on Tennyson's "In Memoriam"* (London: Macmillan, 1929), p. 1.
30. T. H. Huxley, "On Descartes' discourse touching the method of using one's reason rightly and of seeking scientific truth," in *Collected Essays*, vol. I (New York: D. Appleton, 1901), p. 175; "Bishop Berkeley on the metaphysics of sensation," in *Collected Essays*, vol. VI (1902), p. 281; "Descartes," vol. I, p. 194; "On sensation and the unity of structure of sensiferous organs," vol. VI, p. 310.
31. T. H. Huxley, letter to Kingsley, quoted in Leonard Huxley, *Life and Letters of Thomas Henry Huxley*, vol. I (New York: D. Appleton, 1900), p. 237.
32. T. H. Huxley, "Hume," in *Collected Essays*, VI: 70.
33. Samuel Smiles, *Self-Help* (New York: Harper & Brothers, 1900), p. 35.
34. T. S. Eliot, "Arnold and Pater," in *Selected Essays* (1932; rpt. New York: Harcourt, Brace, 1964), p. 387.
35. Walter Pater, *The Renaissance* (1873; rpt. New York: World Publishing, 1961), pp. 222–23.
36. Ibid. pp. 220–21.
37. Ibid. p. 221.
38. Ibid. pp. 221–22.
39. Ibid. p. 223.
40. Ibid. p. 222.
41. Walter Pater, "Style," in *Selections from Pater*, ed. E. E. Hale (New York: Holt, 1901), p. 127.

42. Matthew Arnold, *Culture and Anarchy*, in *The Complete Prose Works of Matthew Arnold*, vol. v (1965), p. 165.
43. Ibid. pp. 170–71.
44. Pater, *Renaissance*, pp. 222–23.
45. Joseph Conrad, *Lord Jim* (1900; rpt. New York: Norton, 1968), p. 18.
46. Ibid. p. 35.
47. Henry James, Preface to *The Ambassadors* (New York: Charles Scribner's Sons, 1909), i: ix.
48. Ibid. p. x.
49. Henry James, Preface to *The Princess Casamassima* (New York: Charles Scribner's Sons, 1922), p. xii.
50. Ibid. pp. vii–viii.
51. Ibid. p. xiii; Conrad, "Preface," pp. xi, ix.
52. Joseph Conrad, *Under Western Eyes* (1911; rpt. Garden City, N.Y.: Anchor–Doubleday, 1963), p. 1.
53. James, "Preface," *Casamassima*, p. viii.
54. Henry James, "The new novel," in *Notes on Novelists* (New York: Charles Scribner's Sons, 1914), p. 348.

2. *Authority*

1. W. B. Yeats, *The Cutting of an Agate*, in *Essays and Introductions* (1912; rpt. New York: Macmillan, 1961), p. 287.
2. T. S. Eliot, "A Foreign Mind," rev. of *The Cutting of an Agate*, by W. B. Yeats, *Athenaeum*, No. 4653 (1919), 553.
3. Ibid. p. 553.
4. Yeats, *Agate*, p. 286.
5. Matthew Arnold, *Culture and Anarchy*, p. 221. Arnold goes on to suggest that by following the free play of consciousness "we shall tend to make good at all points what is wanting to us, and so shall be brought nearer to our complete human perfection."
6. Matthew Arnold, *The Letters of Matthew Arnold to Arthur Hugh Clough*, ed. Howard Foster Lowry (London: Oxford Univ. Press, 1932), pp. 96–97.
7. Matthew Arnold, "The function of criticism at the present time," in Arnold, *Complete Works*, vol. iii (1962), p. 262.
8. Matthew Arnold, "The literary influence of academies," in Arnold, *Complete Works*, iii: 232.
9. Ibid. pp. 255, 245, 248–49, 257.
10. Arnold, *Culture and Anarchy*, pp. 119, 117, 116, 117, 117, 122.
11. Ibid. pp. 123–24.
12. Ibid. p. 134.
13. Ibid. pp. 135, 134, 134, 135, 136, 134.
14. T. S. Eliot, *The Use of Poetry and the Use of Criticism*, 2nd edn (London: Faber, 1933), pp. 103, 105.
15. Irving Babbitt, *The New Laokoon* (Boston: Houghton Mifflin, 1910), p. 251; *Rousseau and Romanticism* (Boston: Houghton Mifflin, 1919), p. xii.

16. Irving Babbitt, *Literature and the American College: Essays in Defense of the Humanities* (Boston: Houghton Mifflin, 1908), p. 6; *Rousseau and Romanticism*, p. xvii.
17. Arnold, "Function of criticism," p. 265.
18. Irving Babbitt, *Masters of Modern French Criticism* (1912; rpt. Westport, Conn.: Greenwood Press, 1977), pp. vii, 368.
19. Ibid. pp. 330, 345, 341.
20. Ibid. p. 345.
21. Babbitt, *Laokoon*, p. xiii.
22. Babbitt, *Masters*, p. 341.
23. Ibid. p. 390.
24. Arnold, *Culture and Anarchy*, pp. 116, 119.
25. Conrad, "*Narcissus*," p. 11.
26. Ibid. p. 154.
27. Arnold, *Culture and Anarchy*, p. 118.
28. Conrad, "*Narcissus*," pp. 174, 173.
29. Conrad, *Lord Jim*, p. 90.
30. Conrad, "*Narcissus*," p. 90.
31. Ibid. pp. 30, 50, 163.
32. Joseph Conrad, *Joseph Conrad's Letters to R. B. Cunninghame Graham*, ed. C. T. Watts (London: Cambridge Univ. Press, 1969), pp. 53–54.
33. Joseph Conrad, *Heart of Darkness* (1899; rpt. New York: Signet, 1950), p. 106.

3 Dating Hulme/parsing modernism

1. Alun Jones reports that at Hulme's death his manuscripts were in the possession of Mrs Ethel Kibblewhite, who passed them on to A. R. Orage, editor of the *New Age*. Orage then arranged for Herbert Read to edit the material. *The Life and Opinions of T. E. Hulme* (London: Gollancz, 1960), p. 147.
2. T. S. Eliot, "A commentary," *Criterion*, 11 (April 1924), 231.
3. Herbert Schneidau, *Ezra Pound: The Image and the Real* (Baton Rouge: Lousiana State Univ. Press, 1969), p. 42.
4. Michael Roberts, *T. E. Hulme* (London: Faber, 1938), p. 12. Roberts is not concerned to deprecate Hulme; he insists that the intellectual borrowing "does not lessen the value of his work" (p. 13).
5. As Hynes has put it, Hulme was "the spokesman of a new point of view though not the creator of it." Samuel Hynes, *Occasions*, p. 123.
6. See, for instance, Graham Hough, *Image and Experience* (London: Duckworth, 1960), pp. 33–35; and Frank Kermode, *Romantic Image* (New York: Macmillan, 1957). Wallace Martin has been alone in recognizing that Hulme's thought must be resolved into a succession of phases. See his discussion of "The origins of Imagism" in *The New Age Under Orage* (Manchester: Manchester Univ. Press, 1967), pp. 145–81.

7. Read says that Hulme was sent down for "indulging in a brawl." See T. E. Hulme, *Speculations*, p. ix. Jones has researched the subject more extensively and reports a series of possible causes: an "escapade on Boat-race night" (in the words of James Fraser), "perpetual rows in his rooms" (according to J. C. Squire) and an attack on a policeman (according to his family). Jones, *Life*, p. 21.

8. William James, "The will to believe," in *The Will to Believe and Other Essays in Popular Philosophy* (New York: Longmans, 1898), p. 3.

9. Quoted in "Notes on Bergson," in T. E. Hulme, *Further Speculations*, ed. Samuel Hynes (Lincoln: Univ. of Nebraska Press, 1962), p. 47.

10. Hulme, *Further Speculations*, p. 53.

11. Ibid. pp. 29–30.

12. T. E. Hulme, "The Philosophy of Intensive Manifolds," in *Speculations*, p. 214; Henri Bergson, *Time and Free Will*, trans. F. L. Pogson (1910; rpt. London: George Allen, 1950), pp. 1–6.

13. Hulme, *Speculations*, p. 174.

14. Ibid. p. 178.

15. Bergson, *Time and Free Will*, p. 240.

16. Henri Bergson, *Introduction to Metaphysics*, trans. T. E. Hulme (London: Macmillan, 1913).

17. Hulme, *Further Speculations*, pp. 23, 26, 26.

18. Ibid. p. 26.

19. F. S. Flint, "The history of Imagism," *Egoist*, II (May 1, 1915), 71.

20. Hulme, "A lecture on modern poetry," in *Further Speculations*, p. 71.

21. Ibid. p. 71.

22. Ibid. pp. 71, 71, 74, 69.

23. Ibid. pp. 73, 72.

24. Ibid. pp. 71–72.

25. Ibid. pp. 74, 75, 78.

26. Ibid. p. 78; "Searchers after reality: Haldane," in *Further Speculations*, p. 10.

27. Hulme, "Searchers: Haldane," p. 10.

28. Hulme, "Notes on language and style," in *Further Speculations*, p. 81.

29. Hulme, "Searchers after reality: Bax," in *Further Speculations*, p. 6.

30. Hulme, "Autumn," in *Speculations*, p. 265.

31. Hulme, "Lecture," p. 73.

32. Hulme, "Searchers: Haldane," p. 10.

33. Hulme, "Notes," p. 87.

34. Hulme, "Bergson's theory of art," in *Speculations*, p. 163.

35. Hulme, "Lecture," pp. 71, 73.

4. Ford: the passing of great figures

1. Ford Madox Ford, "On Impressionism," in *The Critical Writings of Ford Madox Ford*, ed. Frank MacShane (Lincoln: Univ. of Nebraska, 1964), p. 42.

2. See, for instance, Ford's series "The critical attitude" in the *English Review* during the years 1908 and 1909. These were later collected in a volume called *The Critical Attitude* (London: Duckworth, 1911).

3. Ford Madox Hueffer, *Thus to Revisit* (London: Chapman & Hall, 1921), p. 17.

4. Pound, "Ford Madox Hueffer," *New Freewoman*, 1 (Dec. 15, 1913), 251.

5. Richard Aldington, "Reviews," *Egoist*, 1 (July 1, 1914), 247.

6. Pound to Harriet Monroe, May 23, 1914, Letter 45, *The Letters of Ezra Pound 1907–1941*, ed. D. D. Paige (New York: Harcourt, Brace, 1950), p. 37.

7. Ford, "The critical attitude: women's suffrage – the circulating library – the drama – fine arts, etc.," *English Review*, IV (1910), p. 329.

8. Ford Madox Hueffer, *Memories and Impressions* (London: Harper & Brothers, 1911), p. 318.

9. Ibid. p. 299.

10. Ford, "The passing of the great figure," in *The Critical Attitude*, p. 129; Hueffer, *Memories*, p. 320.

11. Hueffer, *Memories*, p. 320.

12. Ford, "Great figure," p. 114.

13. Ford, "On the functions of the arts in the republic," *The Critical Attitude*, p. 28.

14. Ford, "Great figure," p. 115.

15. Ibid. p. 123.

16. Reprinted in *The Critical Attitude*, p. 118.

17. Ford, "Modern poetry," p. 174; "Great figure," p. 126 in *The Critical Attitude*.

18. Ford, "Literary portraits III. Mr. R. A. Scott-James and 'the influence of the press,'" *Outlook*, XXXII (November 22, 1913), 719.

19. Ford, "Functions of the arts," p. 28.

20. Ford Madox Ford, *Henry James* (New York: Albert and Charles Boni, 1915), p. 47.

21. Arnold, *Culture and Anarchy*, p. 148.

22. Ibid. p. 147.

23. Ford, "Great figure," p. 120.

24. Ibid. pp. 119–20.

25. Ford, "Modern poetry," p. 178.

26. Ford, *Henry James*, p. 120.

27. Ford, "English Literature of To-Day – 1" in *The Critical Attitude*, p. 56.

28. Ford, "Modern poetry," p. 175.

29. Ibid. p. 175.

30. Ibid. p. 182.

31. Ibid. p. 179.

32. Ford Madox Ford, "Professor Saintsbury and the English 'Nuvvle,'" *Outlook*, XXXII (November 1, 1913), 605.

33. Ibid. p. 606.

34. Ibid. pp. 606, 605.

35. Ford, *Henry James*, p. 45.

36. Ibid. pp. 29, 103, 28, 68.
37. Hueffer, *Memories*, p. xiii.
38. Ibid. p. xiii.
39. Ibid. pp. xiii–xiv.
40. Ford, "Modern poetry," p. 179.
41. Ford, "Scott-James," p. 718.
42. Hueffer, *Memories*, p. 280.
43. Ibid. p. 281.
44. Conrad, "*Narcissus*," pp. 28, 29.
45. Peter goes on, "No one is going to catch me, lady, and make me a man. I want always to be a little boy and to have fun." J. M. Barrie, *Peter Pan* (New York: Charles Scribner's Sons, 1928), p. 157.
46. R. S. S. Baden-Powell, *Scouting for Boys; a handbook for instruction in good citizenship*, rev. edn (London: C. A. Pearson, 1909), p. 3.
47. Ford Madox Ford, "Literary portraits – XVII: nineteen-thirteen and the Futurists," *Outlook*, XXXIII (January 3, 1914), 15.
48. Ibid. p. 15.
49. Ford Madox Ford, "Literary portraits – XXXV: Les jeunes and 'Des Imagistes,'" *Outlook*, XXXIII (May 9, 1914), 636.
50. Ford Madox Ford, "Literary portraits – XVIII: Mr. A. G. Gardiner and 'Pillars of Society,'" *Outlook*, XXXIII (January 10, 1914), p. 46.
51. Ford, *Henry James*, p. 68.
52. Ford Madox Ford, Letter to Lucy Masterman, Jan. 23, 1913, *Letters of Ford Madox Ford*, ed. Richard M. Ludwig (Princeton: Princeton Univ. Press, 1965), p. 55.
53. Ford Madox Ford, "English literature of to-day – II," in *The Critical Attitude*, p. 102.
54. Ibid. p. 102.
55. Ford, "English literature of to-day – I," in *The Critical Attitude*, p. 64.
56. Hueffer, *Memories*, p. xviii.
57. Ford, "Modern poetry," p. 186.

5. Egoists and Imagists

1. Sidney Hook, quoted in Lawrence S. Steplevich, "Max Stirner and Ludwig Feuerbach," *Journal of the History of Ideas*, 39 (1978), 455.
2. Max Stirner, *The Ego and His Own*, trans. Steven T. Byington (New York: R. Tucker, 1907), pp. 482–83.
3. Ludwig Feuerbach, *The Essence of Christianity*, trans. George Eliot (1841; rpt. New York: Harper & Row, 1957), pp. xxxiii, 33, 27; quoted in Steplevich, "Stirner and Feuerbach," p. 454.
4. Stirner, *The Ego and His Own*, p. 101.
5. Quoted in Ronald Paterson, *The Nihilistic Egoist: Max Stirner* (London: Oxford Univ. Press, 1971), p. 79.
6. Stirner, *The Ego and His Own*, pp. 490, 489.
7. Quoted in Paterson, *The Nihilistic Egoist*, p. 81.

8. Stirner, *The Ego and His Own*, p. 6.
9. On this point, see Paterson, *The Nihilistic Egoist*, and James Huneker, *Egoists: A Book of Superman* (New York: Charles Scribner's Sons, 1909).
10. Victor Basch, *L'Individualisme anarchiste Max Stirner* (Paris: Félix Alcan, 1904), p. i.
11. It had made an earlier, quickly curtailed beginning as the *Freewoman* a year before.
12. "Views and comments," *New Freewoman*, I, 13 (Dec. 15, 1913), 244.
13. Editorial reply to Steven Byington, "Correspondence," *New Freewoman*, I (Dec. 15, 1913), 259; *Egoist*, I (Feb. 2, 1914), 42; "Views and comments," *New Freewoman* I, 6 (Sept. 1, 1913), 104.
14. "Views and comments," *New Freewoman*, I, 1 (June 15, 1913), 4.
15. "Men, machines and progress," *Egoist*, I (Feb. 2, 1914), 42.
16. "Views and comments," *New Freewoman*, I, 13 (Dec. 15, 1913), 244.
17. "Views and comments," *Egoist*, I (Jan. 15, 1914), 25.
18. Remy de Gourmont, "A French view of Nietzsche," *New Age*, XIII, 11 (July 10, 1913), 301.
19. Richard Aldington, *Life for Life's Sake* (New York: Viking Press, 1941), p. 134; Pound to Harriet Monroe, August 1912, Letter 5, *Letters*, p. 10.
20. Pound, "Status rerum," *Poetry*, I, 4 (January 1913), 126.
21. Pound to Williams, December 19, 1913, Letter 31, *Letters*, p. 27.
22. Pound and others, *New Freewoman*, I 13 (December 15, 1913), 244.
23. Pound to Harriet Monroe, December 8, 1913, Letter 30, *Letters*, p. 27.
24. Pound to Amy Lowell, November 26, 1913, Letter 29, *Letters*, p. 26.
25. Pound and others, *New Freewoman*, I, 13 (December 15, 1913), 244.
26. *Poetry*, II, 6 (September 1913), 228.
27. Allen Upward, "The discarded Imagist," *Egoist*, II (June 1, 1915), 98.
28. Donald Davie, *Ezra Pound* (New York: Viking Press, 1975).
29. Allen Upward, *The Divine Mystery: a reading of the history of Christianity down to the time of Christ* (Letchworth: Garden City Press, 1913), p. 3.
30. Ezra Pound, "Allen Upward serious," in *Selected Prose 1909–1965*, ed. William Cookson (New York: New Directions, 1973), p. 407.
31. Pound to Michael Roberts, July 1937, Letter 329, *Letters*, p. 296.
32. Ezra Pound, "Affirmations . . . VI. Analysis of this decade," *New Age*, XVI (Feb. 11, 1915), 411.
33. Quoted in Pound, *Selected Prose*, p. 409; Allen Upward, "The plain person," *Egoist*, I (Feb. 2, 1914), 47; Pound, *Selected Prose*, p. 409.
34. Allen Upward, *The New Word* (New York: Mitchell Kennerly, 1910), pp. 98, 100.
35. Pound, *Selected Prose*, p. 411.
36. Ezra Pound, "The new sculpture," *Egoist*, I (Feb. 16, 1914), 68.
37. Ezra Pound, "The serious artist," in *Literary Essays*, ed. T. S. Eliot (New York: New Directions, 1968), pp. 41, 41, 46, 42, 44, 43, 44.
38. Pound, "Sculpture," p. 68.
39. Manifesto, *Blast*, 1 (June 1914), 7, 148.
40. F. T. Marinetti, "A Futurist manifesto," *New Age*, 15 (May 7, 1914), 16.
41. Wyndham Lewis, "The melodrama of modernity," *Blast*, 1 (June 1914), 143.

42. Ezra Pound, "Vorticism," *Fortnightly Review*, XCVI (1914), 461.
43. Remy de Gourmont, "Tradition and other things," *Egoist*, 1 (July 15, 1914), 262.
44. Pound, Letter, *Egoist*, 1 (March 16, 1914), 117. But Pound, it is worth noting, always remained attracted to specific literary accomplishment of the past. (See, for instance, the essay, "The tradition," in *Poetry* of January 1914.) Foster Damon has suggested that Pound's involvement with Vorticism, with its greater hostility to tradition, created a difficult contradiction in his emerging literary perspective. S. Foster Damon, *Amy Lowell* (New York: Houghton Mifflin, 1935), p. 231.
45. Richard Aldington, "Free verse in England," *Egoist*, 1 (Sept. 15, 1914), 351.
46. Hulme, "Lecture," p. 69.
47. Ford to Lucy Masterman, *Letters*, p. 55.
48. Wyndham Lewis, Vorticist manifesto, "Long live the Vortex," *Blast*, 1 (June 1914), 7.
49. Wyndham Lewis, "Our Vortex," *Blast*, 1 (June 1914), 147.
50. Pound, "Affirmations . . . 1. Arnold Dolmetsch," *New Age*, XVI (Jan. 7, 1915), 246; Lewis, "Futurism, magic and life," *Blast*, 1 (June 1914), 135.
51. Lewis, "Long live the Vortex," p. 7.
52. Stanley K. Coffman, Jr, *Imagism: A Chapter for the History of Modern Poetry* (1951; rpt. New York: Octagon–Farrar, Strauss & Giroux, 1977), p. 212.
53. Ezra Pound, "Edward Wadsworth, Vorticist. An authorised appreciation," *Egoist*, 1 (August 15, 1914), 306.

6. Hulme: the progress of reaction

1. Frank Kermode, *Romantic Image*, pp. 131, 121.
2. Ibid. pp. 130–31.
3. Ibid. p. 129.
4. Donald Davie, *Articulate Energy* (London: Routledge & Kegan Paul, 1955), p. 6.
5. Ibid. p. 13.
6. Babbitt, *Masters*, p. x.
7. Ibid. p. 253.
8. See Babbitt's discussion of Bergson in *Masters of Modern French Criticism*; also Kermode in *Romantic Image* and Pierre Lasserre, *Le romantisme français* (1907; rpt. Paris: Calmann-Lévy, 1920).
9. See, for instance, T. E. Hulme, "A Tory philosophy," in Alun R. Jones, *The Life and Opinions of T. E. Hulme*, pp. 187–201; and T. S. Eliot, "The Action Française, M. Maurras and Mr. Ward," *Criterion*, VII (March 1928), 195–203.
10. Lasserre, *Le romantisme français* (Paris: Calmann-Lévy, 1920), pp. 536–37.
11. Babbitt, *Laokoon*, p. xiii.
12. Babbitt, *Masters*, p. 387.
13. Hulme, "A Tory philosophy," p. 188.

14. Ibid. p. 191.
15. Hulme, "Romanticism and classicism," in *Speculations*, p. 116.
16. Certainly Bergson's view of evolution as the product of an *"élan original"* is closely bound to a traditionally romantic celebration of the will.
17. Hulme, "Romanticism and classicism," p. 116; Hulme, "A Tory philosophy," pp. 189–90.
18. The essay on "Romanticism and classicism," for instance, moves from a defence of the classical spirit to an exposition of Bergsonian theories of art.
19. Pierre Lasserre, "La philosophie de M. Bergson," *L'Action Française*, 27 (March 15, 1911), 174.
20. Ibid. p. 168.
21. Ibid. p. 178.
22. Ibid. p. 178.
23. Ibid. p. 180.
24. The essay on "Romanticism and classicism" begins: "I want to maintain that after a hundred years of romanticism, we are in for a classical revival . . ." Hulme, p. 113.
25. Hulme, "A Tory philosophy," p. 191.
26. Ibid. p. 190.
27. Hulme, "Romanticism and classicism," p. 133.
28. Ibid. p. 114.
29. Ibid. p. 115.
30. *Le Temps* also reported the incident, in its issue of November 4, 1910.
31. T. E. Hulme, "A Notebook," *New Age*, XVIII (Dec. 2, 1915), 112.
32. Hulme, "Notebook," p. 113.
33. Jones, *Life*, p. 68.
34. Edmund Husserl, "A draft of a 'Preface' to the *Logical Investigations*," in *Introduction to the Logical Investigations*, ed. Eugen Fink, trans. Philip J. Bossert and Curtis H. Peters (The Hague: Martinus Nijhoff, 1975), p. 33.
35. Gottlob Frege, "Edmund Husserl's philosophy of arithmetic," *Mind*, 81 (July 1972), 337, 323, 324, 335–336.
36. Ibid. p. 337.
37. Husserl, "Author's abstract to Volume One," *Introduction*, p. 3.
38. Edmund Husserl, *Logical Investigations*, vol. 1, trans. J. N. Findlay (London: Routledge & Kegan Paul, 1970), pp. 43, 121, 125, 122.
39. J. S. Mill, *Examination of Sir William Hamilton's Philosophy*, quoted in John Passmore, *A Hundred Years of Philosophy* (London: Duckworth, 1957), p. 188.
40. Husserl, *Investigations*, 1: 181.
41. Hulme, "Notebook," p. 112.
42. Hulme, "Humanism and the religious attitude," in *Speculations*, pp. 44–45.
43. G. E. Moore, *Principia Ethica* (1903; rpt. Cambridge: Cambridge Univ. Press, 1929), pp. 47–50.
44. Ibid. pp. 6, 20.
45. Ibid. pp. 81–82.
46. Ibid. pp. 83–85.

47. Hulme, "Humanism," p. 9.
48. See Richard Cork's discussion of *Kermesse* and its place in Lewis' development in *Vorticism and Abstract Art in the First Machine Age*, vol. 1: *Origins and Development* (London: Gordon Fraser, 1976).
49. Wilhelm Worringer, *Abstraction and Empathy*, trans. Michael Bullock (New York: International Universities Press, 1953), p. vii.
50. Ibid. p. 5.
51. Quoted in ibid. p. 7.
52. Ibid. pp. 8, 14, 15, 4.
53. "Appendix B," "The plan for a book," in *Speculations*, p. 264.
54. Hulme, "Mr. Epstein and the critics," *New Age*, XIV (Dec. 25, 1913), 251.
55. Hulme, "Epstein," p. 251.
56. Hulme, "Modern art 1. The Grafton group," *New Age*, XIV (Jan. 15, 1914), 341.
57. Hulme, "Modern art and its philosophy," in *Speculations*, pp. 77–78.
58. Sam Hynes, "Introduction," in Hulme, *Further Speculations*, p. xxiii; Jones, *Life*, p. 109. Interestingly, Worringer himself came to recognize and enjoy the polemical function to which his work had been put. In the foreword to the 1948 edition, he referred to "the immediacy with which its theories, which were concerned only with historical interpretation, were transposed so as to apply to contemporary movements in the artistic conflict." *Abstraction*, p. vii.
59. Hulme, "Lecture," p. 72.
60. Cork, *Vorticism*, 1: 140.
61. Raymond Williams, *Culture and Society, 1780–1950* (Garden City, N.Y.: Anchor–Doubleday, 1959), p. 205.
62. Hulme, "Grafton," p. 341, my emphasis.
63. Hulme, "Modern art," p. 84.
64. Hulme, "Humanism," p. 62.
65. Hulme, "Modern art," p. 96.
66. Hulme, "Humanism," pp. 8–9.
67. Hulme, "Modern art," p. 80.
68. Worringer, *Abstraction*, p. 135.

7. *Symbol, impressionism, image, vortex*

1. F. S. Flint, "The history of Imagism," *Egoist*, II (May 1, 1915), 71.
2. The other contributors to the anthology were F. S. Flint, Skipwith Cannell, William Carlos Williams, John Cournos and Ford Madox Ford. For an especially illuminating exposition of the development of Imagism, see David Perkins, *A History of Modern Poetry* (Cambridge: Harvard Univ. Press, 1976), pp. 329–47.
3. Alun Jones, "Notes toward a history of Imagism," *South Atlantic Quarterly*, 60 (Summer 1961), 263, 282.
4. Glenn Hughes, *Imagism and the Imagists: A Study in Modern Poetry* (Stanford: Stanford Univ. Press, 1931), and Stanley K. Coffman, Jr,

Imagism: A Chapter in the History of Modern Poetry (Norman: Univ. of Oklahoma Press, 1951).

5. Kermode, *Romantic Image*, p. 135; Hynes, "Introduction," in Hulme, *Further Speculations*, p. xix; Hughes, *Imagism*, p. 9.

6. Frank MacShane, "'To establish the Facts' a communication on Mr. A. R. Jones and Ford Madox Ford," *South Atlantic Quarterly*, 61 (Spring 1962), 260–65.

7. Ezra Pound, "This Hulme business," in Hugh Kenner, *The Poetry of Ezra Pound* (New York: Kraus Reprint, 1968), p. 307.

8. Schneidau, *Ezra Pound*, p. 38.

9. I am referring, of course, to the late opinions of Hulme: the anti-humanist, rather than the Bergsonian Hulme, two incarnations which, as we have seen, must always be kept distinct.

10. Ezra Pound, "The prose tradition in verse," in *Literary Essays*, p. 377.

11. Ezra Pound, "Ford Madox Hueffer," *New Freewoman*, 1 (December 15, 1913), 251; "The prose tradition," pp. 373, 371.

12. Pound, note to a letter to Harriet Monroe, January 1915, Letter 60, *Letters*, p. 49.

13. Ford, "Modern poetry," p. 187. Cp. Schneidau, *Ezra Pound*, p. 12.

14. Pound, Foreword to *A Lume Spento and Other Early Poems* (New York: New Directions, 1965), p. 7.

15. Pound, "Ford Madox (Hueffer) Ford; Obit," *Nineteenth Century and After*, 126 (August 1939), 179.

16. Ezra Pound, "Status rerum," *Poetry*, 1 (January 1913), 125. Pound goes on to mention that Ford's method risks lapsing into description, but he remains an obvious sympathizer with this side of the question.

17. Ezra Pound, "Vortex," *Blast*, 1 (June 1914), 154.

18. Ford, "On Impressionism," in *Critical Writings*, pp. 34, 37, 36.

19. Ford Madox Ford, *Thus To Revisit* (London: Chapman & Hall, 1921), p. 138.

20. Ford, "Joseph Conrad," in *Critical Writings*, p. 72.

21. Ford, "On Impressionism," p. 44.

22. Ford Madox Ford, "Les jeunes and 'Des Imagistes,'" (Second Notice) *Outlook*, XXXIII (May 16, 1914), 683; and "A jubilee," rev. of *Some Imagist Poets*, *Outlook*, XXXVI (July 10, 1915), p. 46.

23. Ford Madox Ford, Preface to Collected Poems of 1911, in *Collected Poems* (New York: Oxford Univ. Press, 1936), p. 327.

24. Ford, "Modern poetry," in *The Critical Attitude*, p. 187.

25. Pound, "The later Yeats," rev. of *Responsibilities*, by W. B. Yeats, *Literary Essays*, pp. 379, 378. Pound's refusal to identify Yeats as an Imagist did not mean any lessening of his admiration. He continued to acknowledge his great respect for Yeats' poetic accomplishment, while expressing his differences of theoretical opinion.

26. W. B. Yeats, "Magic," in *Ideas of Good and Evil*, in *Essays and Introductions* (New York: Macmillan, 1961), p. 28.

27. W. B. Yeats, *Autobiographies* (New York: Macmillan, 1927), p. 142;

Arthur Symons, *The Symbolist Movement in Poetry* (New York: E. P. Dutton, 1919), p. 9.

28. Yeats, *Ideas*, pp. 155, 116, 164.
29. Pound, "Serious artist," p. 42; "A retrospect," *Literary Essays*, p. 5.
30. Pound, "A retrospect," p. 3.
31. See Graham Hough, *Image and Experience*, pp. 12–14.
32. Ford, "Modern poetry," p. 187; Pound, "In metre," rev. of John Gould Fletcher's *The Dominant City* and *Fool's Gold*, *New Freewoman*, 1 (September 15, 1913), 132; Lewis, "The exploitation of vulgarity," *Blast*, 1 (June 1914), 145.
33. Pound, "Affirmations . . . vi. Analysis of this decade," *New Age*, xvi (Feb. 11, 1915), 410; Mallarmé as quoted in Ian Watt, *Conrad and the Nineteenth Century* (Berkeley: Univ. of California Press, 1980), p. 186.
34. Schneidau, *Ezra Pound*, pp. 21–27.
35. Ford, "Literary portraits – xxxiii: Mr. Sturge Moore and 'The Sea is Kind,'" *Outlook*, xxxiii (April 25, 1914), 559; Ford, *Thus To Revisit*, p. 130.
36. Ford, "Literary portraits – xxxi: Lord Dunsany and 'Five Plays,'" *Outlook*, xxxiii (April 11, 1914), 495.
37. Ford, "Literary portraits – xxxvi: Les jeunes and 'Des Imagistes'" (Second Notice), *Outlook*, xxxiii (May 16, 1914), 683; Ford, "Modern Poetry," p. 189.
38. Ford, "Joseph Conrad," *English Review*, x (Dec. 1911), 77.
39. Pound, "Vorticism," p. 462.
40. Pound, "The Approach to Paris," *New Age*, xiii (October 2, 1913), 662.
41. Ford, "Literary portraits – xxxix: Mr. W. B. Yeats and his new poems," *Outlook*, xxxiii (June 6, 1914), 783.
42. Ford, "On Heaven," *Collected Poems* (New York: Oxford Univ. Press, 1936), p. 13.
43. Ford, "Literary portraits – xlvi: Professor Cowl and 'The theory of poetry in England,'" *Outlook*, xxxiii (July 25, 1914), 109.
44. Ford, "On Impressionism," pp. 34–36.
45. Ford, "'Des Imagistes'" (Second Notice), p. 683.
46. Ford, "'Des Imagistes'" (Second Notice), May 16, 1914, p. 683; "'Des Imagistes,'" May 9, 1914, p. 653.
47. Ford, "Impressionism – some speculations," in *Critical Writings*, p. 150.
48. Ford, "English Literature of To-Day – ii," in *The Critical Attitude*, p. 102.
49. Ford, "Conrad," in *Critical Writings*, pp. 72–73.
50. Ibid. p. 73.
51. Ford, "On Impressionism," p. 40.
52. Ford, "On Impressionism," p. 41. Although this line of reasoning has since lost much of its philosophic plausibility, Ford was writing in a period devoted to the cult of immediacy. Immediate experience was a key concept for philosophers as dissimilar as James and F. H. Bradley – and even more vigorous in this regard was Bertrand Russell. Simultaneously with Ford's Impressionist writings, Russell was developing his central

distinction between "knowledge by description" and "knowledge by acquaintance." He argues that there are certain things with which we can come into direct (perceptual or conceptual) contact – these are the objects of acquaintance – and they provide the basis for all subsequent knowledge. Acquaintance, in brief, is immediate, while description is inferred. Therefore: "All our knowledge, both knowledge of things and knowledge of truths, rests upon acquaintance as its foundation." The connection with Ford should be apparent.

53. David Hume, *A Treatise on Human Nature* (1888; rpt. Oxford: Clarendon Press, 1965), pp. 252–53.
54. Ford, "On Impressionism," p. 43.
55. Pound, "Serious artist," pp. 51, 54, 44, 43, 46.
56. Ibid. p. 46.
57. Pound, "The new sculpture," p. 68.
58. Hugh Kenner, *The Pound Era* (Berkeley: Univ. of California Press, 1971), p. 191.
59. For a detailed discussion of the controversy, see Richard Cork's excellent chapter "The formulation of a rebel group at the October 1913 Exhibition," pp. 102–131.
60. Anthony Ludovici, *New Age*, XIV (Dec. 18, 1913), 215.
61. Hulme, "Epstein," in *Further Speculations*, pp. 108–09.
62. Ludovici, "An open letter to my friends," *New Age*, XIV (Jan. 1, 1914), 279.
63. Ludovici, "Open letter," p. 281.
64. Arthur Hight, "Art," Letter, *New Age*, XIV (Jan. 8, 1914), 319.
65. Lewis, "Epstein and his critics, or Nietzsche and his friends," Letter, *New Age*, XIV (Jan. 8, 1914), 319.
66. Lewis, Etchells, Hamilton, Wadsworth as quoted in Cork, *Vorticism*, p. 94.
67. Hulme, "Grafton," in *Further Speculations*, pp. 115, 114–17, 118.
68. Marinetti, *Observer*, June 7, 1914, p. 7.
69. See his chapter on "Futurism and the arrival of Vorticism," chapter 9 of *Vorticism*, pp. 214–38.
70. Pound, "Sculpture," p. 68.
71. Lewis, "The new egos," *Blast*, 1 (June 1914), 141; *Blasting and Bombardiering* (London: Eyre & Spottiswoode, 1937), p. 110.
72. Wassily Kandinsky, *Concerning the Spiritual in Art* (1912; rpt. New York: George Wittenborn, 1972), p. 67.
73. Henri Gaudier-Brzeska, "Vortex. Gaudier-Brzeska," *Blast*, 1 (June 1914), 155.
74. Pound, "Affirmations/Vorticism," *New Age*, n.s. XVI (Jan. 14, 1915), 277.
75. Pound, "Affirmations . . . 1. Arnold Dolmetsch," *New Age*, XIV (Jan. 7, 1914), 246; Pound, "Vortex," p. 154. The remark about Impressionist passivity, it should be noted, was made in the context of a musical, rather than a literary, argument, but the point readily generalizes.
76. Pound to Harriet Monroe, November 9, 1914, Letter 58, *Letters*, p. 45.
77. Quoted in Cork, *Vorticism*, p. 261.

78. Pound, "Vorticism," p. 465.

79. Ezra Pound, "Dogmatic statement on the game and play of chess," *Blast*, 2 (July 1915), 19.

80. Ezra Pound, letter to Harriet Monroe, April 10, 1915, Harriet Monroe Collection, Univ. of Chicago Library.

81. Pound, "Vorticism," p. 469.

82. Ernest Fenollosa, *The Chinese Written Character as a Medium for Poetry* (San Francisco: City Lights, 1936), pp. 9, 10, 15.

83. Pound, "Affirmations/Vorticism," p. 277.

84. Ford, "'Des Imagistes'" (Second Notice), May 16, 1914, p. 682.

85. Pound, "Vorticism," pp. 468, 464; Kandinsky, *Concerning the Spiritual in Art*, p. 71.

86. Pound, "Vorticism," p. 462.

87. Kermode, *Romantic Image*, p. 151.

88. Pound, *Gaudier-Brzeska*, p. 98.

89. Pound, "Affirmations . . . v. Gaudier-Brzeska," *New Age*, XVI (Feb. 4, 1915), 382.

90. May Sinclair, "Two Notes," *Egoist*, II (June 1, 1915), 88.

91. T. E. Hulme, "Modern art IV. Mr. David Bomberg's show," in *Further Speculations*, p. 144.

92. Bomberg, from the foreword to the catalogue of his show at the Chenil Gallery, July 1914, quoted in Cork, *Vorticism*, p. 202.

93. Pound, "Vortex," p. 154.

94. Pound, "A Retrospect," p. 4.

95. Kenner, *The Pound Era*, p. 179.

96. Pound, "The Wisdom of Poetry," in *Selected Prose* (New York: New Directions, 1973), pp. 361–62; Pound, "The Serious Artist," p. 48; Pound, "Vorticism," p. 467; Pound, "Affirmations . . . IV. As for Imagisme," *New Age*, XVI (Jan. 28, 1915), 349.

97. Pound, "Affirmations/Imagisme," p. 349.

98. Edward Wadsworth, "Inner Necessity," *Blast*, 1 (June 20, 1914), 122.

99. Pound, Letter to Harriet Monroe, January 1915, Letter 60, *Letters*, p. 49.

100. Ezra Pound, "On criticism in general," *Criterion*, 1 (January 1923), 143.

101. Ezra Pound, "James Joyce," *Egoist*, IV (Feb. 1917), 21.

8. The war among the moderns

1. Pound to Amy Lowell, August 1, 1914, Letter 47, *Letters*, p. 38.

2. Pound, "Vorticism," p. 471.

3. Wyndham Lewis, *Blasting and Bombardiering*, p. 40.

4. Ford, *Thus To Revisit*, p. 137.

5. Ibid. p. 140.

6. Lewis, *Blasting*, p. 67.

7. Pound, "A letter from Remy de Gourmont," *Little Review*, IV (December 1917), 7.

8. Hilaire Belloc, *The Servile State* (1912; rpt. New York: Henry Holt, 1946), pp. 19, 3, 126–27.
9. Ford, "Futurists," p. 15; Pound, "The new sculpture," p. 68; Lewis, "The cubist room," *Egoist*, 1 (Jan. 1, 1914), 9.
10. Lewis, "Kill John Bull With Art," *Outlook*, XXXIV (July 18, 1914), 74.
11. Lewis, *Blasting*, p. 35.
12. Ibid. p. 40.
13. Ibid. pp. 81, 80.
14. Ibid. p. 91.
15. Ford, *Thus To Revisit*, p. 62; Lewis, *Blasting*, pp. 90, 95.
16. Pound, "Affirmations/Vorticism," *New Age*, n.s. XVI (Jan. 14, 1915), 277.
17. Pound, "The new sculpture," p. 68.
18. Editorial, *Blast*, 2 (July 1915), 5, 9, 5.
19. Lewis, "Kill John Bull," p. 74.
20. As quoted in *Blast*, 2 (July 1915), p. 78.
21. Lewis, "The London group," *Blast*, 2 (July 1915), 79.
22. Pound to Felix E. Schelling, June 1915, Letter 71, *Letters*, p. 61.
23. Ezra Pound, *Gaudier-Brzeska: A Memoir* (London: John Lane, 1916), p. 5.
24. Pound to John Quinn, March 10, 1916, Letter 85, *Letters*, pp. 73–74.
25. James Douglas, column in the *Star*, July 23, 1915.
26. Pound, *Gaudier-Brzeska*, p. 5.
27. Ford, *Henry James*, p. 120.
28. Ford, *When Blood is Their Argument: An Analysis of Prussian Culture* (London: Hodder & Stoughton, 1915), p. 318.
29. Quoted in Arthur Mizener, *The Saddest Story* (New York: World Publishing, 1971), p. 279.
30. Ezra Pound, "Provincialism the enemy I," *New Age*, XXI (July 12, 1917), 245; "Provincialism the enemy IV," *New Age*, XXI (August 2, 1917), 308; "Provincialism the enemy III," *New Age*, XXI (July 26, 1917), 289; "Provincialism the enemy I," *New Age*, XXI (July 12, 1917), 244, 245.
31. Richard Aldington, *Life For Life's Sake* (New York: Viking Press, 1941), p. 165.
32. See Cork, *Vorticism*, on the consequences of the war for the fine arts: chapter 11, "Vorticism under the shadow of war," pp. 268–96.
33. Pound to Amy Lowell, August 1, 1914, Letter 47, *Letters*, p. 38.
34. Lowell, letter to Harriet Monroe, September 15, 1914, printed in Foster Damon, *Amy Lowell* (Boston: Houghton Mifflin, 1935), p. 237.
35. Pound to Harriet Monroe, January 1915, Letter 59, *Letters*, p. 48.
36. Pound to Amy Lowell, August 1, 1914, Letter 47, *Letters*, p. 38.
37. Pound to Amy Lowell, August 12, 1914, Letter 48, *Letters*, p. 39.
38. Lowell, letter to Pound, November 3, 1914, printed in Damon, *Amy Lowell*, p. 274.
39. Pound to Amy Lowell, August 1, 1914, Letter 47, *Letters*, p. 38.
40. Lowell, letter to Pound, printed in Damon, *Amy Lowell*, p. 275; Damon, *Amy Lowell*, p. 311.
41. Pound to Harriet Monroe, January 1915, Letter 59, *Letters*, p. 48.

42. Pound, "The teacher's mission," in *Literary Essays*, p. 58.
43. In his "Lecture on modern poetry," Hulme had written: "One might say that images are born in poetry. They are used in prose, and finally die a long lingering death in journalists' English. Now this process is very rapid, so that the poet must continually be creating new images, and his sincerity may be measured by the number of his images." Hulme, "Lecture," p. 75. If the process was rapid in 1909, it became still more so in the years after the war. More recently, Irving Howe has formulated the problem in this way: "the dilemma that modernism must always struggle but never quite triumph, and then, after a time, must struggle in order not to triumph." Howe, "The culture of modernism," in *The Decline of the New* (New York: Harcourt, Brace, 1970), p. 4.
44. Pound to Harriet Monroe, September 25, 1915, Letter 74, *Letters*, p. 63.
45. Pound to Harriet Monroe, November 9, 1914, Letter 58, *Letters*, p. 45.
46. *Some Imagist Poets 1915* (Boston: Houghton Mifflin, 1915), p. v.
47. *Some Imagist Poets 1916* (Boston: Houghton Mifflin, 1916), p. vi.
48. Ibid. pp. viii, xii.
49. *Some Imagist Poets 1915*, pp. vi–vii.
50. Pound, "Harold Monro," *Criterion*, 11 (July 1932), 590.
51. T. S. Eliot, "Reflections on vers libre," *New Statesman*, VIII (March 3, 1917), 518.
52. Ibid. p. 519.
53. Ibid. p. 519.
54. J. G. Fletcher, letter, *New Statesman*, VIII (March 24, 1917), 589.
55. Ibid. p. 590.
56. Pound to H. L. Mencken, March 12, 1918, Letter 148, *Letters*, p. 132.
57. T. S. Eliot, *Ezra Pound: His Metric and Poetry* (New York: Alfred A. Knopf, 1917), pp. 5–6, 8.
58. Ibid. pp. 10, 12.
59. Ford, "'Des Imagistes,'" p. 653.
60. Eliot, *Pound*, p. 15.
61. Pound, "Harold Monro," p. 590.
62. Lyndall Gordon, *Eliot's Early Years* (Oxford: Oxford Univ. Press, 1977), pp. 90–91. Gordon writes that "in retrospect, the witty, satiric poems Eliot wrote between 1917 and 1919 seem like a digression from his poetic career."
63. Eliot, "Vers libre," p. 518.
64. Eliot, *Pound*, p. 10.
65. Ezra Pound, "The hard and the soft in French poetry," *Poetry*, XI (Feb. 1918), 264.
66. Hulme, "Lecture," p. 71; Ford, "Modern poetry," p. 185; Conrad, *Heart of Darkness*, p. 68; Virginia Woolf, "Modern fiction," in *Collected Essays*, vol. 2 (London: Hogarth Press, 1966), p. 106.
67. T. S. Eliot, "Reflections on contemporary Poetry," *Egoist*, IV (October 1917), 133; T. S. Eliot, "Contemporanea," *Egoist*, V (June–July 1918), 84.
68. Richard Aldington, "Round/Pond," *Some Imagist Poets 1915*, p. 12.

69. Ezra Pound, "Hard and soft," p. 264.
70. T. S. Eliot, interview in *Writers at Work* (New York: Viking Press, 1963), p. 97.
71. Ezra Pound to Harriet Monroe, January 1915, Letter 60, *Letters*, pp. 48–49.
72. Ezra Pound, "Serious artist," p. 54.
73. Théophile Gautier, Introduction to *Émaux et Camées*, in *The Complete Works of Théophile Gautier*, trans. and ed. F. C. De Sumichrast (London: Postlethwaite, Taylor & Knowles, 1909), pp. 15–16.
74. T. S. Eliot, "The borderline of prose," *New Statesman*, IX (May 19, 1917), 159.
75. Ezra Pound, "A retrospect," in *Literary Essays*, p. 11; Hulme, "Lecture," p. 69.
76. Ezra Pound, "A retrospect," pp. 11, 13; Pound, "Vers libre and Arnold Dolmetsch," *Egoist*, IV (July 1917), 90. The quotation is from a paragraph not reprinted in the essay as it appears in *Literary Essays*.
77. Eliot, "Vers libre," p. 518.
78. *Some Imagist Poets 1915*, p. viii.
79. Pound, "A retrospect," p. 9; Pound, "The serious artist," p. 50.
80. *The New Poetry: An Anthology*, ed. Harriet Monroe and Alice Corbin Henderson (New York: Macmillan, 1925), pp. xxxvi, xxxix.
81. Eliot, "Reflections on contemporary poetry. II," *Egoist*, IV (Nov. 1917), 151.
82. Eliot, "Contemporary poetry," p. 151. "Sincerity" does not disappear from Eliot's critical lexicon, but it takes on more forbidding implications. It does not suggest self-expression so much as a complex negotiation between self and world, along the lines of Gourmont's definition, with which Eliot begins *The Sacred Wood*: "Ériger en lois ses impressions personnelles, c'est le grand effort d'un homme s'il est sincère." *The Sacred Wood* (London: Methuen, 1920), p. 1.
83. Théophile Gautier, "The progress of French poetry," in *The Complete Works of Théophile Gautier*, pp. 267–68.
84. T. S. Eliot, "The possibility of a poetic drama," in *The Sacred Wood* (London: Methuen, 1920), p. 63.
85. T. S. Eliot, "A note on Ezra Pound," in *To-day*, IV (September 1918), 6.
86. Ezra Pound, "Irony, Laforgue, and some satire," in *Literary Essays*, p. 281.
87. Harold Monro, "The Imagists discussed," *Egoist*, II (May 1, 1915), 79.
88. T. S. Eliot, "William Blake," in *Selected Essays* (New York: Harcourt, Brace & World, 1950), p. 278.
89. T. S. Eliot, "London letter," *Dial*, LXXI (August 1921), 214.

9. The Waste Land

1. T. S. Eliot, "London letter," *Dial*, LXX (April 1921), 450.
2. Eliot, "London letter," *Dial*, LXXII (May 1922), 513, 513, 510.

3. Ibid. p. 510.
4. Ibid. p. 511.
5. Ezra Pound to Felix E. Schelling, July 1922, Letter 189, *Letters*, p. 180.
6. T. S. Eliot, "A commentary," *Criterion*, 11 (April 1924), 232.
7. T. S. Eliot, *The Waste Land*, facsimile, ed. Valerie Eliot (New York: Harcourt, Brace, 1971).
8. On the question of "unmerged voices" see Mikhail Bakhtin, *Problems of Dostoevsky's Poetics*, trans. R. W. Rotsel (Ann Arbor: Ardis, 1973), p. 4.
9. See Robert Langbaum's discussion of "shifting references" in *The Mysteries of Identity* (New York: Oxford Univ. Press, 1977), p. 92.
10. Grover Smith, *T. S. Eliot's Poetry and Plays*, 2nd edn (Chicago: University of Chicago Press, 1974), p. 72; James Thomson, *Poems and Some Letters of James Thomson*, ed. Anne Ridler (Carbondale: Southern Illinois Univ. Press, 1963), pp. 72–73.
11. J. G. Frazer, *The Golden Bough*, part IV, *Adonis, Attis, Osiris*, vol. I, 3rd edn (1914; London: Macmillan, 1919), p. 6.
12. F. O. Matthiessen, *The Achievement of T. S. Eliot* (1935; London: Oxford Univ. Press, 1939), p. 20.
13. Eliot, *The Waste Land*, facsimile, p. 113.
14. Ibid. p. 117.
15. T. S. Eliot, *To Criticize the Critic* (New York: Farrar, Straus & Giroux, 1965), p. 42.
16. Conrad, quoted in Eliot, *The Waste Land*, facsimile, p. 3. Since completing this book, I have read a brief but enticing essay by Craig Raine which places due emphasis upon the beginning of the Conrad passage and upon the motif of resurrection. In the context of a Buddhist reading of the poem, Raine cites lines from *The Family Reunion* which should lend greater weight to my suggestion that the opening of the poem evokes the sprouting of a corpse: "Returning the ghosts of the dead/Those whom the winter drowned/Do not the ghosts of the drowned/Return to the land in the spring?/Do the dead want to return?" Craig Raine, "Met him pikehoses: *The Waste Land* as a Buddhist Poem," *TLS* (May 4, 1973), pp. 503–05.
17. Dante Alighieri, *The Divine Comedy*, *Inferno*, trans. Charles S. Singleton (Princeton: Princeton Univ. Press, 1970), pp. 29, 27.
18. Conrad Aiken, "An anatomy of melancholy," in *A Collection of Critical Essays on The Waste Land*, ed. Jay Martin (Englewood Cliffs: Prentice Hall, 1968), p. 57.
19. F. R. Leavis, *New Bearings in English Poetry* (London: Chatto & Windus, 1932), p. 103.
20. Anne Bolgan, "The philosophy of F. H. Bradley and the mind and art of T. S. Eliot: an introduction," in *English Literature and British Philosophy*, ed. S. P. Rosenbaum (Chicago: Univ. of Chicago Press, 1971), p. 252.
21. F. H. Bradley, *Collected Essays*, vol. I (Oxford: Clarendon Press, 1935), p. 216.
22. William James, *Essays in Radical Empiricism*, ed. Ralph Barton Perry (New York: E. P. Dutton, 1971), p. 15.

23. F. H. Bradley, *Appearance and Reality: A Metaphysical Essay* (1893; rpt. Oxford: Clarendon Press, 1930), p. 28.
24. Ibid. p. 460.
25. Ibid. p. 217.
26. F. H. Bradley, *Principles of Logic* (1883; rpt. New York: G. E. Stechert, 1912), p. 533.
27. Quoted in Eliot, "F. H. Bradley," in *Selected Essays* (New York: Harcourt, Brace, 1964), pp. 400–401.
28. On this point see Lyndall Gordon, *Eliot's Early Years* (New York: Oxford Univ. Press, 1977).
29. See James on Bradley in *Essays in Radical Empiricism*, pp. 56–64.
30. Eliot, *Knowledge and Experience*, p. 31.
31. Ibid. p. 148.
32. Pound, "A retrospect," in *Literary Essays*, p. 4.
33. See, for instance, the chapter "The absolute and its appearance" in Bradley, *Appearance*.
34. T. S. Eliot, "Leibniz' Monads and Bradley's Finite Centres," in *Knowledge and Experience*, p. 202.
35. Richard Wollheim makes this point in "Eliot and F. H. Bradley," in *On Art and Mind* (Cambridge: Harvard Univ. Press, 1974), p. 229.
36. Eliot, "Leibniz' Monads," pp. 202, 200.
37. Aldington, "Modern poetry and the Imagists," *Egoist*, 1 (June 1, 1914), p. 202.
38. Harold Monro, "The Imagists discussed," *Egoist*, 11 (May 1, 1915), p. 78.
39. Quoted in Hughes, *Imagism and the Imagists*, p. 62.
40. Eliot, *Knowledge and Experience*, p. 141.
41. Eliot, "Leibniz' Monads," p. 203. The quotation in the *Monist* article includes more of the passage than the note to *The Waste Land*.
42. Eliot, *Knowledge and Experience*, p. 91.
43. Ibid. p. 116.
44. Ibid. p. 126.
45. Ibid. p. 142.
46. Ibid. p. 148.
47. Ibid. p. 142; Eliot, "Tradition and the individual talent," in *Selected Essays*, p. 4.
48. Lewis, "Futurism, magic and life," *Blast*, 1 (June 20, 1914), 135; Monroe and Henderson, *New Poetry*, p. ix.
49. Eliot, "Tradition and the individual talent," p. 5.
50. Eliot, *Knowledge and Experience*, p. 60; Eliot, "Tradition and the individual talent," p. 5 (first two emphases mine).
51. Eliot, "The function of criticism," in *Selected Essays*, pp. 12–13.
52. Leibniz, quoted in Frederick Copleston, S. J., *A History of Philosophy*, vol. 4 (Garden City: Doubleday, 1960), p. 301.
53. Eliot, "Monads and finite centres," in *Knowledge and Experience*, p. 207.
54. Eliot, *Knowledge and Experience*, p. 147.
55. Langbaum, *Mysteries of Identity*, p. 95.

56. Compare Langbaum on the relation of identity and characterization, *Mysteries of Identity*, pp. 83-119.
57. Eliot, *Knowledge and Experience*, p. 155.
58. Ezra Pound to Harriet Monroe, September 1914, Letter 50, *Letters*, p. 40.
59. T. S. Eliot, "Tradition and the individual talent," p. 4. On this period of Eliot's critical career, see William H. Pritchard, *Seeing Through Everything* (New York: Oxford Univ. Press, 1977), pp. 58-62.
60. T. S. Eliot, "War-paint and feathers," rev. of *The Path on the Rainbow: An Anthology of Songs and Chants from the Indians of North America*, ed. George W. Cronyn, *Athenaeum*, no. 4668 (October 1919), 1036.
61. T. S. Eliot, "Blake," "The metaphysical poets," "The 'Pensées' of Pascal," in *Selected Essays*, pp. 277, 247, 364; Eliot, "Tarr," *Egoist*, V (Sept. 1918), 106.
62. Eliot, "War-paint and feathers," p. 1036.
63. Ibid. p. 1036.
64. T. S. Eliot, "London letter," *Dial*, LXXII (October 1921), 453.
65. T. S. Eliot, "Blake," p. 280.
66. Eliot, "Euripides," p. 43.
67. Eliot, "The metaphysical poets," p. 247.
68. T. S. Eliot, "Ulysses, order, and myth," *Dial*, LXXV (November 1923), 483. For pertinent use of the "mythical method" see Anne C. Bolgan, *What the Thunder Really Said* (Montreal: McGill–Queens Univ. Press, 1973), Langbaum, *Mysteries of Identity*, and A. Walton Litz, "*The Waste Land* fifty years after," in *Eliot in His Time*, ed. A. Walton Litz (Princeton: Princeton Univ. Press, 1973).
69. Eliot, "Ulysses," p. 483.
70. T. S. Eliot, "Religion without humanism," in Norman Foerster, *Humanism and America* (New York: Farrar and Rinehart, 1930), p. 112.
71. Eliot, "Tradition and the individual talent," p. 6.
72. Joseph Frank, "Spatial form in modern literature," in *The Widening Gyre* (Bloomington: Indiana Univ. Press, 1963), pp. 10, 13.
73. I. A. Richards, *Poetries and Sciences* (New York: Norton, 1970), p. 64.
74. T. S. Eliot, "Religion and literature," in *Selected Essays*, p. 349.
75. Hugh Kenner, "The Urban Apocalypse," in *Eliot in His Time*, ed. Litz, pp. 23-49.
76. T. S. Eliot, "Lettre d'Angleterre," *La Nouvelle Revue Française*, XVIII (May 1, 1922), p. 623. In this connection, I will allow myself a tentative suggestion which, even if ill-founded, will have the virtue of emphasizing the more general argument. It concerns that elusive monosyllable Da which appears three times in the poem's final section. As has often been noticed, it functions as an ur-syllable, a primitive linguistic root poised between nature and human language. But there is perhaps another implication. In the Spring of 1922, just as he must have been putting the last touches to *The Waste Land*, Eliot wrote an essay called "The Three Provincialities" for Lewis' new journal, *The Tyro*. In it, he writes with some sympathy of Dadaism, observing that "whatever value there may be

in Dada depends upon the extent to which it is a moral criticism of French literature and French life." My tentative suggestion is therefore this: that in the noise of the thunder, Da, there might also sound a playful reference to Tristan Tzara's Dada. Da, then, would signify the most rudimentary utterance and the latest manifestation of the avant-garde, contemporaneity and antiquity yoked together in a single syllable. Whether or not this is a plausible view of Eliot's intention, it dramatizes a general movement in the poem: toward the most distant and the most up-to-date.

77. J. G. Frazer, *The Golden Bough*, Preface to the Third Edition (New York: Macmillan Company, 1935), p. vii.

78. T. S. Eliot, remark cited in *The Waste Land*, facsimile, p. xxv.

79. D. H. Lawrence to Bertrand Russell, December 8, 1915, in *The Collected Letters of D. H. Lawrence*, vol. 1, ed. Harry T. Moore (New York: Viking, 1962), p. 393.

80. Wyndham Lewis, "Manifesto," *Blast*, 1 (June 20, 1914), 30, 33.

81. Frazer, *The Golden Bough*, p. xxv.

82. T. S. Eliot, "The three provincialities," *Tyro*, 2 (1922), 11.

83. T. S. Eliot, "Imperfect critics," in *The Sacred Wood*, p. 37.

84. T. S. Eliot, "A commentary," *Criterion*, II (April 1924), 231.

85. T. S. Eliot, "Syllabus of a course of six lectures on modern French literature," rpt. in A. D. Moody, *Thomas Stearns Eliot: Poet* (Cambridge: Cambridge Univ. Press, 1979), p. 43; "A French romantic," letter to *Times Literary Supplement*, 980 (28 October 1920), 703.

86. T. S. Eliot, "The idea of a literary review," *Criterion*, IV (January 1926), 3.

87. T. S. Eliot, "John Dryden," *Times Literary Supplement*, 1012 (9 June 1921), 361.

88. T. E. Hulme, "Modern art IV. Mr. David Bomberg's show," in *Further Speculations*, p. 144.

89. Eliot, "A commentary," p. 232; Eliot, "Tradition and the individual talent," pp. 4, 6; Eliot, "Ulysses," p. 482.

Epilogue. The editor and the loathed disturber

1. Ezra Pound, "Edward Wadsworth, Vorticist. An authorized appreciation," *Egoist*, 1 (August 15, 1914), 306.

2. T. S. Eliot to Wyndham Lewis, January 31, 1925, in *The Letters of Wyndham Lewis*, ed. W. K. Rose (London: Methuen, 1963), p. 151.

3. Pound, "Monro," p. 590.

4. Ibid. p. 588.

5. Ibid. p. 589.

6. Pound to Harriet Monroe, September 30, 1914, Letter 50, *Letters*, p. 40; Eliot, quoted in Gordon, *Early Years*, p. 68.

7. Eliot, "The method of Mr. Pound," rev. of *Quia Pauper Amavi*, by Ezra Pound, *Athenaeum*, no. 4669 (Oct. 24, 1919), 1065.

8. Pound, "The method of Mr. Pound," Letter, *Athenaeum*, no. 4670 (Oct. 31, 1919), 1163.

9. Eliot, "Mr. Pound and his poetry," Letter, *Athenaeum*, no. 4671 (Nov. 7, 1919), 1163.
10. T. S. Eliot, "Isolated superiority," *Dial*, 84 (January 1928), 4.
11. Ibid. p. 5.
12. Ezra Pound, "Data," *Exile* (Autumn 1928), 106–07.
13. Ibid. p. 106.
14. Wyndham Lewis, *The Enemy* (January 1927), ix.
15. Lewis, *Blasting and Bombardiering*, p. 258.
16. Ezra Pound, "Desideria," *Exile* (Spring 1928), 108.
17. Donald Davie, "Ezra Pound and the English," *Paideuma*, 7 (Spring & Fall 1978), 302.
18. Quoted in Cyril Connolly, "The break-through in modern verse," *London Magazine*, 1 (June 1961), 33.
19. Pound, quoted in Donald Gallup, "T. S. Eliot & Ezra Pound: collaborators in letters," *Atlantic*, 225 (January 1970), 60.
20. Ibid. p. 61.
21. Pound, "The new sculpture," p. 68.
22. Pound to Kate Buss, May 12, 1923, Letter 195, *Letters*, p. 187. See Kenner's interesting discussion of Eliot's invisibility in *The Invisible Poet* (New York: Harcourt, Brace, 1959), pp. ix–xii.

Index